ALL ABOUT
ASSET ALLOCATION

OTHER TITLES IN THE "ALL ABOUT..." SERIES

ALL ABOUT
ASSET ALLOCATION
The Easy Way to Get Started

RICHARD A. FERRI, CFA

McGraw-Hill

New York Chicago San Francisco Lisbon London Madrid Mexico City
Milan New Delhi San Juan Seoul Singapore Sydney Toronto

ISBN 0-07-142958-1

This publication is designed to provide accurate and authoritative information in
regard to the subject matter covered. It is sold with the understanding that the
publisher is not engaged in rendering legal, accounting, or other professional
service. If legal advice or other expert assistance is required, the services of a
competent professional person should be sought.
—*From a Declaration of Principles jointly adopted by a Committee of the American Bar
Association and a Committee of Publishers and Associations*

McGraw-Hill books are available at special quantity discounts to use as premiums
and sales promotions, or for use in corporate training programs. For more
information, please write to the Director of Special Sales, Professional Publishing,
McGraw-Hill, Two Penn Plaza, New York, NY 10121-2298. Or contact your local
bookstore.

 This book is printed on recycled, acid-free paper containing a
minimum of 50% recycled, de-inked fiber.

Library of Congress Cataloging-in-Publication Data

Ferri, Richard A.
   All about asset allocation : the easy way to get started / by Richard Ferri.
       p. cm.
   Includes index.
   ISBN 0-07-142958-1 (pbk. : alk. paper)
   1. Asset allocation. I. Title.
   HG4529.5.F474 2005
   332.6--dc22   2005006147

ℭჳ ყ

To my parents, with love and admiration

CONTENTS

Foreword by William Bernstein   vii

Preface   ix

Acknowledgments   xv

PART ONE: ASSET ALLOCATION BASICS

Chapter 1
Planning for Investment Success   3

Chapter 2
Understanding Investment Risk   19

Chapter 3
Asset Allocation Explained   33

Chapter 4
Multi-Asset-Class Investing   53

PART TWO: ASSET-CLASS SELECTION

Chapter 5
A Framework for Investment Selection   71

Chapter 6
U.S. Equity Investments   83

Chapter 7
International Equity Investments   109

Chapter 8
Fixed-Income Investments   131

Chapter 9
Real Estate Investments   155

Chapter 10

Alternative Investments   171

PART THREE: MANAGING YOUR PORTFOLIO

Chapter 11

Realistic Market Expectations   197

Chapter 12

Building Your Portfolio   221

Chapter 13

How Behavior Affects Asset Allocation Decisions   243

Chapter 14

Investment Expenses and Professional Advice   261

Appendix A

Low-Cost Mutual Fund Providers   279

Appendix B

Research Web Sites   281

Appendix C

Recommended Reading   283

GLOSSARY   285

INDEX   295

In the fall of 1929, Alfred Cowles III had an ordinary, if rather large, problem. Ordinary because, like many other Americans, he had been badly hurt by the recent stock market crash. And large because, not only was he the heir to the *Chicago Tribune* fortune, but he also managed it.

A highly intelligent young man, he took his charge seriously, consuming as much written analysis from the nation's brokerage houses, insurance firms, and financial commentators as he could. Alas, it was in vain; none of them warned him of the impending crash. How could the country's brightest financial stars have been so uniformly wrong?

Cowles's response to the catastrophic stock market decline that wiped out nearly 90 percent of the stock market's value over the next three years, and the Great Depression that it ignited, has thundered down through the financial markets to this very day. Modern investors ignore the lessons learned by Cowles, and those who followed in his footsteps, at their own peril.

For what Cowles and his followers did was nothing less than remove finance from the realm of ignorance and superstition and place it on a scientific footing. With the help of the nation's foremost economists, he founded the Econometric Society, and along with the legendary Benjamin Graham, who had been similarly affected by the 1929 crash, he began to collect and analyze financial data in the most detailed and thoroughgoing way possible. In effect, he, and those who have followed him in the seven decades since, took investing away from the astrologers and the charlatans and gave it to the astronomers and physicists. (This is, in some cases, quite literally true: many of the finest minds of modern finance began their careers in the physical sciences.)

Unfortunately, when you pick up a financial magazine, watch CNBC, or call your broker, you've just traveled back to the pre-1929 era. In fact, you've just accomplished the financial equivalent of betting the farm on the daily horoscope or of taking a rare cancer to a doctor whose main source of recent medical knowledge is *USA Today*.

Like most intellectual revolutions, the modern science of investing is highly counterintuitive. Do you think that it is possible, through careful securities research, to reliably select market-beating portfolios? Wrong: the data show that although many investors do so, in almost all cases this is purely the result of the randomness of the markets—in simple terms, dumb luck. People have also gotten fabulously rich buying lottery tickets; they have also gotten off scot-free without ever wearing a seatbelt. That does not make either activity a good idea. Do you think that by choosing a portfolio of only a few stocks that you hope will score big, you are maximizing your chances of becoming wealthy? Indeed you are, but by doing so, you are also maximizing your chances of a retirement of cat food cuisine. And make no mistake about it: the object of this particular game is not to get rich—it's to not get poor.

All About Asset Allocation will bring you back into the modern era with a comprehensive, yet readable exposition of how to apply to your investment portfolio what seven decades of financial research have taught us about investing.

Building an asset allocation is much like putting up a skyscraper. You will need blueprints—what asset classes to buy, which ones to skip, and how much of each to use. You will also need the construction materials—which building blocks to buy, and who to buy them from. Rick Ferri provides you both of these, in spades.

Unfortunately, in building your financial skyscraper, there is one thing that neither Rick nor I nor any other financial expert can do for you, which is to provide you with the nerve to stick to those blueprints when you find yourself 30 stories up in the naked girders in a howling wind. But with *All About Asset Allocation* by your side, you'll know that you're executing a sound design, using the best materials, and wearing the best safety rope that money can buy.

William Bernstein

The asset allocation strategy outlined in this book provides a no-nonsense, businesslike approach to getting a tough job done. Once an investor understands the importance of asset allocation decisions to the performance of a portfolio, then that investor will be prepared to spend the necessary time designing a portfolio that meets his or her needs.

The portfolio management concepts presented in *All About Asset Allocation* offer a logical investment strategy that is easy to understand and rational in its explanation. Simply stated, asset allocation is a means of spreading your investment risk across many different types of securities, thus reducing overall portfolio risk and subsequently increasing portfolio return.

The strategy is simple to explain and simple to implement, yet it is extremely difficult to maintain. There are too many distractions, too much noise from the financial press and hawkers of investment products. Investors tend to get sidetracked. They forget why asset allocation works. Consequently, they stray from a simple plan that works and move toward an irrational plan that is full of ambiguities. That is not in the best interest of their long-term financial security.

In this age of do-it-yourself finance, many novice investors skip right over the boring asset allocation process and head straight for the sexy stuff: picking stocks, bonds, and mutual funds. That puts the cart before the horse. You cannot build a house without blueprints, and you cannot build a portfolio without an asset allocation plan.

The simplest, most direct approach to managing your portfolio is the best route. When you are driving a car in unfamiliar territory, it is usually best to stay on the main roads. Chances are that by doing so, you will get where you want to go safely and in a reasonable time. The main road may not be the fastest route, but it is the most reliable. Attempting to find a slick little shortcut is more likely to take you someplace you do not want to be. The same philosophy can be applied to your investment portfolio.

Committing to a proven investment strategy is a crucial step on the road to financial security. Those who follow an asset allocation road map subject their portfolios to less risk and less turnover, and ultimately enjoy higher investment performance.

Understanding the fundamental concepts behind building a proper asset allocation is the fabric of which wealth is created. If you have reached the point in life where you are ready for a long-term investment plan, you are reading the right book. *All About Asset Allocation* provides the framework for designing and implementing a prudent and reliable lifelong investment plan.

ADVICE FROM EXPERIENCE

There is an old saying that if you really want to get to know someone, you have to either marry that person or manage his or her money. I have been married to the same wonderful woman for most of my adult life, and I have also had the fortunate experience of getting to know many other people by personally managing their investment portfolios.

As an investment advisor, it is my job to learn about and understand a client's personal financial situation, design a portfolio that fits that individual's financial needs and the needs of dependent family members, implement that portfolio, and maintain it. What I have learned is that every investor is different, and, as a result, every portfolio is uniquely different.

Some financial firms want to fit investors into canned portfolios of mutual funds. That may work well for large investment firms, but it does not work for investors. There are too many issues, too many unique situations. The only way to create an asset allocation is to analyze and consider all the facts before piecing together a prudent and proper investment plan that will work for that situation.

Everyone has different financial needs, different investment experiences, and different perceptions of risk. Those differences make designing portfolios a multifaceted and challenging exercise. Accordingly, the investment recommendations in this book should be viewed as suggestions rather than as hard facts. It is up to you to design the right portfolio to meet your needs.

At its root, asset allocation is a simple idea. Diversifying a portfolio across several unlike markets reduces the risk of the portfolio's losing money while increasing the chance of its making money. Investments in a portfolio may include, but are not limited to, U.S. stocks and bonds, foreign stocks and bonds, and real estate. Your home is also an important investment. Home equity has become an increasing part of retirement planning, and it is likely to become more important for those living in high-cost areas.

Over a person's lifetime, how that person divides investments among stocks, bonds, real estate, and other asset classes will explain more than 90 percent of the investment return. That makes asset allocation decisions the most important decisions in an investor's life, and something that is worth spending considerable time understanding.

DIFFERENT ASSET ALLOCATION STRATEGIES

There are three different types of asset allocation strategies. Two of those strategies require making predictions about future market returns, and one does not. Those strategies are

1. Strategic asset allocation
2. Tactical asset allocation
3. Market timing

Strategic asset allocation focuses on designing a portfolio of investments that is suitable for your needs and sticking with that allocation through all market conditions. Once an asset allocation to stocks, bonds, real estate, and cash is set, it remains in place for a long period of time. Given that markets are always moving up and down, a strategic asset allocation will get off target over time. For that reason, an investor should occasionally "rebalance" the portfolio—that is, put it back on track with the original target mix. Rebalancing keeps a portfolio in line with an investor's goals and objectives, and helps control investment risk.

Tactical asset allocation is a portfolio strategy that allows active departures from a static asset allocation based upon some measure of market valuation. Often called active portfolio management, tactical asset allocation involves forecasting asset-class returns and increasing or decreasing commitment to an asset class based on the forecast. Return predictions may be a function of fundamental variables, such as earnings or interest-rate forecasts; economic variables, such as a forecast of inflation; technical variables, such as recent price trends; or a combination of several variables. Tactical asset allocation means overweighting one asset class and underweighting another based on these predictions.

Market timing is tactical asset allocation taken to the extreme. It involves forecasting asset returns and making "all or none" asset-class bets. A market timing strategy may start the year 100 percent in Treasury bonds and end the year 100 percent in stocks.

Fear and greed make market timing so tempting. No one likes losing money, and no one likes to be out of a bull market. Market timing solves both of those problems. However, a vast array of academic studies prove that market timing does not work. Although some investors may believe that there are strategies that will allow them to successfully weave into and out of the markets, the facts show that few people actually do so, and those people may be lucky rather than good.

The only asset allocation strategy discussed in the body of this book is strategic asset allocation. No one knows which asset classes will perform well and which will not. A well-balanced multi-asset-class portfolio that maintains a strategic allocation over time has a higher probability of long-term success than continually moving money to the asset classes that look attractive at the time.

All About Asset Allocation focuses on selecting the right asset-class mix for your needs, choosing low-cost investments that represent those asset classes, implementing the strategy, and maintaining it. The facts and figures are presented in as straightforward a manner as possible. Some of the data are technical, so I have tried to explain their meaning in easy-to-understand terms. When you have finished reading all the chapters and you understand the important concepts in each chapter, you will possess the knowledge and the tools to put together a sensible portfolio allocation that will serve you well for many years ahead.

A REVIEW OF THE CHAPTERS

All About Asset Allocation is divided into three parts. All three are equally important. Accordingly, the best way to read this book is to start on the first page and read all the way through to the last.

Part 1 explains the need for investment planning and the basic theory behind an asset allocation strategy. Chapter 1 explains why investment planning is important and how asset allocation works in investment planning. Chapter 2 is all about investment risk. Risk is defined in many different ways by many different people, ranging from losing money to the volatility of portfolio returns. Chapter 3 covers the technical aspect of asset allocation, using two asset classes. It includes basic formulas and historical market relationships. Chapter 4 introduces multi-asset-class investing. Adding more asset classes to a portfolio reduces risk and increases long-term return.

Part 2 is a discovery of investment opportunities. Chapter 5 is a discussion of the methodology used to segregate asset classes and asset-class styles. Chapter 6 looks at the U.S. equity market and its various components. Chapter 7 discusses international markets and how diversifying overseas helps U.S. investors. Chapter 8 is an examination of the U.S. fixed-income market and its various components. Chapter 9 covers real estate investing, including home ownership. Chapter 10 is an explanation of alternative asset classes, such as commodities and hedge funds. All chapters provide a sample list of appropriate mutual funds. By the time you have read Part 2, you will have a comprehensive list of potential investments to consider for your portfolio.

Part 3 is all about managing your investment portfolio. Chapter 11 focuses on methods used to forecast various market risks and returns, along with a list of this author's estimates. Chapter 12 covers a life-cycle concept of investing and provides several examples of potential portfolios. Chapter 13 is an interesting chapter on behavioral finance. The right asset allocation is the one that matches both your needs and your personality. Chapter 14 finishes up with a discussion of fees, taxes, index funds, and the pros and cons of hiring professional management. The appendixes have a wealth of information on asset allocation books, helpful investment Web sites, and low-cost mutual fund companies.

ACKNOWLEDGMENTS

I am particularly thankful to Dr. William Bernstein for writing an enlightening foreword. In addition, many thanks to noted authors and investment experts Scott Simon and Bill Schultheis. A special thanks goes to John Bogle, former chairman of the Vanguard Group and founder of affordable mutual fund investing. Appreciation to all those at Vanguard, Morningstar, and Bloomberg for their help in gathering and organizing data. A warm thanks to my cyber friends on the Morningstar.com message boards, particularly the Vanguard Diehards. Credit goes to my coworkers at Portfolio Solutions, LLC, Scott Salaske, Anne Whipple, Ken Carbaugh, and Stavros Bezas, who did an excellent job of reviewing the manuscript. Finally, I wish to thank my wife, Daria, for her love and never-ending support. The Texas ranch is getting closer.

PART ONE

Asset Allocation Basics

Planning for Investment Success

KEY CONCEPTS

- Investment planning is critical to long-term success.
- Asset allocation is the key element of investment planning.
- Discipline and commitment to a strategy are needed.
- There are no shortcuts to achieving financial security.

Successful investing hinges on three steps: the development of a prudent investment plan, the implementation of that plan, and a commitment to follow the plan in good times and bad. A sensible and workable plan provides the road map to fair and equitable investment results.

A major part of any investment plan is portfolio asset allocation. That is the amount of money you invest in each of various asset classes, such as stocks, bonds, real estate, and cash. In the long run, your asset allocation largely determines your rate of return and your level of portfolio risk.

Do you have an investment strategy? Consider the following two investment plans. Which one best resembles your long-term investment plan?

Plan A. Buy investments that are expected to do well in the coming years. If some investments do not make money, sell them and buy others.

Plan B. Buy and hold a well-diversified portfolio of low-cost investments that match my long-term financial needs and are within my tolerance for risk.

If you are like most investors, Plan A looks familiar. The problem with Plan A is that it is not a plan. It is more of a seat-of-the-pants process. Plan A provides no definitive guidelines for what to buy or when to buy it, and there is no mention of risk or risk control. In addition, "making money" is not quantifiable. The statement does not specify how much money is needed to call an investment a success, or how long an investment needs to be held before you can conclude that it is a success or a failure.

As a professional investment advisor, I have talked with thousands of people about their investment portfolios. It is interesting that most people will claim that they have an investment plan, even though their current portfolio shows little evidence of it. Most portfolios are composed of randomly selected investments and residual bits and pieces of securities that were once part of the portfolio.

It is an important step forward for an investor to recognize that he or she needs to design a good investment plan that meets his or her long-term financial objectives. Good planning comes from learning and understanding the basics of the asset allocation decision, and using that information to construct a portfolio that meets a person's needs. Creating a plan takes time, but it is well worth the effort. A good plan does not need to be changed very often.

Once an investment plan has been designed, it must be put in writing. A written plan is not soon forgotten. After implementation of the plan, periodic maintenance is very important. That requires annual reviews of the portfolio to ensure that the investments are still allocated according to the original plan and that the markets have not caused the portfolio to wander too far off its target. The design, writing, implementation, and maintenance of a good plan are the key factors to a financially rewarding portfolio.

Your investment plan and portfolio asset allocation will be unique. It will be based on your needs and your ability to tolerate investment risk. Sellers of investment products have made many attempts to commoditize investment plans, but that does not work. There is no one-size-fits all solution to managing an investment portfolio.

The three parts of this book will give you an understanding and appreciation of asset allocation principles and provide a detailed analysis of various asset classes that might be appropriate for your portfolio. The book covers several different asset classes and includes mutual fund suggestions for those asset classes. In addition, Chapter 13 explains the emotional part of portfolio management, better known as behavioral finance. How you handle market volatility is an important consideration when designing an investment plan. Once you understand the basic concepts of asset allocation and risk tolerance, you will have the tools to confidently design, implement, and maintain a portfolio that has the highest probability of reaching your investment goals.

THERE ARE NO SHORTCUTS

If you are like most people, your financial well-being is always on your mind. We constantly worry about money. Do we have enough? Will we have enough? Will our children have enough? During our working adult years, we struggle to earn enough to cover our living expenses and hopefully save a little for the future. As retirement approaches, we question whether we can afford to retire and still maintain the lifestyle that we have grown accustomed to. In the final years of life, we must decide who gets our unspent money and when those people should get it.

Money matters are stressful. Investing decisions are part of that stress. The earlier in life a person learns to manage money, the better off that person will be, both financially and emotionally. Unfortunately, proper investing principles are not taught to the general public. There are no required courses on investing in high schools or trade schools, and investing is not part of the standard curriculum at colleges, law schools, or medical schools. Generally, when it comes to financial education, most people are self-taught, usually through expensive trial and error.

A serious problem with learning through trial and error is that it takes years of disappointments and poor results before you are able to discern good information among all the noise. During the learning period, most people slip so far behind the market averages that it is impossible for them to catch up. You could try going to a professional for advice, but that is a hit-or-miss proposition. A large majority of investment advisors have an ulterior motive, namely, selling investment products that pay them commissions and fees.

Some investors who realize that they have fallen behind decide to become more aggressive in an attempt to get their portfolio back up to speed. That approach typically backfires. Investors cannot simply decide that they are going to start making money in the markets by being more aggressive. Newspapers regularly print stories of people who decided to swing for the fence and ended up losing much of their life savings.

During 2001 and 2002, newspapers and magazines routinely ran stories about the fate of workers in high tech, telecommunications, and other rapidly growing industries. Many of those folks staked their life savings on their employer's stock purchase programs. When the Nasdaq market fell over 80 percent and several large companies filed for bankruptcy protection, thousands of middle-aged workers at those companies not only lost most of their retirement and life savings, but also lost their jobs.

Enron Corporation was a highly publicized disaster that ruined the financial plans of many people nearing retirement age. You could not pick up a newspaper or popular magazine without seeing an article about a former Enron employee who lost nearly all his or her savings as a result of the company's collapse. Some former Enron workers were considering selling their homes to pay bills. Others were so devastated by the event that they did not know what would become of them. The stories typically included photographs of the victims depicted in a state of despair.

Due to the magnitude of the loss, Enron become the poster child for everything that was wrong with owning too much stock in one company. However, Enron was just the tip of the iceberg. There were hundreds of bankruptcies and near bankruptcies during the same period that claimed the retirement savings of tens of thousands. Some of those companies had been household names for generations.

In 2004, the *New York Times* reported on the fate of workers at Corning, Inc. This old-line company is an established and respected producer of glass and glass products. In addition to making other glass products, however, Corning was a major producer of fiber-optic cable for the telecommunications industry. During the 1990s, there was a race on between telecom companies to lay fiber-optic cable in every city and every town across the nation. Corning sold fiber-optic cable to everyone in the race, and sales skyrocketed. Corning's stock skyrocketed as well, to the benefit of people like Gordon Casterline. Machinist Gordon Casterline and many other long-time hourly workers figured that they could retire early by investing most of their savings in company stock.

Casterline's dream of early retirement vanished when telecommunication stocks collapsed in the early 2000s. The market for fiber-optic cable virtually disappeared overnight. Buyers canceled orders, and those in bankruptcy did not pay their past debts. The price of Corning stock slid from $113 to pennies per share in less than one year. The meltdown happened so fast that a local bartender observed that people would have been better off investing in a case of beer and redeeming the can deposits than buying Corning stock. Gordon Casterline and his friends lost almost everything. They will be working at Corning for many more years in an attempt to make up some of their losses, if they retain their jobs amid the company's cutbacks.

Some people believe that they can avoid investment mistakes by seeking professional advice. Let the buyer beware. Regrettably, the investment advice business is not the most professional or ethical industry in the world. There are only a few regulatory requirements that must be met to become a paid investment advisor, and none of those requirements have anything to do with skill in the field of investment management. Consequently, many people who are licensed as investment advisors are poorly trained, and some are downright incompetent.

At the peak of the stock market in early 2000, a local Prudential Securities representative invited several retiring East Ohio Gas Company employees to a seminar on the forthcoming rollover of their retirement funds. According to the *New York Times*, the young man recommended that members of the audience invest their retirement money in a portfolio of stocks that would soon increase rapidly in value. He said that this portfolio of technology, health care, financial services, and other rapidly growing companies was destined to benefit significantly from a shift in the country's demographics.

The broker managed to convince about a dozen East Ohio Gas retirees to open rollover accounts and place all their retirement money in this exciting strategy. You can guess what happened.

Over the next two years, the average return on those accounts was minus 60 percent. One retiree lost over 85 percent of his nest egg. The new retirees were paralyzed. By the time they acted to stem the losses, there was not enough money left in their accounts to pay their monthly expenses.

The imprudent investment recommendations of the Prudential Securities broker led to several lawsuits. Retirees who settled with Prudential were forbidden under the agreement to talk about the settlement. However, securities settlements rarely equal more than 60 percent of the loss, and that is before legal fees and other costs. It is also fair to say that because of their emotional stress, the Ohio Gas retirees lost much more than their money. The legal battle cost them at least a couple of years of happy retirement.

Aside from being born into wealth, there are no easy shortcuts to financial security. People who look for shortcuts tend to find failure instead. It takes only one bad investment decision to wipe out years of prudent saving and investing. The headlines carry the big riches-to-rags stories; however, we do not read about the huge number of investors who make small errors in judgment every day, resulting in lower account values. Those small mistakes can accumulate into big shortfalls, especially when the person does not know that he or she is making mistakes.

SUPERIOR INVESTMENT SKILL IS RARE

There is a simple reason why the Prudential Securities broker mentioned earlier could not deliver superior investment performance: superior performance requires both access to superior information and the skill to use that information profitably. Most professional advisors, such as the Prudential representative, do not have superior information. They get the same information at the same time as everyone else. In fact, I believe that people who sit at home watching CNN and other financial news networks are probably

more informed than most stockbrokers, who spend their time selling investment products. But even if a professional advisor did
have access to a new piece of market-moving news, few advisors
have the skill to recognize the information as superior and to make
money from it.

During the 2004 Berkshire Hathaway shareholders' meeting
in Omaha, Charlie Munger, the legendary investor and vice chairman of the company, gave his explanation of why Warren Buffett
has been successful in picking winning stocks over the years.
Munger said that Buffett had the natural ability to sift through
thousands of pieces of information and pick out the one or two
items that had market-moving relevance. Munger went on to
explain that the typical investor (including professionals) spends
too much time researching irrelevant facts and either misses
the important information or is not skilled enough to make a
profit from it.

There are ways in which people can make money from superior information without having a lot of trading skill. We all
remember Martha Stewart and the jail time she did for lying about
the inside information that she profited from. If someone receives
inside information that would have a material effect on a security
price, that individual is prohibited from using the information to
profit personally and cannot pass it on to someone else who would
use it to make a profit. Even indirect benefits derived from passing
along inside information are against the law. Those include
business benefits and social benefits.

Securities law explicitly states that all relevant investment
news must be released by a company to all investors at the same
time. Typically this is done through one of the large news release
services. The relevance of newly released information is almost
immediately reflected in the security price. Unless you hear the
news before anyone else, it is very difficult to use the information
to make a quick profit.

It is easy to make money in retrospect. All we need to do is
pick the next big and profitable company. So, how do you do that?
Back in the early 1980s, only a handful of people predicted that
home computers would become a household appliance. The name
"Microsoft" could easily have been confused with that of a brand
of bathroom tissue. Who would have guessed that Microsoft

Corporation would be one of the most successful companies in the twentieth century? At the same time Microsoft was forming, *Popular Science* magazine predicted that personal aero-cars would replace the family automobile by the twenty-first century. These carlike flying machines would take off and land in your driveway, thereby eliminating traffic jams. Today, there are no aero-cars in driveways, while Microsoft makes the world's best-selling software and is the most valuable company in the United States.

HOT MONEY AND COLD RETURNS

Some investors try to predict the future of mutual funds by looking at fund ratings. In fact, the number one mutual fund selection criterion used by investors and advisors is to select funds on the basis of their Morningstar ratings. The idea is that mutual fund managers who get high ratings must be smart, and it is a good idea to buy the best. Many studies have concluded that an overwhelming majority of new mutual fund contributions flow into those funds that have recently received a five-star Morningstar rating for past performance.

Unfortunately, five-star ratings typically do not persist for a long period, especially after a lot of new money flows into a fund. Some of this year's best-performing funds will be next year's worst. Chasing hot investment performance has become such a large problem that the Securities and Exchange Commission mandates that every mutual fund advertisement that gives past performance numbers must clearly state that *past performance is not an indication of future results.*

Trend following is also very risky. When technology stocks soared in the late 1990s, people clamored for more. The higher those stocks went, the more the public bought. Investors believed that the future performance of "new economy" stocks would continue to shine indefinitely. The investment experts on financial news shows insisted that the old stock valuation models no longer worked, and that we all needed to adjust to a "new paradigm." Few investors stopped to think that if one sector of the market had tripled in value recently, there was *more* risk in that sector, not less risk.

There is no secret about what happened next. Between 2000 and 2002, technology stocks lost over 80 percent of their value.

Small investors across the nation suffered terribly. Most wild-eyed Wall Street analysts did lose their jobs, but only after cashing multimillion-dollar bonus checks for fostering the largest transfer of wealth in the nation's history.

WHO HAS THE SKILL?

A majority of stockbrokers and professional investment advisors will try to convince you that they have Warren Buffett–type skill and can determine what is important and what is not. That is plain nonsense. There are hundreds of thousands of people managing investments and selling investment products. They range from registered stockbrokers to independent investment advisors to mutual fund money managers, trust account managers, and hedge fund managers. A few of these people may have access to superior information and the skill to use it, but it is a small minority. The rest are all smoke and mirrors. The problem is, you cannot tell which is which.

In 1998, Federal Reserve Chairman Alan Greenspan cautioned against buying into the new concepts designed to beat the market. The following statement was given before the Committee on Banking and Financial Services of the U.S. House of Representatives:

> This decade is strewn with examples of bright people who thought they had built a better mousetrap that could consistently extract an abnormal return from financial markets. Some succeed for a time. But while there may occasionally be misconfigurations among market prices that allow abnormal returns, they do not persist.
>
> Indeed, efforts to take advantage of such misalignments force prices into better alignment and are soon emulated by competitors, further narrowing, or eliminating, any gaps. No matter how skillful the trading scheme, over the long haul, abnormal returns are sustained only through abnormal exposure to risk.[1]

Beating the market is tough, especially without taking on more risk. There are people who have done it, but that does not mean that you will or that your mutual fund managers will. Warren Buffett can talk all day long about how he beat the market, and you can take copious notes as he talks, but that does not mean that you can go out and invest like Buffett. The world does not work that way. Superior investment performance requires superior information and the skill to invest based on that information, and neither you nor I have that information or skill.

Beating the market is not easy. If fact, over a lifetime of investing, only a handful of people have actually done it. Most of those people were very lucky, and a few, like Warren Buffet, have proven skill. For the rest of us, there is asset allocation.

A GREAT BUT BORING SOLUTION

The asset allocation information in this book offers an easy-to-understand, easy-to-maintain, reliable long-term investment plan. That being said, asset allocation is not without major drawbacks. First, asset allocation is a boring strategy. You learn the basics, invest your money, diligently follow the plan, and grind out investment gains. It is a no-nonsense, businesslike approach to portfolio management that will definitely put you to sleep. There are no home runs, no bragging rights at the club, no exciting stories to tell. Second, it is never the number one strategy for the year. Some other strategy always beats it, but no one knows what that strategy will be on a year-to-year basis.

Are you ready to be bored? Can you settle for second place year after year? If you adopt the strategy in this book, you will not have much to talk about in social circles. Your portfolio will never be the best-performing or the worst-performing; it will always be a good-performing portfolio. That is not something that gets attention, but it does make money. Asset allocation means being the tortoise in the race between the tortoise and the hare. The slow and steady tortoise always wins, but the hare is much more exciting to watch.

Over the years, your asset allocation portfolio is likely to outpace all of your friends' portfolios, and that should give you something to brag about eventually. The best part may be explaining to your friends that the reason you did better is that your friends invested poorly, not that you invested brilliantly. Once you decide that it is better to have more money than to be the center of attention, asset allocation becomes your lifelong investment strategy.

TIME CHANGES INVESTMENT PRIORITIES

As we advance through life, our financial needs change and our attitude toward investing changes. Accordingly, the asset allocation of your portfolio may need to be adjusted to accommodate those changes. The following paragraphs touch on some of those issues and adjustments that occur during life. Chapter 12 covers the topic of life-cycle investing in more detail.

Young investors have the luxury of time on their side. They can try various investment strategies and make mistakes because they have plenty of time ahead to make up any losses. In addition, younger people have the luxury of not having much to lose. A $3,000 loss on a $10,000 account at age 25 is much easier to overcome than a $30,000 loss on a $100,000 account at age 55.

As time passes, youthful dreams are gradually replaced by midlife realities. Careers are progressing, families are formed, and daily life becomes more predictable and routine. By midlife, people tend to have a good idea of their career potential and what their long-term financial picture looks like. For the first time they can envision how they might live in retirement, and that allows them to develop a more refined savings and investment plan to reach that goal.

When people reach their late fifties and early sixties, they should be in the peak earning years. By this time, their children are either finishing college or already on their own. At this stage, most people refocus their energy on their own personal lives and make definite plans to retire. At that point, a person should have accumulated enough retirement assets to forecast a retirement date. The asset allocation of a portfolio should be reviewed and changes made to prepare for retirement.

Life is not forever. As a person enters his or her senior years, the portfolio may need to be looked at again. Asset allocation at this point may look beyond the grave. If a person has more money than will be needed during the remainder of life, he or she may consider investing a portion of the excess based on the needs and ages of heirs. As a result, it is common for asset allocation to become slightly more aggressive during the late stages of life.

Asset allocation is at the center of portfolio management in every phase of life. Younger investors may develop an asset allocation that is different from that of an older investor, but that does not mean that a young investor should have a more aggressive allocation than an older person. It depends on each person's unique situation. Asset allocation is personal. There is a correct allocation for your needs and tolerance for risk at every stage in life.

HOW ASSET ALLOCATION WORKS

Asset classes are broad categories of investments, such as stocks, bonds, real estate, and money market funds. Each asset class can be divided into categories. For example, stocks can be categorized into U.S. stocks and foreign stocks. Bonds can be categorized into taxable bonds and tax-free bonds. Real estate can be divided into owner-occupied residential real estate, rental residential real estate, and commercial real estate.

The subcategories can be further divided into investment styles and sectors. Examples of styles include growth and value stocks, large and small stocks, and investment-grade bonds and non-investment-grade bonds. Sectors can mean many things. Investments can be divided by industry sectors, such as real estate stocks; or they can be geographically divided, such as Pacific Rim and European stocks; or they can be based on issuers, such as mortgage bonds, corporate bonds, and Treasury bonds. A well-diversified portfolio will hold all asset classes, many asset-class styles, and several asset-class sectors.

Successful investors study all asset classes and their various components in order to understand the differences among them. They recognize how the returns on one asset class move with those on other classes, then they weigh the advantages and disadvantages of including each class in their portfolio. The tax efficiency of each investment may also be a consideration. Investors should be aware of which asset-class styles and sectors are better placed in tax-sheltered accounts and which ones are suitable for taxable accounts.

Asset allocation is the cornerstone of a prudent investment plan and is the single most important decision that an investor will make in regard to a portfolio. Once the fundamentals of asset allocation are understood and all the various styles and sectors of each asset class have been examined, a person can select proper investments for the portfolio to put the plan in place.

Asset allocation largely determines the risk and rate of return that a portfolio is expected to experience over time. If your portfolio has the right asset allocation for your needs, it is well on its way to fulfilling your financial goals with an acceptable amount of risk.

THE ACADEMICS WEIGH IN

In the January/February 2001 issue of the *Financial Analysts Journal*, Roger Ibbotson, a Yale finance professor and chairman of Ibbotson Associates, and Paul Kaplan, vice president and chief economist at Ibbotson Associates, published a landmark study entitled "Does Asset Allocation Policy Explain 40, 90 or 100 Percent of Performance?"[2] The study was conducted to answer the hotly debated question of whether it was the asset allocation of a portfolio or a manager's skill in picking stocks and bonds that drove portfolio performance. The study overwhelmingly concluded that more than 90 percent of a portfolio's long-term variation in return was explained by its asset allocation. Only a small portion of the variation in return was explained by the manager's individual stock or bond selections.

The Ibbotson/Kaplan report builds on two studies by Gary Brinson, L. Randolph Hood, and Gilbert Beebower, who looked at the same question 15 years earlier. In 1986, the three analyzed the returns of 91 large U.S. pension plans between 1974 and 1983.[3] At the time, they concluded that asset allocation explained a significant portion of portfolio performance. Brinson, Beebower, and Brian Singer published a follow-up study in 1991 and essentially confirmed the results of their first paper: more than 90 percent of a portfolio's long-term return characteristics and risk level are determined by the asset allocation.[4] Both of those studies were also published in the *Financial Analysts Journal*.

There is overwhelming evidence that a large percentage of a portfolio's performance is determined by the percentage of money that an investor places in stocks, bonds, real estate, and money market funds. To a much lesser extent, the performance of a portfolio is affected by the individual's investment selection within those asset classes. *All About Asset Allocation* is a guidebook to help you decide the important 90 percent: what portion of your portfolio should be allocated to various asset classes, styles, and sectors.

INVESTMENT SELECTION

The establishment of a proper investment plan is a two-step process. First, since asset allocation explains more than 90 percent of portfolio performance over time, it follows that people should spend a considerable amount of time understanding how asset allocation works and selecting an asset allocation mix that is best for their needs. Second, individual investments that best represent those asset classes, styles, and sectors must be selected.

In addition to asset allocation, investment cost is a major driver of return. The less you pay in fees and commissions, the higher your annual return is expected to be. Accordingly, appropriate investments not only should have broad diversification within the asset class you are seeking, but also should be low in cost.

Mutual funds are a perfect fit for an asset allocation strategy. They give you broad diversification in a selected investment style at a reasonable cost. However, you need to be very selective in the mutual funds you buy. There are vast differences in cost. One mutual fund may be managed identically to another except that the fees are significantly higher. Avoid mutual funds that charge high management fees and commissions.

Another consideration when selecting a fund is how the fund is managed. You can select a passive fund, where the manager attempts to match the performance of a particular market index, or an actively managed mutual fund, where the manager is trying to beat a particular market. On average, actively managed funds are three times more expensive than passive funds. Rarely do active managers have enough skill to overcome the fees and commissions charged by the funds they manage.

Since the data from indexes are used in the study and design of asset allocation strategies, an excellent choice among low-cost passive mutual funds is an index mutual fund that tracks the performance of a particular stock or bond market. The low cost, wide diversification, low tracking error with the index, and high tax efficiency of index funds make them ideally suited to an asset allocation strategy. There are a large and growing number of index funds on the market today that track many different asset classes, styles, and sectors. Several of these funds are highlighted at the end of each chapter in Part 2. For more information on index mutual funds, see *All About Index Funds*, published by McGraw-Hill in 2002.

DON'T OVERANALYZE

The information presented in this book will get you thinking deeply about how to optimize an asset allocation for your needs. That is exactly the intent of this book. You should spend some time thinking about how the strategy works before you design a portfolio and implement a plan.

I will warn you that there can be a tendency to overanalyze the data in an attempt to find the perfect asset allocation. Consequently, the undertaking becomes never-ending. You can never know everything about every asset class, style, and sector. Even if you were to become very knowledgeable about asset classes and how they work together, you still could not know for certain how the portfolio will act in the future. You can only develop a portfolio that has a high probability of success. No portfolio can guarantee success.

The greatest enemy of a good plan is the dream of a perfect plan.

von Clausewitz

Take the time to establish a prudent investment plan for your needs, implement that plan, and begin to maintain it. Do not wait to take action on a good plan while you strive for perfection. There will always be time to tweak the plan at a later date if needed. Putting a good plan into action today is much better than searching for a perfect plan that cannot be known in advance.

CHAPTER SUMMARY

Successful investing requires the design, implementation, and maintenance of a long-term investment strategy that is based on your unique needs. Asset allocation is a central part of that plan. The strategy shifts the focus of investing from trying to pick winners to being diversified in many unlike investments at all times.

No one knows what will happen in the financial markets next week, next month, or next year, but we still need to invest for the future. Asset allocation solves a problem that all investors face, namely, how to manage your investments without knowing the future. Asset allocation eliminates the need to predict the future direction of the markets and eliminates the risk of being in the wrong market at the wrong time. It also eliminates the risk of others giving you bad advice.

We have only a finite amount of time in life to build a portfolio that will sustain us during retirement, and it does not take many mistakes before that goal is put in jeopardy. You do not want to be the next person we read about who has lost your retirement savings by taking inappropriate risk. Develop a good asset allocation plan, implement the plan, maintain the plan, and make adjustments as your needs change. Asset allocation is not an exciting investment strategy, but when it comes to making money, boring can be very profitable.

NOTES

[1]"Private-Sector Refinancing of the Large Hedge Fund, Long-Term Capital Management," Testimony of Chairman Alan Greenspan before the Committee on Banking and Financial Services, U.S. House of Representatives, October 1, 1998.

[2]Roger G. Ibbotson and Paul D. Kaplan, "Does Asset Allocation Policy Explain 40, 90 or 100 Percent of Performance?" *Financial Analysts Journal*, January/February 2000.

[3]Gary P. Brinson, L. Randolph Hood, and Gilbert L. Beebower, "Determinants of Portfolio Performance," *Financial Analysts Journal*, July/August 1986.

[4]Gary P. Brinson, Brian D. Singer, and Gilbert L. Beebower, "Determinants of Portfolio Performance II: An Update," *Financial Analysts Journal*, May/June 1991.

CHAPTER 2

Understanding Investment Risk

KEY CONCEPTS

- Investment returns are directly related to investment risk.
- There are no risk-free investments after taxes and inflation.
- Practitioners view risk as investment volatility.
- Individuals view risk as losing money.

One of the oldest axioms on Wall Street is, *there is no such thing as a free lunch.* You do not get something for nothing. If your investment goal is to earn a rate of return that is higher than inflation and taxes, there will always be some risk involved.

There is a long-standing relationship between risk and return in the financial markets: the greater the uncertainty of investment return, the higher the expected return on the investment. Investments with less risk have lower expected returns. Although investment risk cannot be eliminated, it can be controlled in a portfolio through proper asset allocation.

An asset allocation strategy combines different types of investments, each with its own risk and return characteristics, into one portfolio that has unique risk and return characteristics unlike those of the individual investments. A properly designed portfolio is expected to have a higher "risk-adjusted" return than each of the individual investments that make up the portfolio. Once you learn the mechanics behind asset allocation and accumulate information on different asset classes, you are ready to design a portfolio that has an expected return and an acceptable level of risk to meet your unique financial needs.

THE MYTHICAL RISK-FREE INVESTMENT

The lowest-risk investment in the U.S. financial markets is a U.S. Treasury bill (T-bill), a government-guaranteed investment that matures in one year or less. Treasury bills are sold at a discount from face value and don't pay interest before maturity. The interest is the difference between the purchase price of the bill and the amount that is paid to you either at maturity (this amount is the face value) or when you sell the bill prior to maturity.

The U.S. Treasury issues T-bills weekly, and the interest rate is set by an auction system. Since T-bills are used quite frequently as an investment in money market funds, the current rate is a good proxy for the interest an investor will earn in a money market fund.

In the financial world, T-bills are often referred to as a "risk-free" investment because of their short maturity and government guarantee. However, *risk-free* may be an inappropriate choice of words. T-bills provide a reliable positive return; however, that return is subject to the corrosive effects of taxes and inflation.

Figure 2-1 highlights the year-over-year rate of return of T-bills minus the inflation rate. The return is not always positive. There have been several periods in which the rate of return on T-bills has not kept pace with inflation, most recently from 2001 to 2004. If short-term interest rates are below the inflation rate, investors in T-bills and money market funds are losing purchasing power. That means that money invested in T-bills will buy fewer goods and services one year from today than it does now.

Taxes are also a big drag on investment return. Depending on a person's federal income tax rate and the rate of inflation, the "risk-free" T-bill return can easily be negative. For example, the compounded 30-day T-bill return in 2004 was 1.2 percent. The after-tax return was 0.8 percent, assuming that an investor pays 25 percent income tax. Inflation was 3.3 percent in 2004. That meant that investors who owned T-bills lost 2.5 percent after taxes and inflation.

FIGURE 2-1

Annual Treasury Bill Returns after Taxes and Inflation

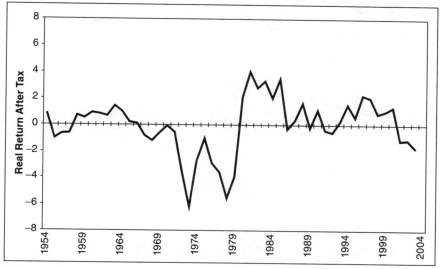

Source: Federal Reserve.

Figure 2-2 illustrates the compounded after-tax and after-inflation return of $100 that was continually reinvested in 30-day Treasury bills since 1955. The chart assumes that 25 percent federal income tax was paid each year on the return.

The lowest point on Figure 2-2 was in 1980. The value of the $100 starting amount had dropped to $75.26. It took it 21 years to climb back to the original $100 in 2001. Then it began to drop again. Over the entire 50-year period, the buying power of $100 invested in T-bills fell to $96.44.

There are a couple of Treasury investments that are protected from the corrosive effect of inflation. Treasury Inflation Protected Securities (TIPS) and I-bonds are a relatively new type of Treasury security that protects principal and interest from rising inflation. The maturity value of those bonds increases in value in direct proportion to an increase in the inflation rate. The interest paid during the period also increases with inflation.

FIGURE 2-2

Cumulative 30-Day T-Bill Return after Taxes and Inflation,
Assuming a 25 Percent Tax Rate, from December 31, 1954

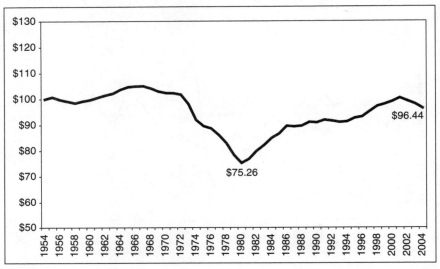

Source: Federal Reserve.

Since inflation is factored out of inflation-protected bond returns, some people believe they are a better representation of a risk-free rate than T-bills. However, those securities are not without risk. First, TIPS are publicly traded securities. As a result, they fluctuate in value as interest rates rise and fall. After intermediate-term interest rates jumped about 1 percent in the third quarter of 2004, the total return on the Lehman Treasury Inflation Notes Index fell about 3 percent. Second, neither TIPS nor I-bonds escape taxation. Both the interest payments and the inflation adjustment gain are eventually taxed as ordinary interest income. More information on inflation-protected securities can be found in Chapter 8, "Fixed-Income Investments."

Risk-free investments are a myth. They do not exist. If one were created, it would need to have a government guarantee, stable daily value, and inflation protection, and to be completely tax-free. As of this writing, there is no such animal.

DEFINING INVESTMENT RISK

Investment risk means different things to different people. To some, it is the volatility of prices. To others, it is the amount that can be lost during a specific period of time. Still others believe that risk is not meeting one's financial objectives.

Academics define risk as the volatility of periodic investment returns. Volatility can be measured over different periods of time. The monthly up and down movement in prices is generally the standard measurement. Large monthly changes in value equate to high volatility and high risk, whereas small changes equate to low volatility and low risk.

Large pension fund trustees view investment risk as the uncertainty that future pension obligations will be met. Defined-benefit pension funds are managed so that the future payments to retirees are matched by the future expected value of the pension fund. An actuarial assumption of pension obligations is compared to a forecast plan value based on an estimated return on assets. If the forecast plan value is equal to the obligation, the plan is fully funded. If the forecast value is less than the plan's obligations, there is an underfunding. Underfunded pension plans represent a financial risk to employers. An underfunded pension obligation means that the employer will have to commit more resources to the fund to maintain its solvency.

Mutual fund managers see risk as the underperformance of their fund compared to other funds in the same category. If a large growth fund manager does not perform well in relation to other large growth fund managers, then that fund manager will lose favor with investors, which results in assets flowing out of the fund. A manager who performs poorly for too long may lose his or her job.

Individual investors define risk as losing money. Nothing gets people's attention faster than when the value of their account begins to fall. The S&P 500 was up about 36 percent for the year through September 1987, and then it fell apart. On Friday, October 16, stocks unexpectedly fell by 9 percent. The following Monday, prices came crashing down another 23 percent. Investors were shell-shocked. Despite the collapse in October, the market still stood in positive territory at the end of the month, and by year-end the S&P 500 was up a respectable 5 percent. Investors who had money in the stock market for the full year in 1987 made money, but that is not what people remember about the year of "the Crash."

No one wants to lose money. However, in order to earn real inflation-adjusted returns after tax, you need to take risk in a portfolio, and that means losing money on occasion. All of the broadly diversified portfolios outlined in this book have inherent risk and will go down in value once in a while. There is no free lunch on Wall Street. That being said, proper asset allocation in a portfolio can reduce the frequency of losing periods and the amount lost during those periods. Asset allocation is a risk-reduction strategy.

THE REAL RISK IN EVERY INVESTOR'S LIFE

Pension fund managers have the most practical definition of risk, namely, not having enough money to pay retirement benefits in the future. That is also a good definition for individual investors to adopt. Running out of money in retirement is everyone's fear. The thought conjures up images of living out your days miserably in substandard housing and getting by on government support. Thus, the real risk for individual investors is the probability of outliving their money.

Every pool of capital is accumulated for some reason. Usually, the assets are going to be used to pay for a liability, such as income needs during retirement. Fortunately, people are catching on to the basic idea that funding a liability is the ultimate investment goal of a portfolio. People have long-term cash needs. If an investor saves enough while working and earns a high enough return on those assets during his or her life, then that investor's retirement income liability may be matched.

There is a minimum dollar amount that each person needs in order to be financially secure. That amount can be thought of as a personal financial liability. The risk we all have in life is not accumulating enough assets to cover that liability. Therefore, it is beneficial to know what amount is necessary to attain financial security. By the way, this figure is not the amount that people need in order to feel secure; it is the amount they actually need to sustain their lifestyle. All too often, investors overestimate the amount of money it takes to be financially secure. Consequently, they will work their fingers to the bone and never spend a fraction of what they have accumulated before passing on.

Figuring out how much you need in order to be financially secure is not difficult. The amount is based on a combination of factors, including your age, health, spending habits, lifestyle decisions, taxes, pension income, Social Security benefits, rental income, and other items. It sounds like a lot of work, but you need to do the detailed analysis only once. Chapter 12 explains the calculation in more detail.

VOLATILITY AS RISK

Losing money is one definition of risk. Not matching future needs is another. Both of these financial risks can be controlled once you have a clear understanding of where they originate. For that, a discussion of volatility is appropriate.

Portfolio volatility, or the up-and-down movement in the value of an investment, is the definition of risk used by most academics and researchers. Volatility can be measured using any interval of time—minutes, days, weeks, months, or years. Monthly volatility is most noticeable to individual investors. This is because they receive monthly statements from their brokerage firms and see firsthand the actual gains and losses in the account.

Volatility is measured in units of standard deviation; the larger the variation in value, the greater the standard deviation. Standard deviation (expressed as σ) basically measures the average amount of movement around the midpoint of the data being measured. For example, assume that an investment has an average return of 5 percent and a standard deviation of 10 percent. Based on a "normal distribution," there is a 68 percent chance that the return will fall between −5 percent and +15 percent. Figure 2-3 illustrates this concept.

The standard deviation of asset-class returns is not static. There are times when the returns are more volatile than others. Figure 2-4 shows the rolling five-year standard deviation of returns for various asset classes. Small stocks have had the highest amount

FIGURE 2-3

Normal Distribution

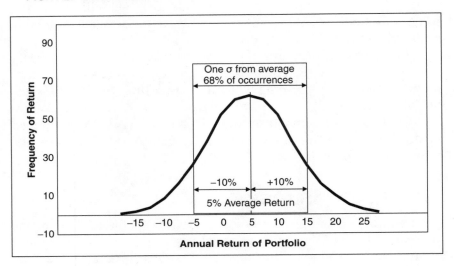

of variation over the years, followed by large stocks, corporate bonds, and Treasury bills.

A jump in volatility tends to be associated with falling returns for that asset class, and lower volatility is associated with higher returns. The increase in volatility in the corporate bond market during the early 1980s was directly related to rapidly increasing interest rates during that period. The fall in stock volatility during the 1980s and 1990s occurred during one of the longest bull markets in history.

Despite changes in volatility, the range of volatility for an asset class tends to be fairly consistent over time. For example, in Figure 2-4, the average standard deviation of small stocks is about 20 percent, the average standard deviation of large stocks is about 15 percent, and the average standard deviation of long-term corporate bonds is about 8 percent.

In the financial world, risk is the primary driver of return. The average standard deviation gives investors an idea of the relationship between the historic risk and return of one investment and the historic risk and return of another. It should be no surprise that

FIGURE 2-4

Rolling 60-Month Volatility of Various Asset Classes

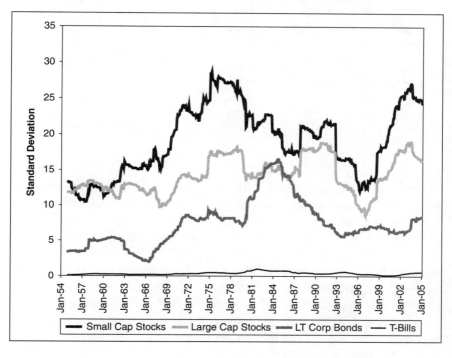

investments that have had a higher σ have had a higher long-term return than investments with lower risk. Table 2-1 illustrates this phenomenon.

Table 2-1 has two return columns. The simple average return column on the left is computed by summing the returns of all years and dividing by 50. The compounded return on the right is derived by linking the return in one year to that in the next in a continuous chain. The compounded return is also known as the annualized return.

Notice that the simple average return on small stocks is almost 3 percent higher than its compounded return. The reason small stocks have a wider spread between their simple and compounded return is the high standard deviation of small-stock

TABLE 2-1

Asset-Class Data from 1955 to 2004

Asset Class	Simple Average Return	Standard Deviation (σ)	Compounded Return
Small U.S. stocks	15.8%	20.1%	12.9%
Large U.S. stocks	12.5%	14.6%	10.9%
Long corporate bonds	7.3%	8.4%	6.8%
Treasury bills	5.3%	0.8%	5.3%

returns (σ = 20.1 percent). Greater variation in returns reduces long-term compounded returns. The simple average return on T-bills is the same as the compounded return because T-bills had a very small standard deviation of returns (σ = 0.8 percent).

Volatility creates lower returns and thus is a risk. For that reason, if you can reduce the risk in an investment or a portfolio of investments, the compounded return comes closer to the simple average return. That is what proper asset allocation can do.

We need to go through some math to get an understanding of how volatility affects compounded returns. To illustrate how variability of returns reduces account value, refer to Table 2-2. Four portfolios are presented, each with a starting value of $10,000.

An analysis of the four portfolios in Table 2-2 shows that all the accounts had a simple average return of 5.0 percent, yet each one had a different compounded return. Portfolio A ended with a 1.1 percent higher compounded return than Portfolio D. The reason for the difference in the compounded return is the difference in *how* the portfolios earned a 5.0 percent simple average. Portfolio A had no variability of return (+5 percent, +5 percent), while Portfolio D had the highest variability (+20 percent, −10 percent). Consequently, while the simple averages of Portfolio A and Portfolio D were the same, Portfolio A compounded to the highest value and Portfolio D compounded to the lowest.

Standard deviation is sometimes difficult to envision. Think of standard deviation as the "average miss" from the portfolio's simple average return. A portfolio may have a simple average of

TABLE 2-2

Four Portfolios with Different Standard Deviations

	Calendar Year Return	Portfolio Value
Portfolio A		
Year 1	+5%	$10,500
Year 2	+5%	$11,025
	Simple average = 5.0%	Compounded = 5.0%
Portfolio B		
Year 1	+10%	$11,000
Year 2	0%	$11,000
	Simple average = 5.0%	Compounded = 4.9%
Portfolio C		
Year 1	+15%	$11,500
Year 2	−5%	$10,925
	Simple average = 5.0%	Compounded = 4.5%
Portfolio D		
Year 1	+20%	$12,000
Year 2	−10%	$10,800
	Simple average = 5.0%	Compounded = 3.9%

5 percent even though it never actually earns 5 percent any given year. The average miss around the 5 percent average is the portfolio's standard deviation.

Table 2-3 illustrates how an "average miss" is computed. Note that an observant math wizard will quickly realize that the data in Table 2-3 do not represent the exact standard deviations of the portfolios, but for illustrative purposes, they are close enough.

It is interesting to note in Table 2-3 that as the standard deviations of the portfolios increased evenly in 5 percent increments from 0 percent to 15 percent, the compounded return difference between the portfolios increased exponentially from one portfolio to the next. To illustrate, there was a 5 percent difference in standard deviation between Portfolios A and B and a 0.1 percent difference in compounded return, a 5 percent difference in standard deviation between Portfolios B and C and a 0.4 percent difference in compounded return, and a 5 percent difference in

TABLE 2-3

Calculating Standard Deviation

Portfolio	Year 1 Return	Missed the Simple Average of 5% by	Year 2 Return	Missed the Simple Average of 5% by	Average Miss (approximately σ)
A	+5%	0%	+5%	0%	0%
B	+10%	5%	0%	5%	5%
C	+15%	10%	−5%	10%	10%
D	+20%	15%	−10%	15%	15%

standard deviation between Portfolios C and D and a 0.6 percent difference in compounded return.

The lesson we learn from Tables 2-2 and 2-3 is that the greater the volatility of return in a portfolio, the lower the compounded return on that portfolio. Thus, any strategy that lowers the return volatility of the portfolio without lowering the simple average return will increase the compounded return.

Reducing the risk of a portfolio though asset allocation has a second benefit: it ensures commitment to the investment plan. Investors do not like to lose money, especially a large amount of money. Reducing the standard deviation in a portfolio increases the probability that an investor will continue to stick with the investment plan. By selecting a proper asset allocation, an investor lowers the variability of returns, which increases the probability that the person will maintain a long-term commitment to the investment plan in bad markets.

CHAPTER SUMMARY

There is a long-standing relationship between risk and return in the financial markets. The higher the expected return on an investment, the greater the uncertainly of that return occurring. Once the risk and return of individual asset classes are understood and accepted, that knowledge can be used to build a portfolio that has an acceptable level of risk based on your unique financial circumstances.

There are no risk-free investments. Every portfolio that attempts to earn an excess rate of return over taxes and inflation carries some risk of loss. Temporary loss of money in an account is not enjoyable; however, it can be controlled. Risk can be managed by using a well-diversified asset allocation strategy. Developing and maintaining a long-term investment plan reduces risk and increases the probability of financial success.

CHAPTER 3

Asset Allocation Explained

KEY CONCEPTS

- Diversification reduces the chance of a large loss.
- Rebalancing a portfolio annually controls risk.
- Low correlation between asset classes is essential.
- Correlations between asset classes are not static.

Diversification is the time-honored practice of spreading financial risk across several different investments to reduce the probability of a large loss in a portfolio. Asset allocation is a mathematical approach to diversification. It involves estimating the expected risk and return on various investments, observing how those investments interrelate to one another under different market conditions, and then methodically constructing a portfolio that has a high probability of achieving your goals with the lowest level of expected portfolio risk.

Academics have done a good job quantifying the benefits of asset allocation. There are literally hundreds of papers on the subject, each one complete with an abundance of formulas, equations, acronyms, and industry jargon. You will see some of those terms and formulas in this chapter and throughout the book. These items are explained as they are introduced. If you are unsure of a term, a glossary is provided at the end of the book.

ASSET ALLOCATION: A SHORT HISTORY

In 1952, a 25-year-old graduate student from the University of Chicago named Harry Markowitz wrote a revolutionary research paper entitled "Portfolio Selection." That 14-page paper would eventually change the way most investment professionals managed their clients' portfolios.

Markowitz's paper explored the idea that financial risk is not only necessary but desirable in portfolio management in order to achieve a high rate of return. However, portfolio risk can be controlled through proper diversification of investments. He argued that the risk of each individual investment is not as important as how all the investments work together to reduce overall portfolio risk. Using formulas borrowed from mathematicians, Markowitz quantified the risk-return relationship achieved through proper asset allocation within a portfolio.

Markowitz's research paper was submitted to and published in the prestigious *Journal of Finance*. Initially, "Portfolio Selection" was little noticed. It was considered too basic by many academic authorities. None of Markowitz's professors at the University of Chicago dreamed that over the next 50 years that small report would become one of the most widely cited papers in finance.

In 1959, Markowitz expanded his research in a book entitled *Portfolio Selection: Efficient Diversification of Investments.* The work earned Markowitz wide recognition in the financial economics field and eventually earned him The Bank of Sweden Prize in Economic Sciences in Memory of Alfred Nobel—i.e., a Nobel Prize.

Markowitz's idea was called Modern Portfolio Theory (MPT) in academia, and today Markowitz is known as the father of MPT. It took several years for MPT to catch on. The math relied on advanced computing power to generate efficient portfolios. Thus, most people were not able to use Markowitz's research effectively until the late 1970s, when computing power became more affordable.

By 1980, asset allocation research had expanded rapidly in universities, bank trust departments, and large private money management firms. Today the methodology is so prevalent that every individual investor has access to free basic asset allocation software on the Internet. It can be found on the Web site of nearly every major mutual fund company and brokerage firm. You can even find simple investment portfolio recommendations based on MPT research in most homemaker magazines.

The asset allocation information that blankets the public domain is a good start in explaining the strategy; however, it is only a start. Serious investors need to know much more to design a truly effective portfolio.

REBALANCING EXPLAINED

In the long run, all of the investments selected for a well-diversified portfolio are expected to generate a certain minimum rate of return, given the inherent level of risk in each of those investments. If you did not expect a higher return from the higher-risk investments, then you would not make those investments (see Chapter 11 for more information on the expected risks and returns of various asset classes and categories).

The problem with using long-term return estimates to build a portfolio is that those forecasts do not help you in the short term because the short-term performance of financial markets is unpredictable. Some investments may be performing well while others are performing poorly.

You could build a perfect portfolio if you knew in advance which investments would perform well and which ones would perform poorly. However, investors who have any experience at all know that it is not possible to predict when each investment will move up or down, or by how much. As a result, it is not prudent to attempt to switch and swap asset classes based on short-term market predictions. While that might work on occasion, you will eventually make a big mistake that will cost you more than you ever gained. Instead, wise investors maintain a position in all investments all of the time.

One practice that separates asset allocation from simple portfolio diversification is the *rebalancing* that occurs in asset allocation strategies on a regular basis. Rebalancing is the means by which you get the portfolio back to its original asset allocation target, thereby remaining adequately diversified. It is accomplished by selling a portion of the investment that is over its target allocation and buying more of the investment that is under its target allocation. For example, assume that your target allocation is 50 percent in stocks and 50 percent in bonds. Assume that after one year, the markets have moved the portfolio to 60 percent in stocks and 40 percent in bonds. Selling the extra 10 percent in stocks and buying 10 percent in bonds gets the portfolio back to its original asset allocation target of 50 percent in stocks and 50 percent in bonds. Rebalancing can also be done when new money is added or withdrawn from an account and when dividends and interest are paid.

Rebalancing hinges on a theory called *regression to the mean*. Simply stated, regression to the mean assumes that all investments have a specific risk and return profile, and that over time all investments fall in line with those natural tendencies. Rebalancing takes advantage of overly optimistic and overly pessimistic pricing discrepancies in the marketplace. It forces the sale of a small portion of the portfolio that has gone up in value and forces a purchase in the portion that did not perform as well. Even though rebalancing may feel counterintuitive, the process basically follows the logic that it is better to sell high and buy low than the other way around.

Rebalancing is an essential component of all the asset allocation examples provided in this book. When analyzing the charts, tables, and data in this chapter and others, assume that the investments are rebalanced annually at the beginning of each year.

Table 3-1 offers a hypothetical example of how annual rebalancing works to reduce portfolio risk and increase return. The table assumes that two different investments are held over a two-year period of time. The first portfolio in Table 3-1 assumes that there is no annual rebalancing. The money placed in each investment at the beginning of Year 1 is allowed to "ride" to the next year. The second portfolio assumes rebalancing after one year. Money from the investment that went up is shifted to the investment that went down, so that both investments have an equal amount at the beginning of Year 2. Notice how differently the rebalanced portfolio behaves compared to the "let it ride" portfolio.

Individually, both Investment 1 and Investment 2 earned a 3.9 percent compounded return over the two-year period. That means that the "let it ride" portfolio with 50 percent in each investment to start also earned 3.9 percent. However, a rebalanced portfolio that maintained 50 percent in Investment 1 and 50 percent

TABLE 3-1

Annual Rebalancing Example

Investments	Return in Year 1	Return in Year 2	Compounded Return
Investment 1	+20%	−10%	3.9%
Investment 2	−10%	+20%	3.9%
Hypothetical Portfolios			
50% Investment 1 and 50% Investment 2, no rebalancing (let it ride)	5.0%	2.9%	3.9%
50% Investment 1 and 50% Investment 2, rebalanced	5.0%	5.0%	5.0%

in Investment 2 both years eliminated the volatility of returns, and that increased the compounded return of the portfolio to 5.0 percent.

Diversifying across many investments that are dissimilar and rebalancing those investments to their original target at the end of the year reduces the annual volatility of the portfolio and increases the return. The "free lunch" from rebalancing is the essence of Modern Portfolio Theory.

There are different methods of rebalancing. The two most popular ones are based on the calendar or on a percentage. When using a calendar method, investors choose to rebalance after a specific period of time, such as annually, quarterly, or monthly. Other investors prefer to use asset-class percentage targets. When a portfolio is off the target allocation by a certain percentage, it is rebalanced, regardless of when the last rebalancing took place.

A rebalancing strategy based on percentages has delivered slightly higher returns and slightly less portfolio risk than the calendar method; however, percentage strategies require significantly more time to monitor and implement, and I do not believe they are worthwhile for individual investors to pursue. Therefore, annual rebalancing is the method used in this book. Annual rebalancing is simple and cost-effective, and takes only a little time each year to implement.

CORRELATION EXPLAINED

Annual rebalancing helps capture a diversification benefit by selling some of an investment that did well and buying more of an
investment that did not do as well. Of course, this assumes that the
investments in a portfolio do not all act the same way. Therefore,
the method of selecting investments that do not act the same way
is as important as rebalancing itself.

Selecting investments that do not go up and down at the same
time can be made easier with *correlation* analysis. This is a mathematical measure of the tendency of one investment to move in
relation with another. The correlation coefficient is a mathemati-
cally derived number that measures this tendency toward
co-movement. If two investments move in the same direction at the
same time, they have a *positive correlation*. If they move in opposite
directions at the same time, they have a *negative correlation*. If
the movement of one investment is independent of the movement
of the other, they are *noncorrelated*.

The challenge facing investors is to find investments that have
negative correlation, noncorrelation, or at least low positive correlation with each other. Once those investments have been identi-
fied, investors should place an appropriate percentage of their
portfolio in each one, and rebalance those investments annually.

There is no benefit gained by purchasing investments that
have a consistently high positive correlation with other investments already in a portfolio. Nonetheless, this is a very common
mistake that people make. During the late 1990s, many investors
thought they were diversifying their portfolios by purchasing
several different growth mutual funds; however, all those funds
were heavily weighed in the same group of technology and communications stocks. When the technology and communications
sectors of the economy fell between 2000 and 2002, all growth
mutual funds collapsed concurrently.

Figure 3-1 illustrates the movement in the returns of two
mutual funds that have a consistently high correlation with each
other. Figure 3-1 assumes a portfolio of 50 percent in Fund A and
50 percent in Fund B, rebalanced annually.

Since Fund A and Fund B are highly correlated, there would
be no diversification benefit from owning both in a portfolio.

FIGURE 3-1

Perfect Positive Correlation
Year-over-Year Returns

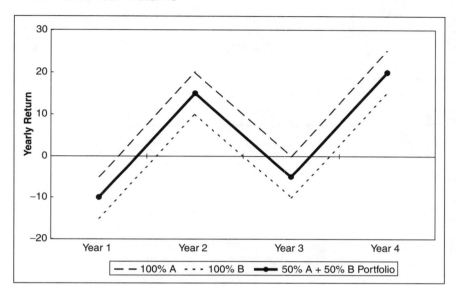

Ideally, you would like to invest in two mutual funds that have a negative correlation. Figure 3-2 shows that Fund C and Fund D move in opposite directions, which means that the two funds have negative correlation. A portfolio of 50 percent in Fund C and 50 percent in Fund D, rebalanced annually, will result in a return that is less volatile than the return on either of the two investments individually. Negative correlation is ideal when selecting investments for a portfolio, but it is very difficult to find.

Correlation is measured using a range between +1 and −1. Two investments that have a correlation of +0.3 or greater are considered positively correlated. When two investments have a correlation of −0.3 or less, this is considered negative correlation. A correlation coefficient between −0.3 and +0.3 is considered noncorrelated.

When two investments are noncorrelated, either the movement of one does not track the movement of the other or the

FIGURE 3-2

Perfect Negative Correlation
Year-over-Year Returns

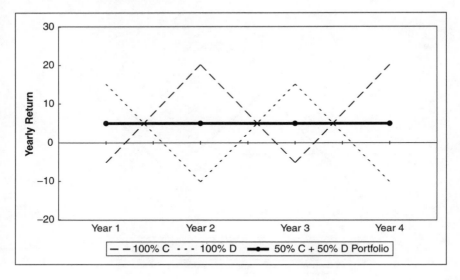

tracking is inconsistent and shifts between positive and negative. Figure 3-3 represents two investments that are noncorrelated; sometimes they move together and sometimes they do not. There is a diversification benefit from investing in noncorrelated assets.

Table 3-2 is a summary of the diversification benefits from correlation. The table assumes that all three portfolios have a simple average return of 5 percent per year, although they have different compounded returns because of the volatility of each portfolio. Portfolio 1 held two investments with negative correlation, and it produced the lowest risk and the highest return. In contrast, Portfolio 3 held two investments with positive correlation. That portfolio had more risk and achieved the lowest return.

Developing a portfolio that holds assets that have negative correlation or noncorrelation with one another is very beneficial. The problem is finding those investments. They are rare. Just when you think you may have found a good noncorrelating investment, something changes and the investment becomes positively correlated. You will see many charts and tables throughout this book

FIGURE 3-3

Noncorrelation
Year-over-Year Returns

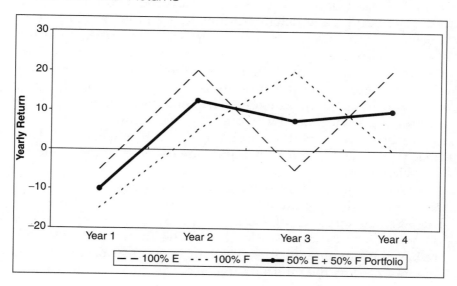

showing the correlations of investments shifting rapidly and without explanation.

Since it is so difficult to find investments that are negatively
correlated, in practice most portfolios are composed of investments
that either are noncorrelated or have a low positive correlation
with one another. Investments that have low positive correlation
do have some diversification benefit.

TABLE 3-2

The Relationship between Correlation and Portfolio Return

Portfolio	Correlation of Assets	Simple Average Return	Compounded Return	Standard Deviation
1: 50% C + 50% D	−1.0	5.0%	5.0%	0%
2: 50% E + 50% F	0.0	5.0%	4.6%	10%
3: 50% A + 50% B	+1.0	5.0%	4.2%	14%

THE TWO-ASSET-CLASS MODEL

Finance professors begin teaching asset allocation techniques using two asset classes. The students learn about correlation, risk reduction, and the efficient frontier in a simple model of two investments that have low correlation with each other. After the students have mastered an understanding of the benefits of asset allocation using two investments, the professor expands the exercise into a multiasset portfolio by adding a third, fourth, fifth, and sixth investment category. The remainder of this chapter follows the same path by explaining asset allocation using a two-asset-class portfolio consisting of U.S. stocks and U.S. Treasury bonds. Chapter 4 expands the discussion into a multi-asset-class model.

The two asset classes examined in this chapter are a U.S. large-stock index and an intermediate-term Treasury-note index. The S&P 500, an index of 500 leading U.S. corporations, is used as a proxy for U.S. large-stock returns. The Treasury-note returns are based on two data series. Prior to 1973, the Treasury return is represented by the return on five-year Treasury bonds. Starting in 1973, the Treasury-note returns represent the performance of the Lehman 1-10 Year Treasury Index, which is a diversified portfolio of short- to intermediate-term U.S. Treasury securities.

RISK-AND-RETURN FIGURES

In this chapter and for the remainder of the book, portfolio risk and return are illustrated using charts and tables. Figure 3-4 represents a classic risk-and-return frontier. The vertical axis in Figure 3-4 represents the compounded annualized return of a series of portfolios, and the horizontal axis is the risk as measured by the standard deviation of those annual returns.

At one end of the chart is the risk-and-return for the first investment in a portfolio, and at the other end is the risk-and-return for the second investment. The points in between represent the risks and returns of portfolios using various asset allocations, spaced using 10 percent intervals. The points on a risk-and-return chart are linked together to form a line that represents all the different combinations of the two asset classes. Depending on

FIGURE 3-4

Classic Risk-and-Return Frontier

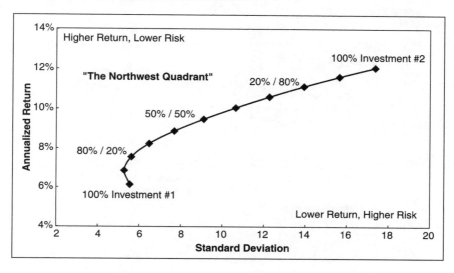

which two asset classes are used, the line curves upward and to the left to varying degrees.

The vertical y axis is easy to understand because high returns are always better than low returns. However, an equally important factor in the chart is the risk measure on the horizontal x axis. The more volatile the annual returns of a portfolio, the further to the right on the horizontal x axis the points are. Points far to the right on the x axis depict very aggressive portfolios. Clearly, the preferable place on the chart is the area in the upper-left portion, depicting high returns with low risk. This area of the chart is often referred to as the *Northwest Quadrant*.

Turn your attention to Figure 3-5. A portfolio of 100 percent Investment A has the lowest return and the lowest risk. On the other hand, a portfolio of 100 percent Investment B has the highest return and the highest risk. What would you expect the risk and return of a portfolio that is 50 percent in Investment A and 50 percent in Investment B to be?

FIGURE 3-5

Risk-and-Return Chart Showing Diversification Benefit of
Asset Allocation

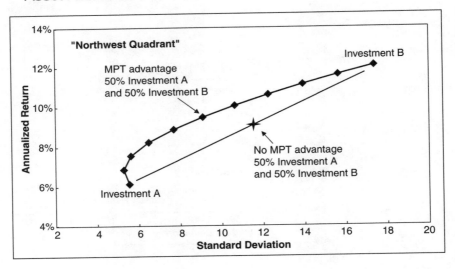

One might expect that a portfolio of 50 percent Investment A
and 50 percent Investment B would have a return and risk level
where the star is located, which is halfway between the two investments. However, because of the benefits of rebalancing, the actual
risk of 50 percent in Investment A and 50 percent in Investment B
was much lower than expected, and the return was higher.

Let's put some names to those two investments. Investment A
is actually the annualized return and standard deviation of the
intermediate-term Treasury notes from 1950 to 2004. Investment B
is the annualized return and standard deviation of the S&P 500
from 1950 to 2004. Each point on the line represents portfolios
using 10 percent increments of the two asset classes. This can be
seen in Figure 3-6.

Based on the return data calculated for Figure 3-6, there was
an MPT advantage in the intermediate-term Treasury notes and
S&P 500 portfolio during the period measured. Table 3-3 quantifies
what the advantage was.

FIGURE 3-6

Risk and Return Using 10 Percent Increments, 1950–2004
Intermediate-Term T-Notes and S&P 500

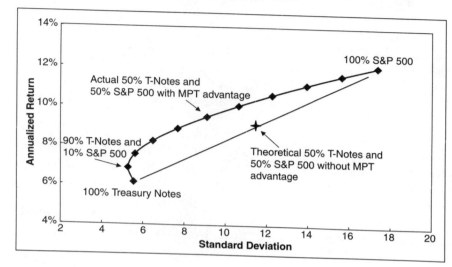

Reducing portfolio risk increases portfolio return. The 50 percent intermediate Treasury notes and 50 percent S&P 500 Index portfolio had an increase in return of 0.4 percent per year created by a reduction in return volatility of 2.4 percent per year.

TABLE 3-3

Portfolio Returns, 1950–2004

Portfolio Characteristics	Annualized Return	Risk (Standard Deviation)
100% intermediate T-notes	6.1%	5.6%
100% S&P 500	12.1%	17.4%
Expected return and risk of a 50% T-notes and 50% stock mix (no MPT)	9.1%	11.5%
Actual return and risk of a 50% T-notes and 50% stock mix	9.5%	9.1%
MPT advantage	0.4%	(2.4%)

CORRELATIONS ARE NOT CONSISTENT

Finding asset classes that have low correlation with each other is not easy. Simply looking at past correlations does not solve the problem because correlations are constantly shifting.

Financial articles and books frequently give tables or matrixes using a single long-term historic correlation number between different asset classes. Then the author suggests using the matrix to make investment selections. That is not enough.

Observing a single long-term correlation number between two asset classes provides some useful information to investors; however, it also gives a false impression of what the future could hold. Past correlations are not a reliable indicator of future correlations. They can change quite frequently and without warning. Some asset classes become more correlated with each other, and others become less correlated.

Figure 3-7 is a visual representation of the shifting 36-month correlation between intermediate Treasury notes and the S&P

FIGURE 3-7

Rolling 36-Month Correlation
Intermediate-Term Treasury Notes and S&P 500

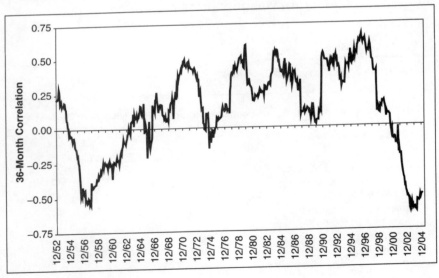

FIGURE 3-8

Diversification Benefit over Five Independent 10-Year Periods, 1955–2004
Intermediate-Term T-Notes and S&P 500

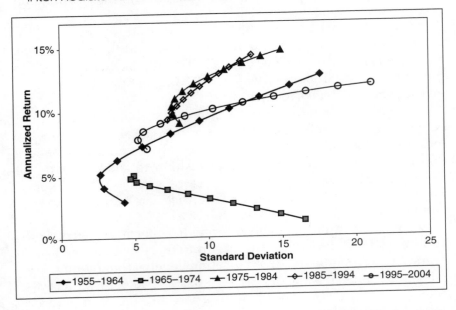

exemplify this phenomenon are 1955–1964 and 1995–2004. In both periods, negative correlation between intermediate-term Treasury notes and the S&P 500 lowered portfolio risk by 3 percent or more and increased returns by over 0.4 percent annualized.

TABLE 3-4

Benefits of Diversification over Independent Periods

Period	Correlation during the Period	Reduction in Portfolio Risk	Increase in Return (MPT)
1955–1964	−0.7	−3.5%	0.43%
1965–1974	0.0	−2.1%	0.36%
1975–1984	+0.2	−2.4%	0.24%
1985–1994	+0.7	−0.6%	0.08%
1995–2004	−0.2	−3.0%	0.60%

Figure 3-9 illustrates how one period can be vastly different from the next. During the 1975–1984 period, there was noncorrelation between intermediate-term Treasury notes and the S&P 500. That reduced the risk in the portfolio by 2.4 percent and increased the annualized return by 0.24 percent. In contrast, during the 1985–1994 period, there was a high positive correlation of +0.7 between the two investments. As a result, there was only a 0.6 percent reduction in portfolio risk and a meager 0.08 percent annualized return gain.

It is almost impossible to find asset classes that are negatively correlated over all periods of time. However, it is possible to find a few asset classes that are consistently noncorrelated with each other, and more that have low positive correlation during most 10-year periods. A well-diversified portfolio includes several of

FIGURE 3-9

Diversification Benefit Difference between Two Independent Periods
Intermediate-Term T-Notes and S&P 500

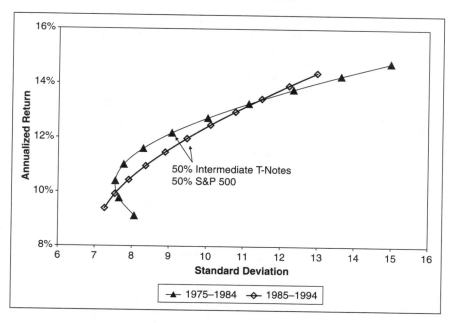

these investments (see Part 2 for details on investment selection). No one knows when the assets in a portfolio will begin to become more correlated or less correlated, which is why it is prudent to have several dissimilar investments in your portfolio. Some of those investments will be moving out of sync with the rest of the portfolio. The diversification will provide the overall MPT benefit you are looking for.

ASSET ALLOCATION IS NOT INFALLIBLE

By studying correlations and employing an asset allocation strategy, you will reduce the chance of portfolio loss, but you will not eliminate it. You cannot eliminate all risk from your portfolio, even if you have several investment categories in your portfolio. There will be periods of time when even the most diversified portfolios will lose money. When those periods occur, there is nothing an investor can do short of abandoning the entire investment plan, which is not a good idea. Trying to guess when down periods will occur and adjusting your portfolio accordingly will probably lose you more money than keeping to your plan and rolling with the punches.

Figure 3-10 provides an example of how returns fluctuate over different periods. Figure 3-10 is a histogram of portfolio returns for the 55 years from 1950 to 2004. The portfolio is composed of 50 percent intermediate-term Treasury notes and 50 percent S&P 500, rebalanced annually.

Notice in Figure 3-10 that in 10 out of 55 years, the return on a 50 percent bond and 50 percent stock portfolio was negative. In 3 of those 10 years, the loss was greater than 5 percent. Table 3-5 quantifies these results in more detail.

The worst return year for the 50 percent bond and 50 percent stock mix was 1974, when the portfolio lost 9.6 percent. More recently, in 2002, the same portfolio lost 6.4 percent. Asset allocation goes a long way toward reducing the losses in a portfolio, but it cannot eliminate all the risk.

A single-year loss in a portfolio does not signal the failure of an asset allocation strategy. Rather, losses must be expected to occur on occasion. However, for those who expect to make money every year, losing periods such as those that occurred in 1974 and

FIGURE 3-10

Annual Return Frequency Distribution
50% Intermediate-Term Treasury Notes and 50% S&P 500,
1950–2004

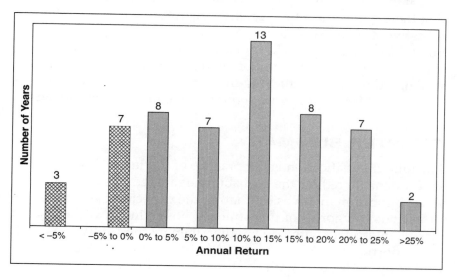

TABLE 3-5

Distribution of Returns for Stocks, Bonds, and Blend

Return Distribution	50% T-Notes and 50% S&P 500	Intermediate T-Notes	S&P 500
<−10	0	0	6
−10% to −5%	3	0	4
−5% to 0%	7	6	3
0% to 5%	8	21	3
5% to 10%	7	16	6
10% to 15%	13	9	5
15% to 20%	8	2	6
20% to 25%	7	1	8
>25%	2	0	14
Lowest year	−9.6%	−1.8%	−26.5%
Highest year	27.7%	25.0%	52.6%
Annualized return	9.5%	6.1%	12.1%

2002 can lead to the failure of the entire investment plan. By failure, I mean that the investor abandons his or her long-term strategy because he or she has lost money.

If there is one thing that is certain in the financial markets, it is that there will come a time again in the future when even the best investment plan loses money. Asset allocation is a good strategy, but it does not always make money. If you implement an asset allocation strategy and fully understand its limitations, then you are well on your way to achieving the hidden diversification benefits that Harry Markowitz wrote about more than half a century ago.

CHAPTER SUMMARY

Portfolio diversification is the practice of buying several different investments to reduce the probability of a large loss in a portfolio. Asset allocation involves estimating the expected risk and return of various categories of investments, observing how those asset classes interrelate with one another, then methodically constructing a portfolio of investments that have a high probability of achieving your goals with the lowest level of expected portfolio risk.

No asset allocation plan can be perfect. Correlations between asset classes change over time, which causes the results of asset allocations to vary. There may be periods when the diversification effect is small, and there are times when the benefits are large. No one knows when correlations will change or by how much. Sometimes investments in a portfolio become less correlated with each other, and other times they become more correlated. Thus, it is wise to hold several different types of investments in a portfolio at all times.

CHAPTER 4

Multi-Asset-Class Investing

KEY CONCEPTS

- Owning several asset classes is better than owning just a couple.
- Each new asset class reduces overall portfolio risk.
- Low correlation between asset classes is essential.
- There are good asset allocations, but no perfect portfolios.

In Chapter 3 we looked at the way two different asset classes can work together to form a lower-risk and higher-return portfolio. Multi-asset-class investing involves adding several different investment types and styles to a portfolio to further reduce portfolio risk and increase the potential for higher return.

> *Let every man divide his money into three parts, and invest a third in land, a third in business, and a third let him keep in reserve.*

> Talmud saying, circa 1200 BC–500 AD

It is not possible to know which types of investment will perform well at any given time; thus, it is important to have all types of investments in the portfolio at all times, and to rebalance annually. Broad diversification is the essence of multi-asset-class investing.

In this chapter, we expand the number of asset classes from two to five and analyze how those additions affect portfolio risk and return. The three new asset classes analyzed in this chapter are Pacific Rim stocks, European stocks, and corporate bonds.

EXPANDING THE ENVELOPE

If the new assets you choose are fundamentally different from the other investments in your portfolio, there is a diversification benefit. Figure 4-1 demonstrates how adding multiple asset classes shifts the characteristics of the portfolio to lower risk and higher return.

Adding multiple asset classes pushes the portfolio risk and return toward the *Northwest Quadrant*. The Northwest Quadrant is an investment utopia. It is the optimal portfolio that investment managers dream about and attempt to construct, and it is the type of portfolio you should seek for yourself, using a correct set of individual investments based on your needs. It represents a portfolio with consistently high returns and consistently low risk.

Now for the bad news—utopia does not exist. The Northwest Quadrant is a myth. There are no perfect portfolios holding a combination of investments that consistently achieve higher returns with low risk. Although multi-asset-class investing does shift the

FIGURE 4-1

Moving Northwest with Multi-Asset-Class Portfolios

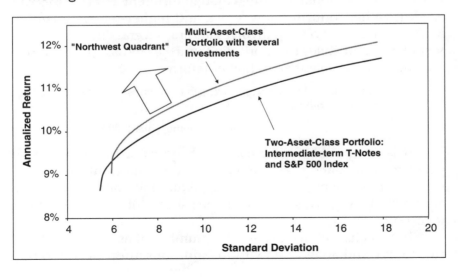

risk and return characteristics of a portfolio *toward* the Northwest Quadrant, no asset allocation eliminates all risk while producing a consistently high return.

INTERNATIONAL STOCKS

Of the three new asset-class categories introduced in this chapter, the first two are international equity indexes. Foreign stocks have historically offered several benefits for U.S. investors. First, foreign stocks do not always move in correlation with the U.S. equity markets, which creates a diversification opportunity. Second, international stocks trade in foreign currencies. That offers investors a hedge against a decline in the U.S. dollar. Both are important reasons to have some foreign stock exposure in a portfolio.

Roger C. Gibson, CFA, CFP, is a well-known author on the subject of asset allocation. His first book, *Asset Allocation: Balancing Financial Risk* (McGraw-Hill), is a classic work on the subject. In March 1999, Gibson published an award-winning article in the *Journal of Finance* entitled "The Rewards of Multiple-Asset-Class Investing." The article articulates the benefits of investing internationally:

> Diversification across two major forms of equity investing with dissimilar patterns of returns further reduces the equity risk. The result is a balanced portfolio, tilted toward equities, appropriate for an investor with a longer investment time horizon who is simultaneously concerned about risk and return. It is a remarkably elegant and powerful asset allocation strategy.

International equities include all publicly traded companies headquartered outside of the United States. The list includes large companies in developed nations, such as Sony Corporation of Japan, and small companies in emerging countries, such as Danubius Hotel of Budapest, Hungary. In all, there are more than 20,000 international companies that trade on foreign exchanges.

Several index providers cover the world's financial markets. They offer individual country indexes, regional indexes, and global indexes. For example, Morgan Stanley Capital International (MSCI) offers country indexes on dozens of markets. In addition, MSCI packages countries together into regions. The MSCI Pacific

Rim Index includes Japan, Singapore, Australia, and New Zealand. The MSCI European Index includes the United Kingdom and several continental European countries, including Germany, France, Spain, Italy, Sweden, and Switzerland.

International indexes are available in both the local country currency and U.S. dollars. It is important to understand the difference. Local currency indexes are the returns that local people receive in local currency, and dollar indexes are what U.S. investors receive after converting the currency to U.S. dollars. There can be big differences between the two, depending on the movement of the dollar. The news media in the United States generally publish returns only in U.S. dollars, which distorts the actual performance of the underlying stocks.

Rather than using a total European index for the study, I created an index that is composed of two equally weighted indexes, the MSCI Europe excluding the United Kingdom and the FTSE All Share Index (a U.K. index). That provides more even coverage across the two geographical areas. The two indexes are rebalanced annually to maintain an equal allocation.

The Pacific index used in this chapter is composed of two equally weighted Far East indexes, the MSCI Japanese Large Company Index (formally an index of the largest stocks on the Tokyo Stock Exchange) and the MSCI Pacific Rim Index excluding Japan. The two Pacific indexes are rebalanced annually to maintain an equal allocation. No emerging countries indexes are included in this chapter.

Table 4-1 is a sampling of large-cap equity returns from the three global areas: the United States, Europe, and the Pacific Rim. The shaded cell represents the geographical region that had the highest-returning index for that year. It is evident that the region of the world with the highest return is not consistent. The highest-returning region moves in an unpredictable manner, and so does the lowest.

Placing all three geographical indexes into a portfolio creates a better risk-adjusted return than having only U.S. equities. Figure 4-2 shows a risk-and-return diagram for U.S. and international stocks. The international index is a mix of 25 percent in Japan, 25 percent in the Pacific Rim without Japan, 25 percent in the United Kingdom, and 25 percent in continental Europe. The international composite index dates back to 1973.

TABLE 4-1

U.S., European, and Pacific Rim Stocks

	S&P 500	European Index	Pacific Rim Index
1985	32.2	75.1	30.7
1986	18.5	42.6	70.1
1987	5.2	13.4	23.0
1988	16.8	15.4	33.0
1989	31.5	26.9	9.0
1990	−3.2	−1.0	−23.2
1991	30.6	14.7	22.7
1992	7.7	−3.6	−7.1
1993	10.0	29.5	52.7
1994	1.3	2.4	4.0
1995	37.4	22.7	7.1
1996	23.1	23.8	2.8
1997	33.4	21.8	−27.2
1998	28.6	24.4	−0.5
1999	21.0	19.2	52.5
2000	−9.1	−10.1	−21.6
2001	−11.9	−18.7	−19.3
2002	−22.1	−17.2	−8.0
2003	28.7	39.0	41.6
2004	10.9	22.7	17.6

It is interesting that the returns on the S&P and the international stock mix were about equal over the period, yet diversifying into both created a portfolio that had higher returns than either one of the indexes, with less risk. Thus, in the long run, international stock diversification increased portfolio return and lowered risk.

Multi-asset-class investing does not always work. There have been periods of time when adding international stocks reduced returns and added risk. Figure 4-3 breaks down the risk-and-return chart into independent 10-year periods starting in 1975.

Figure 4-3 shows that from 1995 to 2004, investing in international stocks was a losing proposition. During that period, the

F I G U R E 4-2

S&P 500 and International Mix, 1973–2004

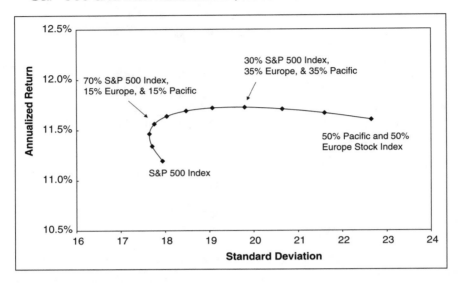

F I G U R E 4-3

S&P 500 and International Stocks: Risk and Reward, Various 10-Year Time Periods

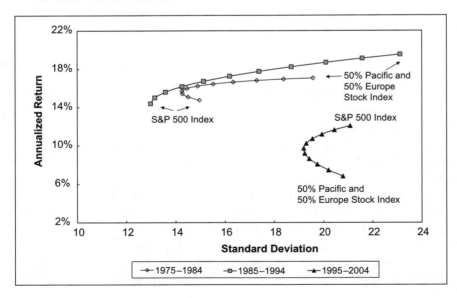

U.S. stock portion returned 12.1 percent annually, while the international portion returned only 6.8 percent. Both asset classes had about the same risk over the 10-year period.

During the period from 1995 to 2004, some investment icons suggested avoiding international stocks altogether. I disagree with that opinion. A single independent 10-year period of time is not a reason to be out of international stocks for a lifetime. The returns on asset classes change from period to period, and correlations between asset classes also change. There have been and will be periods when international stocks reduce risk and increase return, and times when they do not. However, over the long term, international equity investing has added diversification benefits and should be expected to add benefits in the future.

CORPORATE BONDS

Thus far, intermediate-term Treasury bonds have been the only fixed-income asset class we have used in a portfolio. The second fixed-income class we will use is an index of U.S. intermediate-term investment-grade corporate bonds. The index includes bonds issued in the United States by predominantly U.S. corporations and a few bonds issued by large foreign corporations that are issued in the United States and denominated in U.S. dollars.

Table 4-2 is a sampling of period returns from the Lehman 1–10 Year Treasury Index and the Lehman 1–10 Year Credit Index. For all practical purposes the word *credit* means "corporate." The reason the word *credit* is used is a matter of semantics. Corporations do issue all of the bonds in the Lehman 1–10 Year Credit Index; however, some of the bonds in that index are asset-backed securities. Asset-backed bonds are backed by receivables rather than by the corporation that issued the bond. They are a different entity that has its own credit rating. If an asset-backed bond were to default, the company that issued the bond would not be obligated to make up the loss.

Table 4-2 represent the annual returns of the Treasury index and the credit index. The shaded cell each year represents the highest-returning index for that year. Intuitively, one would expect corporate bonds to return more than Treasuries because the interest rate on corporate bonds is higher (see Chapter 6). Yet this is not

TABLE 4-2

Treasury and Corporate Bond Indexes

Year	LB 1–10 T-Notes	LB 1–10 Credit Index	Credit Less T-Notes
1985	18.0	18.5	0.5
1986	13.1	13.5	0.4
1987	3.6	3.9	0.3
1988	6.4	8.0	1.6
1989	12.7	12.9	0.2
1990	9.6	7.6	−2.0
1991	14.1	16.6	2.5
1992	6.9	8.2	1.3
1993	8.2	11.1	1.9
1994	−1.7	−2.6	−0.9
1995	14.4	19.2	4.8
1996	4.1	4.0	−0.1
1997	7.7	8.4	0.7
1998	8.5	8.3	−0.2
1999	0.5	0.2	−0.3
2000	10.5	9.5	−1.0
2001	8.4	9.8	1.4
2002	9.6	10.1	0.5
2003	2.3	6.9	4.3
2004	2.0	4.1	2.1

always the case. Over the sample 20-year period from 1985 to 2004, Treasury bond returns were higher than the returns on corporate bonds in 6 out of 20 years.

As the difference in returns between corporate bonds and Treasury notes changes, the "yield spread" between government-guaranteed Treasuries and nonguaranteed corporate bonds widens or narrows. The yield spread is the difference in income between the indexes. When corporate spreads narrow, corporate bonds perform well. When the spread increases, government bonds are outperforming.

There are a number of factors that explain why the yield spread increases and decreases. Those factors tend to revolve around the earnings cycle of corporations, which corresponds to

Intermediate-Term T-Notes and Intermediate Corporate
Bonds: Risk and Reward

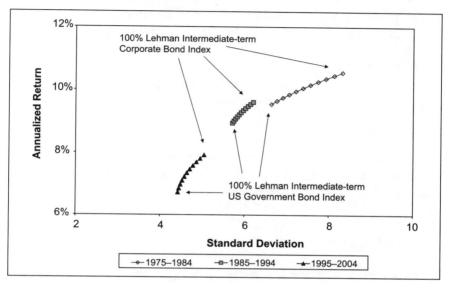

the boom-bust cycle of the economy. More information on
the behavior of credit spreads and bond investing in general is
available in Chapter 8, "Fixed-Income Investments."

The correlation between the Treasury index and the credit index
is typically high, about +0.9, although the returns do not always
move in unison. For that reason, there is some diversification benefit
gained from having corporate bonds and Treasury bonds. Corporate
bonds produced higher returns during all the 10-year periods
illustrated in Figure 4-4, while the added risk was acceptable.

BUILDING A MULTI-ASSET-CLASS
PORTFOLIO

When building a multi-asset-class portfolio, keep these three
thoughts in mind:

- The future risks, returns, and asset-class correlations
  cannot be known with any degree of certainty.

Consequently, the perfect portfolio cannot be known in advance.

- A portfolio with more asset classes is better than a portfolio will fewer asset classes. That being said, after about 12 different investments, the diversification benefits diminish and the maintenance required increases.
- The best portfolio you can design is one that fits your needs. If you are comfortable with the allocation, you will maintain it over a long period of time and during all market conditions. That is what really counts.

The enemy of a good plan is the quest for a perfect plan because the quest for a perfect plan is an endless journey. The minutiae bog people down. They start to suffer from analysis paralysis, and nothing gets accomplished. Fight the urge to be perfect. Instead, design a good plan, implement that plan, and maintain the plan. You will be much further ahead by doing so.

A MULTI-ASSET-CLASS EXAMPLE

The following is an example of a multi-asset-class portfolio using the five asset classes covered in this chapter:

- U.S. large-cap equities (S&P 500 Index)
- Large Pacific Rim equities
- Large European equities
- Intermediate U.S. Treasury notes
- Intermediate U.S. dollar–denominated corporate bonds

For purposes of illustration, the following global equity allocation and a U.S. fixed-income allocation are used:

- Global equity = 70 percent S&P 500 Index, 15 percent Pacific index, 15 percent Europe index
- Fixed income = 50 percent LB 1–10 Year Treasuries and 50 percent LB 1–10 Year Credit Index

Figure 4-5 illustrates the difference in risk-and-return characteristics between a two-asset-class portfolio and a multi-asset-class portfolio. The two-asset-class portfolio holds U.S. stocks and

FIGURE 4-5

Multi-Asset-Class Portfolio versus Two-Asset-Class Portfolio, 1973–2004

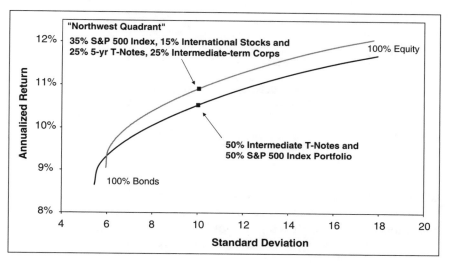

Treasuries, and the multi-asset-class portfolio consists of the global equity mix and fixed-income mix given earlier.

Table 4-3 quantifies the increase in return and the decrease in risk from using a multi-asset-class approach during the 1973–2004 period. Adding three more asset classes pushed the risk-and-return line toward the desirable Northwest Quadrant. Over that period of time, the return was increased by 0.4 percent annualized without any increase in risk.

For such a small increase in return, you may be wondering, why bother with multi-asset-class investing? First, the example includes only five asset classes. You will probably use more. Second, contrary to the investment hype that proliferates in the media and in conversation, meaningful portfolio gains are measured in fractions of a percentage point, not in big percentages. An extra return of 0.4 percent may not sound like much, but over a period of 32 years, a 0.4 percent increase in return on a $10,000 investment earns an extra $24,600.

Wesley Branch Rickey (December 20, 1881–December 9, 1965) was an innovative Major League Baseball executive who is best

TABLE 4-3

Portfolio Returns 1973–2004

S&P 500 + T-Note	100% Treasuries	50/50 Mix	100% S&P 500
Total return	6.1%	10.0%	11.2%
Standard deviation	5.5%	10.0%	17.9%
Multiasset	**100% U.S. Bond**	**50/50 Global Mix**	**100% Global Equity**
Total return	8.6%	10.4%	11.6%
Standard deviation	5.9%	10.0%	17.8%

known for helping break baseball's color barrier and creating the framework for the modern minor league system. Rickey once commented, "Baseball is a game of inches." In that same light, *asset allocation is a game of inches.* If you can make extra money without taking extra risk, then do it.

Figures 4-6 to 4-8 illustrate the risk-and-return characteristics of the five-asset-class portfolio versus the two-asset-class portfolio over three different 10-year periods of time. The series of charts is provided to illustrate how asset-class returns and correlations can change. An asset allocation strategy that worked well during one period may not work as well during the next. Multi-asset-class investing requires a lot of patience and a long-term commitment. Once you go down this road, it is for life.

As illustrated in Figure 4-6, from 1975 to 1984, multi-asset-class investing in international stocks worked beautifully. The strategy generated an extra 0.7 percent in return using the multi-asset-class portfolio, and a 1.6 percent per year reduction in risk.

The diversification benefit continued between 1985 and 1994, as illustrated in Figure 4-7. The return was still 0.7 percent higher using the multi-asset-class portfolio during the period; however, there was no reduction in risk.

Asset allocation strategies work well most of the time, but not all of the time. Between 1995 and 2004, investing internationally was a disappointment. As illustrated in Figure 4-8, there was about

FIGURE 4-6

Multi-Asset-Class Portfolio versus S&P 500 and
Intermediate-Term T-Notes, 1975–1984

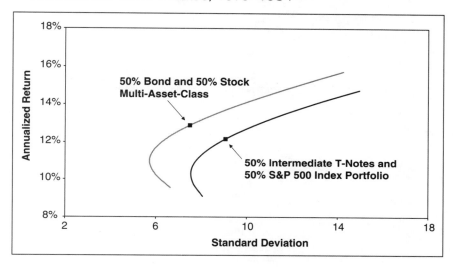

FIGURE 4-7

Multi-Asset-Class Portfolio versus S&P 500 and
Intermediate-Term T-Notes, 1985–1994

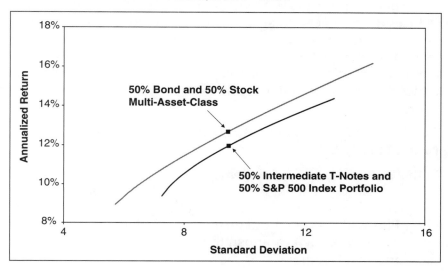

FIGURE 4-8

Multi-Asset-Class Portfolio versus S&P 500 and
Intermediate-Term T-Notes, 1995–2004

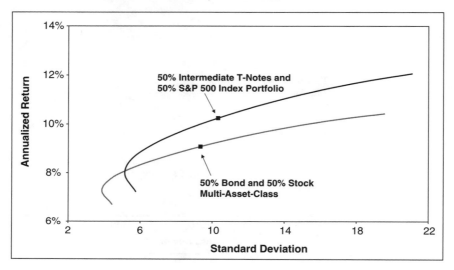

a 1.1 percent decrease in return using the multi-asset-class portfolio, although there was a 1.0 percent decrease in risk.

There are no perfect portfolios. Modern portfolio theory
reduces the number and size of unpleasant outcomes, but it does
not eliminate them. Multi-asset-class investing is designed as a
long-term strategy for long-term investors. That is why it is important to develop a proper portfolio that you are comfortable with
under all market conditions.

CONTINUING THE JOURNEY TO THE NORTHWEST

In this chapter, we added three new asset classes to the portfolio:
European stocks, Pacific Rim stocks, and U.S. corporate bonds.
However, the quest for a multi-asset-class portfolio is just beginning. Part 2 of this book establishes parameters for discovering
new asset classes that can push the efficient frontier further into
the Northwest Quadrant.

As a prelude to Part 2, here are three points about the correlation between asset classes to consider:

1. It is very rare to find low-cost investable asset classes that are negatively correlated or even noncorrelated with each other. Most of the asset classes you investigate and ultimately use have some positive correlation with each other.

2. The correlation between asset classes can change. Investments that were once noncorrelated may become correlated in the future, and vice versa. Past correlations are a guide, not a guarantee.

3. During a time of extreme volatility, when you want low correlation between asset classes, positive correlation can increase dramatically. After the World Trade Center was attacked on September 11, 2001, all stock markets around the world fell by more than 5 percent. No amount of global stock diversification helped a portfolio during that horrific time.

In the real world, asset allocation requires just as much common sense as it does quantitative number crunching. Accordingly, your study of this strategy does not stop here. There are a number of books, Web sites, and computer programs that can assist you. Roger Gibson's book, *Asset Allocation: Balancing Financial Risk* (McGraw-Hill), is a good start, along with *The Intelligent Asset Allocator,* by William Bernstein (McGraw-Hill). Bernstein also has an informative Web site where he posts free analysis and commentary each quarter. The Web address is www.efficientfrontier.com.

A FINAL WORD ABOUT MULTI-ASSET-CLASS INVESTING

There are several ways to design a multi-asset-class portfolio. Some people rely on standard questionnaires that lead to asset-class selection via a computer model. The problem with computers is that they are purely mathematical. They cannot factor in human behavior, which is a large part of successful investing. As a result, a subjective approach is also needed. However, if only subjectivity is used, an asset allocation tends to become skewed toward those asset classes that have performed the best in recent years.

The approach advocated in this book is to consider both the mathematical side of the equation and the subjective side. Each investor has unique needs, experiences, and circumstances. Mathematical models should be used to assist in understanding how asset classes have moved together in the past, and then common sense should take over. Investors should design a portfolio that offers the potential return they need in order to reach their financial goals while staying within their risk tolerance level. More information on asset-class selection and the process of portfolio design are covered in Part 2 and Part 3.

CHAPTER SUMMARY

Multi-asset-class investing reduces portfolio risk and increases the potential for higher return. Owning several dissimilar asset classes is better than owning a few. Each new asset class reduces overall portfolio risk. By adding several different asset classes and sectors in a portfolio, you can create an efficient set of investments that work together to achieve your financial goals with less risk and higher expected return.

Finding asset classes that have low correlation with each other is a challenge. Correlations between asset classes can change significantly between time periods. Consequently, a methodology should be used to determine if an asset class is suitable for inclusion in your portfolio. That is the goal of Part 2.

The enemy of a good asset allocation is the quest for a perfect one. Fight the urge to be perfect. It is not possible. Instead, design a good multi-asset-class portfolio, implement the plan, and maintain the plan. You will be glad you did.

PART TWO

Asset-Class Selection

CHAPTER 5

A Framework for Investment Selection

KEY CONCEPTS

- At its core, asset allocation is risk diversification.
- Investments with unique risks make good diversifiers.
- Ideal investments are fundamentally different from each other.
- Ideal investments are expected to have low correlation with each other.

Asset allocation is a simple concept: Diversify a portfolio across several unlike investments to reduce the overall risk of the portfolio, while potentially increasing the long-term return. The challenge is finding investments that have different characteristics from those of other assets in a portfolio and are available for investment.

At its core, asset allocation is a three-step process:

1. Determine the portfolio's overall equity and fixed-income mix based on an investor's needs and tolerance for financial risk.

2. Develop a portfolio of fundamentally different investments that are expected to have a low correlation with one another and are expected to deliver a fair rate of return given each investment's inherent risk.

3. Rebalance the investments annually to control overall portfolio risk and increase long-term return.

The starting point of a portfolio is its equity and fixed-income mix. The equity/fixed-income mix has the greatest bearing on portfolio risk and return. Accordingly, most U.S. investors start with a broad U.S. stock fund and a broad U.S. investment-grade bond fund as the cornerstones of a portfolio. Then they add on from there.

Ideally, investors would like to add investments that are negatively correlated with U.S. stocks and bonds. Negatively correlated investments would smooth out portfolio volatility caused by the U.S. stock and bond markets.

Unfortunately, finding investments with negative correlation with both U.S. stocks and U.S. bonds is nearly impossible. Just when you think you may have found a negatively correlated asset class, something changes and the correlation unexpectedly shifts to neutral or positive.

Usually a correlation shift occurs at exactly the point in time when you do not want it to. For example, during October 1998, Russia defaulted on its foreign debt obligations. That event caused a domino effect that led to a crisis in the global financial markets. Initially the Asian markets collapsed. Within a week, European and U.S. markets fell. There was no place to hide from the contagion. A second unexpected shift in correlation occurred after the September 11, 2001, terrorist attack on the World Trade Center and the Pentagon. The U.S. stock market closed for a week before opening significantly lower. But that did not stop all other major international markets from falling sharply.

In an unpredictable world, correlations between investments change suddenly and without notice. As a result, it is impossible to design a portfolio that completely neutralizes risk during every market cycle.

It is rare to find an investment that has a consistently negative correlation with the U.S. stock and bond markets and is also expected to deliver a fair rate of return given the risk. However, there are many investments that have varying periods of negative and positive correlation. These investments should be looked at closely. It is not possible to predict which of these investments will have a low or negative correlation next, although if you have enough of these varying-correlation investments in your portfolio, something will be working in your favor most of the time.

Part 2 of this book is all about isolating specific asset classes and categories that may fit your needs and objectives. Your objective when reading this section is to build a list of these investments for possible inclusion in your portfolio. Whether you actually use those investments is the subject of Part 3.

GUIDELINES FOR ASSET SELECTION

The broad asset classes considered in the following chapters include stocks, bonds, real estate, commodities, and collectibles. Categories within those asset classes include, but are not limited to, U.S., European, and Pacific Rim stocks; government bonds, mortgages, and corporate bonds; residential and commercial real estate; and gold, coins, and fine art. Asset-class categories can be further divided into styles such as growth and value stocks, large and small stocks, investment-grade and non-investment-grade bonds, and many other categories.

The purpose of this chapter is to give you a set of guidelines for isolating potential investments. These guidelines will be applied to broad asset classes, their subcategories, and styles within categories. By the end of Part 2, you should have a list of investments for possible inclusion in a broadly diversified portfolio. That is not to say that all these investments should be included in your portfolio, or that other investments that are not on the list should be excluded. It is simply a good reference point to work from.

Potential investments for inclusion in your portfolio should have three important characteristics:

1. The underlying assets of the investment are fundamentally different from the underlying assets of other investments in the portfolio.
2. Historically, there have been periods of negative correlation, noncorrelation, or low positive correlation with other investments in the portfolio. Investments with varying correlation also qualify.

3. The investments are accessible. They may be purchased
    by all investors through liquid, low-cost, and broadly
    diversified funds, such as an index mutual fund, an
    exchange-traded fund (ETF), a no-load actively
    managed mutual fund, or an inexpensive unit
    investment trust (UIT).

FUNDAMENTAL DIFFERENCES

At its root, asset allocation is risk diversification. In order to
have risk diversification, investments in a portfolio have to be
fundamentally different from one another. Accordingly, the first
criterion for selection is that an investment under consideration
be quantifiably different from all other investments. Sometimes
the difference between investments is obvious, and sometimes it
requires significant analysis.

It is easy to isolate fundamental differences between major
asset classes. Stocks and bonds are uniquely different. They have
different obligations from the issuer, have different income
streams, and are even taxed differently.

Owning stocks means that you own a part of a company and
are entitled to your fair share of the profits through dividends and
share price appreciation. Consequently, equity investors have earnings risk. If there are no earnings, the value of the company stock
falls. Stock investors are also the last to receive anything in the
event of corporate liquidation.

Bond investors lend money to a company or other entity that
is obligated to make regular interest payments, plus pay back the
loan on time. Interest payments must occur whether the company
has profits or not. An issuer's obligation to bondholders is spelled
out to investors in an agreement called a bond covenant. The
biggest risk a bondholder faces is default risk, which is the risk that
an issuer will not meet its financial obligations under the bond
covenant. In that respect, the overall financial health of the issuer is
important to both stock and bond investors.

Within an asset class, differentiating between some categories
is also straightforward. A European equity index consists of
companies with their headquarters in Europe. That makes it fundamentally different from a U.S. equity index, which consists of

companies with their headquarters in the United States. By definition, European stocks and U.S. stocks are *mutually exclusive*. Membership in one index precludes membership in the other. For example, a company that has its worldwide headquarters in Europe cannot have its worldwide headquarters in the United States. It is either a European company or a U.S. company, not both.

Finding unique investments among category styles is more complicated. Styles are segments within categories rather than separate categories. For instance, there is not much fundamental difference between large U.S. stocks and small U.S. stocks. The accounting is the same, the exchange they trade on is the same, and the taxes are the same. Nonetheless, the U.S. stock market can be divided so that a large-stock index is mutually exclusive from a small-stock index. Then the two indexes can be annualized to see if they exhibit significantly different risk-and-return characteristics. If large and small stocks are different, then an allocation between those subcategories may be appropriate. Value stocks and growth stocks can also be considered as mutually exclusive segments of the same market. While there are no fundamental differences between the reporting procedures or taxation of growth stocks and value stocks, they can be examined separately to see if they exhibit significantly different risk-and-return characteristics over market cycles.

SECURITIES OVERLAP

One reason to analyze the fundamentals of an investment is to avoid or minimize securities overlap. When security overlap occurs, it means that two investments generally hold the same securities and therefore are prone to be highly positively correlated with each other. Some overlap of securities may be unavoidable in a widely diversified portfolio. In fact, overlap may be desired if you are trying to gain more exposure to a certain category style. Those situations are discussed later in this section. At this point, investment overlap will be discussed as a detriment to diversification.

In the late 1990s, technology and telecommunications stocks were soaring in value. The best-performing mutual funds at the time were growth funds that were heavily invested in those sectors. Investors reacted to the surge by overweighing their portfolios in growth funds that were doing well. According to the Investment Company Institute (ICI), starting in late 1998, quarterly money flow into growth funds began to outpace the amount flowing into value funds. By the time growth stocks peaked in early 2000, investors were transferring billions of dollars out of value funds and into growth funds. Figure 5-1 illustrates this massive transfer of capital.

Mutual fund companies were quick to deliver new funds that whetted investors' appetites. Figure 5-2 illustrates the large number of new growth funds opened during the late 1990s compared to the small number of conservative value funds.

When growth stocks fell sharply between 2000 and 2002, portfolios that held several overlapping growth funds were devastated. Investors in those funds realized that diversification does not simply mean owning several mutual funds with different names. The underlying assets in those funds need to be examined and diversified.

FIGURE 5-1

Quarterly Money Flow into Growth Funds and Value Funds

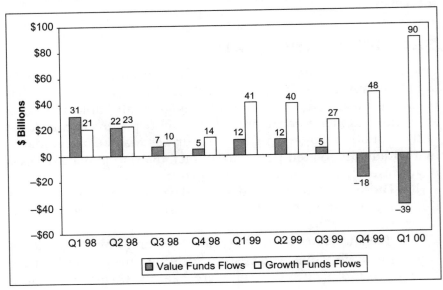

FIGURE 5-2

Number of New Growth and Value Funds, 1997–2000

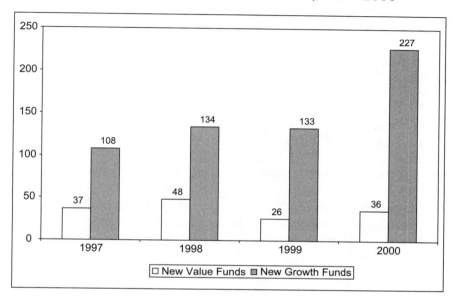

As mentioned earlier, some securities overlap is okay as long as you know it exists and understand how it will affect your investment performance. For example, the S&P 500 is composed of predominantly large-company stocks, although there are several mid-cap stocks and a few small stocks in the index. If a person were to invest in both an S&P 500 Index fund and a small-cap index fund such as the Vanguard Small Cap Index Fund, there would be some overlap of stocks. The question is, how much? For all practical consideration, the effect of the small-cap stocks on the return of the S&P 500 Index is negligible. As a result, you can add the Vanguard Small Cap Index Fund to an S&P 500 Index fund without adding measurable securities overlap in the portfolio.

LOW OR VARYING CORRELATION

After fundamental analysis, a second criterion for including an asset-class category in your potential list of investments is correlation. You are looking for investments that have negative correlation, noncorrelation, low correlation, or varying correlations with other investments on the list.

Correlation is measured using a numerical range between +1 and −1. When two investments generally move up and down in unison, they have *positive* correlation. The range is normally between +0.4 and +1.0. When two investments move in opposite directions, they have a *negative* correlation, in a range between −0.4 and −1.0. When two investments do not move in sync with each other, they are considered noncorrelated. Normally, the correlation range for noncorrelation is between −0.3 and +0.3.

Correlations shift over time. Two investments that are positively correlated in one period can become noncorrelated or negatively correlated the next. As a result, a single long-term correlation measurement between two investments is of limited use. Nevertheless, there are several books and financial studies that cite a single long-term correlation as their only point of reference for building a portfolio. In this book, "rolling" correlations are used as a reference for study rather than a static long-term number. Rolling correlations allow you to see when and how correlations between asset classes shift.

It is not necessary for two investments to always have negative correlation, noncorrelation, or consistently low correlation with other investments for them to be useful in asset allocation. As long as two investments do not have consistently high positive correlation with each other, they will both help reduce long-term portfolio risk and increase long-term return.

Figure 5-3 illustrates the stark difference in correlation that can occur between asset classes. Between 1955 and 1964, the S&P 500 Index and intermediate-term U.S. Treasury notes had a −0.7 correlation with each other. However, correlations shifted 180 degrees over the next 30 years. Between 1985 and 1994, the correlation between the S&P 500 and T-notes was +0.7. By 2004, the 10-year correlation had shifted back to negative. Despite the shifting correlation, the two assets have provided good diversification in a portfolio over the long term. If you need further help with the concept of correlation, please refer to Chapter 3.

FIGURE 5-3

S&P 500 and Intermediate-Term Treasury Note Portfolio
Independent 10-Year Correlations

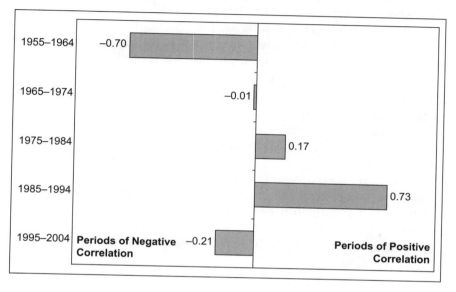

LOW-COST AVAILABILITY

When you find an asset-class category that you would like to include on your investment list, that asset-class category must be "investable." That means that there are low-cost marketable securities available that represent that asset class, such as a no-load mutual fund. Specifically, look for mutual funds that have low expense ratios and no redemption fees. Recall that asset allocation strategies require annual rebalancing, and redemption fees diminish the benefits of rebalancing.

The investment vehicle selected to represent an asset class or category in a portfolio should also provide enough diversification *within* the fund. Broad diversification within a fund ensures that the correlation between the investment vehicle and the asset-class category you studied is very high. For example, the correlation between most indexes of large U.S. stocks and the Vanguard 500 Index fund is over +0.99. Accordingly, the Vanguard 500 Index is ideally suited as a potential investment to represent the large-cap U.S. stock category in a portfolio.

Some asset-class categories are available only in the form of expensive packaged products that are not well suited for individuals. Those investments generally take the form of a limited partnership (LP). LPs are typically expensive, illiquid, tax-inefficient, loosely regulated, secretive, and oversold by Wall Street hawks. Frankly, unless you really know what you are doing, or you have social passion for being with the "in" crowd and several million dollars to tie up in illiquid investments, stay away from these oversold products. That includes hedge funds, commodity trading funds, private equity funds, and venture capital pools. For more information, see Chapter 10, "Alternative Investments."

There are also asset-class categories that have no means of investment. For example, most people reading this book will not be trading museum-quality oil paintings by Old Masters. Except for the curious-minded, it does not matter how they have performed. Spend your time investigating asset classes that are available to you.

THE GLOBAL MARKETS

Asset allocation works best when the investments in a portfolio are fundamentally different from one another and have low or varying correlation with one another. The world is a very big place, and there are many different asset classes, categories, and styles to consider, as can be seen in Figure 5-4. With over 50 percent of the world's tradable securities, the United States still holds a preeminent place in the global capital markets. But that percentage is getting smaller every year and is likely to shrink more quickly in the future. Emerging countries are becoming an increasingly important source of new securities. These include securities from China, India, and several former Soviet satellite countries.

In the last few years, several mutual fund companies have introduced low-cost index funds that cater to investors seeking instant global diversification across broad swaths of the global marketplace. Each year, fund providers create more investable securities covering asset classes and categories with the fundamental characteristics we are looking for.

FIGURE 5-4

Total Investable Assets in the Global Capital Markets
$64 Trillion as of 2000

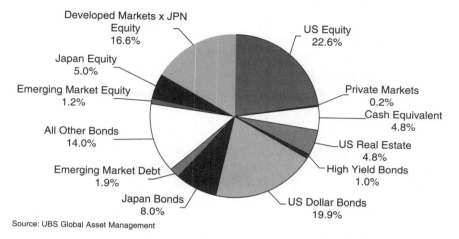

Source: UBS Global Asset Management

The remaining five chapters in Part 2 analyze the asset classes and categories highlighted in Figure 5-4, plus several others. Here is a summary of the asset classes, categories, and styles that are covered:

- Chapter 6: U.S. Equity Investments
  - Total U.S. stock market construction
  - Size analysis (large and small)
  - Style analysis (growth and value)
- Chapter 7: International Equity Investments
  - Developed markets
  - Emerging markets
  - Size and style indexes
- Chapter 8: Fixed-Income Investments
  - U.S. investment-grade fixed income
  - U.S. non-investment-grade fixed income
  - International fixed income

- Chapter 9: Real Estate Investments
  - Home ownership as an investment
  - Rental property as an investment
  - Real estate investment trusts (REITs)
- Chapter 10: Alternative Investments
  - Collectibles as investments
  - Commodities and publicly traded commodity funds
  - Limited partnerships, including hedge funds

A list of potential investments is provided at the end of each chapter. Each of those investments best represents the asset classes and categories discussed in that chapter. These funds are provided for information only and should be considered only after further analysis, including reading the prospectus.

Which investments from the following chapters will actually make it into your portfolio is difficult to say. That is a function of many factors, including your time horizon, income need, risk tolerance, tax situation, and a variety of other factors. Those considerations and others are discussed in Part 3 of this book.

CHAPTER SUMMARY

At its core, asset allocation is a strategy of risk diversification. Different asset classes and categories have different risks that are not related to one another. Holding fundamentally different investments in a portfolio reduces overall portfolio risk and increases return.

Finding investments with unique risk-and-return characteristics is a challenge. The best diversifiers have different fundamental characteristics and have low or varying correlation with other investments. Different fundamentals mean that the asset classes represent mutually exclusive markets or different types of securities within markets that have distinguishable characteristics.

A list of potential investments from each asset class is included at the end of the chapter covering that asset class. Those lists are designed to be a guide. Each investor is unique, and that means that each portfolio will be different.

U.S. Equity Investments

KEY CONCEPTS

- U.S. stocks have produced real returns averaging 6 percent.
- The stock market is divided into many different categories.
- Diversifying among categories can increase return and reduce risk.
- Total stock market funds and small value funds are recommended.

U.S. equities are a core position in a balanced investment portfolio. Approximately 150 million Americans own U.S. equities today, either directly or indirectly. We own them directly through stock purchase and indirectly through mutual funds, employer retirement accounts, insurance annuities, and other pooled investment vehicles.

This chapter advocates that investors approach the U.S. market in a couple of different ways. Depending on the complexity of the U.S. stock position you wish to build in your portfolio, you might hold the entire stock market in the form of a total market index fund or build a self-styled index using different categories of U.S. stocks within the total market index. U.S. equities can be divided into different categories based on company size, industry, and fundamentals (growth or value).

Interestingly, not all categories of U.S. equities are highly correlated with one another. Within the stock market, some categories may be performing well while others are performing poorly. Thus, it is important to understand how the U.S. stock market is constructed to possibly gain a diversification advantage within this asset class.

A HISTORY OF U.S. EQUITY RETURNS

Over the long term, an investment in U.S. equities has delivered exceptionally good returns. As America prospered during the twentieth century, established companies grew and new companies in new industries were established. U.S. industry enjoyed steady earnings growth, even through two major world wars. As a result, U.S. companies paid reliable dividends, stocks increased in value, and shareholders profited.

From 1950 to 2004, the broad market for U.S. stocks returned 12.1 percent annually. That handily beat the 6.2 percent return on five-year Treasury notes and the 3.9 percent level of inflation. Table 6-1 is an after-inflation rate of return over different periods of time. The inflation-adjusted return is also known as the *real* return because it is the amount of purchasing power the investment created.

Real returns reinforce the fact that inflation is an invisible tax on all investments. The portion of return that is related to inflation cannot be counted as investment gain. When creating an asset allocation for your portfolio, you should always consider the expected real return of the investments you are considering.

TABLE 6-1

Real U.S. Stock and Bond Returns

	1950–2004	1968–1982	2000–2004	Historic Average over Inflation
U.S. stocks	8.2%	0.2%	−4.9%	5% to 7%
U.S. five-year T-note	2.3%	0.3%	5.1%	1% to 2%

Sources: Standard & Poor's; St. Louis Federal Reserve.

It is not always easy to make a real return in the U.S. stock market. There have been several periods of time between 1950 and 2004 when U.S. equities did not perform well. For 15 years, from 1968 to 1982, the inflation-adjusted return of U.S. equities was barely above the rate of inflation. From 2000 to 2004, U.S. stocks lost 4.9 percent annually after accounting for inflation. If U.S. stocks average a real return of 5 percent from 2005 to 2010, over the entire 10-year period from 2000 to 2010, stock returns will return slightly greater than zero percent after inflation, and negative after income taxes.

Investors must expect periods of time when equities do not make money after inflation. That is the nature of investment risk. However, patience is a virtue. In the long run, equities have outpaced inflation by a wide margin, and they are expected to be one of the investments with the best real return in the future.

U.S. EQUITY MARKET STRUCTURE

When a company sells stock to the public for the very first time, it is distributed through a tightly controlled initial public offering (IPO). Investment bankers are hired to bring the company public and promote the shares. Investors who get the new shares tend to be large institutions that do significant business with the investment banker and friends of the officers of the company that is coming public. Individual investors who do relatively little business with large Wall Street firms and have no influence with management generally do not get access to the hottest IPOs. This is not the fairest system of distribution, but that is the way it works.

Once a stock is issued under the IPO process, it begins trading on the secondary market. Which stock exchange carries a new company depends on the company's financial history and the value of the company. There are about 8,000 U.S. stocks that trade actively in the U.S. equity market; however, only about half meet the criteria to trade on a major exchange. Companies must meet certain listing requirements to be eligible to trade on the New York Stock Exchange (NYSE), the American Stock Exchange (AMEX), or the National Association of Securities Dealers Automatic Quote System (Nasdaq). Companies that do not qualify for listing on the NYSE, AMEX, or Nasdaq are called bulletin board stocks or pink sheet companies.

TABLE 6-2

Approximate Number of Stocks on Each Exchange

Stocks Sorted by Exchange	Number of Companies	Percent of Total Market Value
New York Stock Exchange	1,665	80%
American Stock Exchange	375	<1%
Nasdaq	3,015	19%
Bulletin board stocks	3,500+	<1%

Source: Wilshire Associates.

Table 6-2 is a breakdown of where stocks trade in the United States. The table includes only individual U.S. common equities. It does not include listed bonds, preferred stocks, exchange-traded mutual funds, or foreign stocks listed on U.S. exchanges.

You can buy bulletin board stocks through a broker that has access to that dealer market. Years ago, dealers who were members of the National Quotation Bureau (NQB) would publish weekly bid and ask prices on bulletin board stocks on long sheets of pink paper, thus the name pink sheets. The list would be distributed to all brokerage firms. Brokers now refer to electronic pink sheets if one of their clients wants to buy or sell a nonlisted security.

THE BROAD STOCK MARKET

Wilshire Associates is a privately owned investment firm with headquarters in Santa Monica, California. Since its founding in 1972, the company has developed a wide variety of U.S. indexes, one of which is the Dow Jones Wilshire 5000 Composite Index. The Wilshire 5000, as it is commonly known, was the first U.S. equity index to capture the return of the entire market of listed U.S. stocks. Those are the companies that are listed on the NYSE, AMEX, and Nasdaq. Bulletin board stocks are not included in Wilshire indexes.

When originally introduced in 1974, the Wilshire 5000 Index held 5,000 stocks, thus the name. Today, the number of stocks in the index depends on the number of stocks trading on the major U.S. stock markets, which equals about 5050.

The major criteria for inclusion in the Dow Jones Wilshire 5000 Composite Index are as follows:

- The company must be headquartered in the United States. Nondomiciled U.S. stocks and foreign issues (ADRs) are excluded.
- The stock must trade in the United States on the New York Stock Exchange, the American Stock Exchange, or Nasdaq.
- The stock must be the primary equity issue for the company.
- Common stocks, REITs, and limited partnerships are included.
- Bulletin board issues are excluded.

The Dow Jones Wilshire 5000 Composite is the most complete broad market index; however, there are several other broad market indexes. They include the MSCI US Broad Market Index (~3,800 stocks), Russell 3000 (~3,000 stocks), Dow Jones Total Market Index (~1,625 stocks), Morningstar Total Market (~2,000+ stocks), and Standard & Poor's 1500 (~1,500 stocks). There are several low-cost index funds available that attempt to match the return of these broad market indexes. A partial list of those funds is available at the end of this chapter.

SIZE AND STYLE OPPORTUNITIES

An investment in a total U.S. stock market fund is a solid foundation on which to base a stock allocation. From there, you can analyze various sectors of the U.S. stock market to possibly find an opportunity to add greater diversification through selectively overweighting one or more sectors. To do sector analysis, investors need a system for segmenting the market so that the sectors do not overlap.

Morningstar, Inc., in Chicago is a widely respected mutual fund and stock research company. The company has developed a comprehensive strategy for categorizing stocks that includes 97 percent of the U.S. equity market. The system is called the Morningstar Style Box. The nine-box grid divides stocks into three distinct size factors and three valuation factors. See Figure 6-1 for

FIGURE 6-1

Morningstar Style Box Methodology with Micro-Cap Added

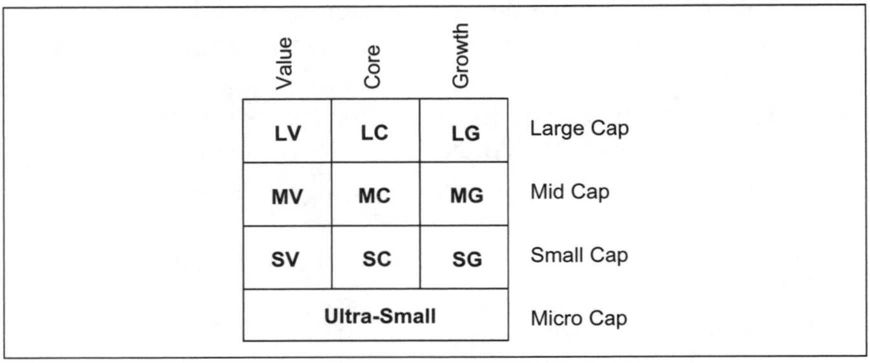

an illustration of the style box methodology. For a complete description of Morningstar's methodology, refer to the *Rulebook* at http://indexes.Morningstar.com.

One limitation of Morningstar Style Box methodology is that it covers only about 2,000 of the largest stocks, thus overlooking more than 3,000 very small "micro-cap" issues that trade on U.S. exchanges. Accordingly, Figure 6-1 adds an extra micro-cap stock portion to the bottom of the Morningstar box to increase the coverage to 99 percent of the U.S. equity market.

THE MORNINGSTAR SIZE CLASSIFICATION SYSTEM

The Morningstar size classification system categorizes companies according to their "free float" market value. The free float market value is defined as a company's total outstanding market value less private block ownership. In other words, the free float market value of Microsoft stock does not include the value of the shares owned by Bill Gates. Free float is a common method of index construction that is widely becoming the standard for index providers.

The three Morningstar size classifications plus an extra micro-cap size cover 99 percent of the stock on the U.S. market. The four categories are:

- Large cap = largest 70 percent of investable market cap
- Mid cap = next 20 percent of investable market cap (70th to 90th percentile)
- Small cap = next 7 percent of investable market cap (90th to 97th percentile)
- Micro cap = remaining 2 percent of investable market cap (97th to 99th percentile)

As a reminder, the micro-cap portion is not a Morningstar style. I took the liberty of adding the box to show where that size category would fit if it were included in the Morningstar classification system. The micro-cap box completes the classification system so that it includes all stocks listed on the NYSE, AMEX, and Nasdaq. The only stocks not included are bulletin board stocks.

THE MORNINGSTAR STYLE CLASSIFICATION SYSTEM

All index providers classify companies by style as well as size. Different index providers determine value and growth using different methodologies. Some providers divide their indexes between growth and value. Morningstar divides theirs into three categories depending on fundamental characteristics. These categories are value, core, and growth. Morningstar categorizes companies using a "multifactor" model that consists of five variables. Table 6-3 highlights those five factors. The most influential factors

TABLE 6-3

Variables and Weights Used by Morningstar in Style Analysis

Value Factors	Growth Factors
• Price/projected earnings (50.0%)	• Long-term projected earnings growth (50.0%)
• Price/book (12.5%)	• Historical earnings growth (12.5%)
• Price/sales (12.5%)	• Sales growth (12.5%)
• Price/cash flow (12.5%)	• Cash flow growth (12.5%)
• Dividend yield (12.5%)	• Book value growth (12.5%)

in the equation are the stock's price compared to its past earnings and price compared to projected earnings.

Morningstar first calculates a company's value score, then its growth score, and finally its overall style score by subtracting the value score from the growth score. If the result is strongly positive, the company is classified as "growth." If the result is strongly negative, the company is classified as "value." If the value score minus the growth score is not sufficiently different from 0, the stock is classified as "core."

Breakpoints for value, growth, and core are set so that over a three-year rolling period, each style represents one-third of the investable universe within each capitalization class. That keeps a nearly equal number of stocks in each style box. Morningstar reconstitutes each index twice annually (adding or removing stocks). It also rebalances the indexes quarterly (adjusting constituent weights).

Based on this methodology, the Wilshire 5000 Composite Index falls roughly into the boxes illustrated in Figure 6-2. Each box contains the number of stocks in that particular box and the percentage of the index represented by the box.

FIGURE 6-2

Average Number of Stocks in the Morningstar Style Boxes

Value 626–33%	Core 685–34%	Growth 659–33%	
81 23%	76 24%	68 23%	Large Cap 225–70%
203 6%	230 7%	239 6%	Mid Cap 672–20%
342 2%	379 3%	352 2%	Small Cap 1073–7%
3080–3%			Micro–3%

Source: Morningstar.

The large-cap row holds 225 stocks, which is only 5 percent of the stocks in the Wilshire 5000 Composite Index. Yet those 225 stocks represent 70 percent of the free float market value of the entire listed U.S. stock market. The remaining 4,825 stocks make up the remainder of the stock market. It is interesting to note that it takes more than 3,000 micro-cap stocks to make up 3 percent of the listed market.

PERFORMANCE BY SIZE

The weighted-average market value of the stocks in an index has a profound effect on that index's long-term performance. In the late 1970s, two academic researchers, Rolf Banz and Marc Reinganum, independently found that micro-cap stocks had a long-term return close to 5 percent per year higher than large-cap stocks.[1] That fact was not a great revelation, since smaller stocks had much higher volatility than large stocks and were expected to return more. However, using new financial models of risk and return developed by William Sharpe, researchers Banz and Reinganum found that micro-cap stocks had higher-than-expected returns even after accounting for the extra volatility. Something else was going on in the micro-cap marketplace that was not being picked up by the return volatility numbers.

It was also interesting to Banz and Reinganum that sometimes the prices of micro-cap stocks moved in the opposite direction from large-cap stocks. That meant that the return on micro-cap stocks did not always correlate with the returns on the rest of the market. As a result, there may be a diversification benefit to owning micro-cap stocks in greater weight than the 3 percent position inherent in a total stock market index fund.

Table 6-3 offers excellent insight into the difference in return between the broad market and micro-cap stocks. The Russell 3000 Index is composed of the largest 3,000 stocks traded in the United States. The micro-cap index in Table 6-4 is derived by the Center for Research in Security Prices (CRSP). The CRSP Stock File Indices contain historical market summary data on all stocks traded on the NYSE, AMEX, and Nasdaq back to 1926.

Notice the large differences in return between the CRSP Micro Cap Index and the Russell 3000 during 1998, 2001, and 2003.

TABLE 6-4

Comparing Micro-Cap Stocks to the Broad Market

	Russell 3000 Index	CRSP Micro Cap Index	CRSP Micro Cap Return minus the Russell 3000
1995	36.8	33.3	−3.5
1996	21.8	19.1	−2.7
1997	31.8	24.1	−7.7
1998	24.1	−7.9	−32.0
1999	20.9	32.2	11.3
2000	−7.5	−13.4	−5.9
2001	−11.5	34.2	45.7
2002	−21.6	−14.1	7.5
2003	31.6	78.4	46.8
2004	12.5	16.8	4.3

Those differences are surprising considering that both indexes hold thousands of publicly traded U.S. companies. Generally, academics believe that in a broadly diversified portfolio, individual company risk is diversified away, leaving only market risk. Therefore, a random portfolio of 3,000 stocks diversified across several industries is expected to return very close to the same performance as another portfolio of 3,000 stocks diversified in the same manner. Clearly, that is not the case when one portfolio is made up of only micro-cap stocks. Micro-cap indexes have a unique risk factor above and beyond indexes of larger stocks than cannot be diversified away by adding more micro-cap stocks.

Figure 6-3 reflects the 36-month rolling correlation between the CRSP Total U.S. Market return, CRSP mid-cap stocks, and CRSP micro-cap stocks. The CRSP Total U.S. Market returns are almost exactly the same as those for the Dow Jones Wilshire 5000 Index, only the data go back further. The CRSP Mid-Cap Index is highly correlated with the broad market. Consequently, a separate portfolio of mid-cap stocks has not been a good diversifier for investors who own a total stock market index fund. Micro caps are a different story. At times there is high positive correlation between

FIGURE 6-3

CRSP Total Market Index Correlations with the Micro-Cap
Index and Mid-Cap Index
36-Month Rolling Correlations

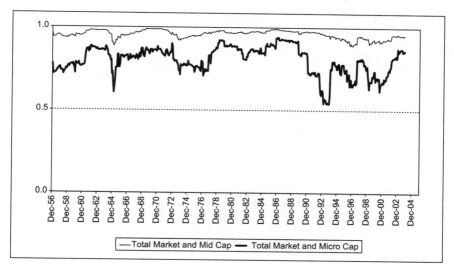

micro caps and the total stock market, and at other times the correlation is lower. The varying correlation signals diversification potential.

A portfolio that has an overweighting in micro-cap stocks acts differently from a total stock market portfolio. Figure 6-4 illustrates the theoretical diversification benefit that was achieved by adding 10 percent increments of CRSP micro-cap stocks to a total stock market index fund.

Had it been possible, over the 30-year period from 1975 to 2004, a portfolio of 80 percent in a total stock market index fund and 20 percent in a micro-cap index fund would have increased U.S. returns by 1.1 percent with a small increase in risk. However, the returns in Figure 6-4 are theoretical because there were no total market index funds or micro-cap index funds in 1975. That is not the case today. You can now purchase a low-cost no-load total stock market index fund and a micro-cap index fund.

FIGURE 6-4

Return Characteristics of Adding Micro-Cap Stocks to a
Total Market Fund, 1975–2004

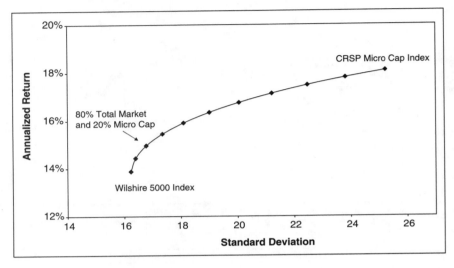

The more than 3,000 micro-cap stocks that trade actively on U.S. exchanges count for only 3 percent of the value of the entire listed market. Accordingly, the performance of micro-cap stocks does not have a large impact on the performance of the broad market. Overweighting micro-cap stocks in a portfolio as a separate U.S. stock category has had diversification benefits in the past and may add diversification benefits in the future.

FINDING A MICRO CAP FUND IS DIFFICULT

Now the bad news: It is very difficult to find a low-cost broadly diversified micro-cap fund that is still open to the public. Most micro-cap index funds are closed to new investors or are available only through a paid investment advisor. Sometimes a closed fund will reopen to the public for a short period of time. When that occurs, you have to be ready to invest. That means monitoring certain funds for potential opening dates.

There are micro-cap funds that are open to all investors all the time, but be careful in your selection. Some of these funds have a high sales commission, others have exorbitant management fees, and still others invest only a portion in micro-cap stocks and the rest in small- and mid-cap stocks.

If a brand new fund is open, make sure the average market weight of the companies in the fund is less than $300 million and that it will be widely diversified, with at least 500 companies. Also ensure that the total expense is below 1 percent and that there is no commission to buy or sell shares.

U.S. EQUITY PERFORMANCE BY STYLE

The practice of categorizing stocks into style categories is as old as stock trading itself. Years ago, investors mainly used dividend yield to categorize growth and value stocks. Stocks paying high dividends were considered value plays, while stocks paying low dividends were growth plays. As more financial information became available, in part as a result of mandatory SEC reporting, investors became more sophisticated. Researchers created and compared ratios such as price/earnings ratios (P/E ratios) and the P/E to earnings growth. In addition, a company's market price/book value became a leading dividing line. It was widely believed that earnings and book value ratios gave clues to finding profitable investment opportunities. Stocks with low price/earnings and price/book ratios were considered better values than stocks with high ratios. In 1934, Benjamin Graham and David Dodd wrote guidelines that quantified these ratios in their timeless investment book *Security Analysis*. The book is still one of the most widely distributed investment classics of all time.[2]

Not much has changed since Benjamin Graham and David Dodd wrote the book on fundamental investing over 70 years ago. Today, investors still analyze the same fundamental factors and price ratios, and they still look for value using earnings and book value. Granted, there have been some changes in the way people analyze the data and the amount of information available to the public. However, the speed and accuracy of computers has made the analysis hundreds of times faster, even after an increase in the amount of data.

As security valuation progressed over the years, analysts and academic researchers began to agree on standard labels for categories of stocks based on fundamental ratios. Companies that had a high market price relative to their fundamentals were labeled "growth" companies, and those that had a low market price relative to their fundamentals were labeled "value" companies. Some companies such as Morningstar use a third category called "core" or "style neutral" to describe those stocks whose valuations fell in the middle range between growth and value.

As style categorization became popular and computers made number-crunching faster, it was natural for researchers to go back in history and reconstruct indexes based on style methodology. In the 1970s, researchers were able to compare historic style returns going back to the early 1900s with a high degree of accuracy. What those historic data showed was that value stocks outperformed growth stocks by several percent over the long term, and outperformed during most independent 10-year periods of time.

In addition, researchers have found that the value premium exists in foreign markets as well, suggesting that the same factors that drive U.S. value stock returns drive value stock returns in all countries everywhere. That observation begged the question, "Will the opportunities for returns be higher in global value stocks than in global growth stocks in the future?"

Growth advocates pounced on the relevance of the value premium. Some people called the value effect an anomaly that was not likely to occur in the future. Others questioned the accuracy of the studies. Still other said that the data were accurate in theory, but that when they were applied to real portfolios, trading costs and liquidity constraints eroded away any value premium in the marketplace.

However, in June 1992, Eugene Fama and Ken French fired another volley in defense of the value effect when they published the most comprehensive paper on the subject in the *Journal of Financial Economics*. The paper was entitled, "The Cross-Section of Expected Stock Returns."[3]

Fama and French (FF) put forth the notion that the performance of a broadly diversified U.S. stock portfolio relied on three primary risk axes to determine its return. Those three risk factors were the basic risk of the market itself (market risk or beta), the percentage of small-cap stocks in the portfolio by market weight (size), and the percentage of value orientation by market weight (the latter defined by price/book ratio—BtM).

When FF measured how much exposure a widely diversified portfolio had to the three risk factors of beta, size, and BtM, they could determine with 95 percent accuracy how that portfolio performed in relation to the stock market *without knowing the actual return of the portfolio*. That meant that 95 percent of a portfolio's return is the result of the amount of risk taken in the three factors, and very little of a portfolio's return is the result of stock selection within the portfolio. The results were a blow to active portfolio managers, who until this time had the public believing that it was their stock-picking prowess that had generated most of the portfolio's investment return.

Here is an abbreviated explanation of the three FF factors that explain 95 percent of the return of a diversified U.S. stock portfolio:

1. *Market risk factor.* Commonly referred to as beta (β). All diversified stock portfolios move up or down to some extent with the overall total stock market. Beta is a measurement of the movement of a particular portfolio that is a result of movement in the broad market. On average, about 70 percent of the return of a broadly diversified portfolio is explained by β, making that factor the most influential in explaining portfolio returns.

2. *Size risk factor.* FF confirmed earlier studies' findings that small stocks have higher returns than the broad market and do not always move in correlation with the broad market. The size factor cannot be diversified away by adding more small stocks; therefore, it is its own unique risk factor. The greater the percentage of small stocks by market weight in a portfolio, the greater the size factor effects on a portfolio.

3. *Value risk factor.* FF quantified earlier studies showing that value stocks have had higher returns than the broad market, and that value stocks do not always correlate with growth stocks. Like the size risk, the value factor cannot be diversified away by adding more value stocks; hence, value has its own unique risk factor.

Based on these findings, FF proceeded to create a set of indexes that measure size and style factors. Their indexes are available as a free download on Kenneth French's Web site at Dartmouth College.[4]

THE VALUE FACTOR CONTINUED

Tables 6-5 through 6-7 are comparisons of style returns using two separate index providers. FF provides the first set of returns, and Frank Russell and Company provides the second. The FF indexes go back to 1926, whereas the Russell indexes originate in 1979. The comparison given here uses 25 years of data from the inception of the Russell indexes.

Before discussing the results of the study, an explanation of the methodology is needed. There are large differences in stock selection methods in the FF value indexes and the Russell value indexes.

First, Fama and French use only one fundamental ratio to separate growth from value. Specifically, FF use book-to-market as a proxy. Russell uses a multifactor model to separate growth and value. Second, the FF style indexes are mutually exclusive; meaning that if a stock is in one style, it is not in the other. Russell uses a graduated scale to make the transition from growth to value. If a stock in the Russell index has both value and growth characteristics, its market value could be divided into both segments. For example, a stock could have 60 percent of its market value attributed to growth and 40 percent to value. Third, FF neutral indexes are mutually exclusive from their value and growth indexes, whereas the Russell indexes do not have a neutral or core category.

TABLE 6-5

Comparing Large-Cap Funds, 1979–2004

	FF Large Growth	FF Large Neutral	FF Large Value	Russell 1000 Growth	Russell 1000	Russell 1000 Value
Annualized return	13.0	14.2	14.3	12.3	13.6	14.6
Standard deviation	16.8	15.7	15.5	18.1	15.4	14.3

TABLE 6-6

Comparing Small-Cap Funds, 1979–2004

	FF Small Growth	FF Small Neutral	FF Small Value	Russell 2000 Growth	Russell 2000	Russell 2000 Value
Annualized return	11.0	17.5	19.3	10.5	13.5	16.1
Standard deviation	24.4	17.4	18.7	23.8	19.6	16.5

Table 6-5 compares the difference in risk and returns between large growth stocks, large value stocks, and large core holdings of both the FF large-cap indexes and the Russell large-cap indexes.

Although there are large differences in the style methodology of the two index providers, over the past 25 years the results are similar using both the FF large-cap style indexes and the Russell 1000 large-cap style indexes. Using both methodologies, the performance of large-cap value stocks was higher than the performance of growth stocks, and the risk as measured by standard deviation was less for value stocks than it was for growth stocks.

Table 6-6 is a similar comparison of the FF small-cap style indexes and Russell 2000 small-cap style indexes. The data reveal a wide difference in return between small-cap value and small-cap growth returns.

The excess return of small-cap value stocks over small-cap growth was greater than 5 percent annually for the 25-year period. That was more than twice the excess return of large-cap value stocks over large-cap growth stocks. In addition, the risk of small-cap value stocks as measured by their standard deviation was considerably less than that of small-cap growth stocks. The implication of the data is that the value premium is much stronger in the small-cap sector of the market than in the large-cap sector. That point will be important later in the chapter.

Table 6-7 compares the value premium across the broad market. The FF composite indexes are composed of 85 percent large-company stocks and 15 percent small-company stocks. That is roughly the market weighing. The Russell 3000 is an actual index of the 3,000 largest U.S. stocks, adjusted for free float.

TABLE 6-7

Comparing Total Market Funds, 1979–2004

	FF Composite Growth	FF Composite Neutral	FF Composite Value	Russell 3000 Growth	Russell 3000	Russell 3000 Value
Annualized return	12.8	14.7	15.1	12.1	13.6	14.7
Standard deviation	17.5	15.5	15.6	18.3	15.5	14.3

As you might have expected, the broad value stock indexes outperformed broad growth stock indexes while exhibiting less volatility of return. Figure 6-5 provides a visual presentation of the difference in return between the Russell 3000 Index and the Russell 3000 Value Index from 1998 to 2004.

FIGURE 6-5

Annual Difference in Return between the Russell 3000 Index and the Russell 3000 Value Index

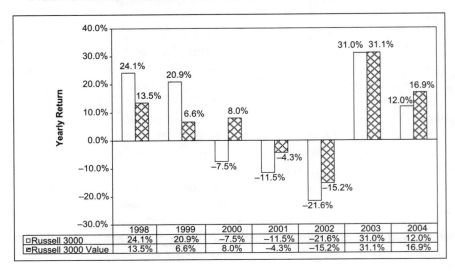

	1998	1999	2000	2001	2002	2003	2004
Russell 3000	24.1%	20.9%	−7.5%	−11.5%	−21.6%	31.0%	12.0%
Russell 3000 Value	13.5%	6.6%	8.0%	−4.3%	−15.2%	31.1%	16.9%

FIGURE 6-6

Total Market Index and Fama/French Value Composite
36-Month Rolling Correlations

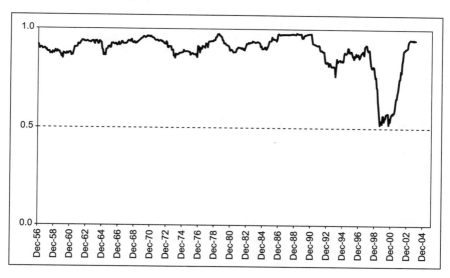

Figure 6-6 illustrates the rolling 36-month correlation between the Dow Jones Wilshire 5000 Composite and the FF Value Composite described earlier. Notice the sharp decrease in correlation between value stocks and the composite index during the late 1990s. That event resulted from the rapid run-up in the valuation of large-cap growth stocks, especially technology stocks, which tended to dominate the Wilshire 5000 Index at the time.

Figure 6-7 is an interesting 30-year risk-and-return chart that combines a broad market index and a value index. At the bottom left of the chart is the Wilshire 5000 Composite Index, and at the top right is the risk and return of a Fama/French value index composite using 85 percent of the FF Large Value Index and 15 percent of the FF Small Value Index. Starting with the Wilshire 5000, each subsequent point on the chart adds a 10 percent position in the FF value composite. The hypothetical portfolios were rebalanced annually.

The point on Figure 6-7 representing a hypothetical portfolio of 60 percent in the Wilshire 5000 and 40 percent in the FF value

FIGURE 6-7

Return Characteristics of Adding Value Stocks to a Total Market Fund, 1975–2004

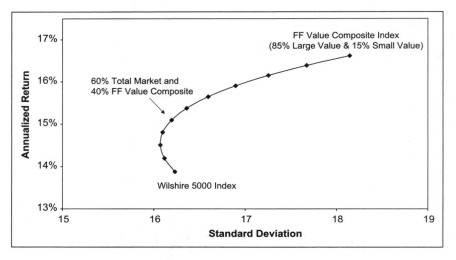

index composite is an important place on the chart. It represents a portfolio that produced a 1.2 percent greater return than a portfolio invested 100 percent in the Wilshire 5000 Composite Index without an increase in volatility. Based on this knowledge, an extra amount of value stocks added to a total stock market portfolio is worth consideration.

SMALL-CAP VALUE DIVERSIFIES A TOTAL MARKET FUND

We have observed that small stocks exhibit higher expected rates of return than larger stocks, albeit with a higher standard deviation of returns, and we have observed that value stocks have exhibited higher rates of return than growth stocks, although the extra risk of owning value stocks must be something other than higher standard deviation.

There have been many explanations for the value effect in the market, but no one has pinpointed exactly why the phenomenon exists all over the world. Perhaps it is a poor earnings outlook for

TABLE 6-8

The Difference in Return between the Total Market and Small Value Stocks

	Wilshire 5000 Index	FF Small Value	FF Small Value Minus the Wilshire 5000
1995	36.5	27.7	−8.8
1996	21.2	20.7	−0.5
1997	31.3	37.3	6.0
1998	23.4	−8.6	−32.1
1999	23.6	5.6	−18.0
2000	−10.9	−0.8	10.1
2001	−11.0	40.2	51.2
2002	−20.9	−12.4	8.5
2003	31.6	74.7	43.1
2004	12.5	26.6	14.1

value companies. Perhaps it is overly pessimistic scenarios by Wall Street analysts. Perhaps no one cares about these unglamorous companies. Whatever the reason, according to Eugene Fama and Ken French, it is assumed that value stocks have additional fundamental or economic risk someplace that is not picked up by the standard deviation of value index returns. That is the reason those stocks have higher returns.

Armed with this information on size and style factors, we turn our attention to a small segment of the stock market that has both a size premium and a value premium. The category of small-cap value represents approximately 3 percent of the capitalization of the broad U.S. market. As expected, with both size and style factors affecting the return of this category, the year-over-year performance of small-cap value stocks deviates substantially from the performance of the total stock market. Table 6-8 documents the return data.

The FF Small Value Index represents only about 3 percent of the Wilshire 5000 Index. With such a small overlap, small value stocks can have large differences in return from the total market. Figure 6-8 illustrates the historic rolling 36-month correlation between small value stocks and the broad market. The inconsistency

FIGURE 6-8

CRSP Total Market Index and Fama/French
Small-Cap Value Index
36-Month Rolling Correlations

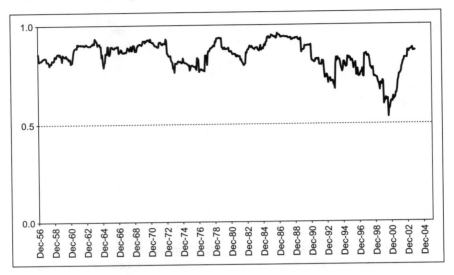

of correlation between the broad market and small value stocks creates potential for the creation of a more efficient U.S. stock portfolio.

An interesting point on Figure 6-8 is the downward spike
in correlation that occurred during the late 1990s. During that
period, small-cap value stocks performed poorly in relation to the
predominantly large-cap growth-oriented Wilshire 5000. The trend
reversed between 2001 and 2002, when small value stocks cata-
pulted over 100 percent and the Wilshire 5000 fell sharply.

Investors who followed a broadly diversified asset allocation
that included a total market fund and a small value index fund
would have faired very well during the 10-year period from 1995
to 2004. Unfortunately, as discussed in Chapter 5 and highlighted
in Figure 5-2, the late 1990s was a time when many investors
abandoned value stocks in favor of glamour growth stocks, only to
watch those stocks meet their demise.

FIGURE 6-9

Return Characteristics of Adding Small Value Stocks to a
Total Market Fund, 1975–2004

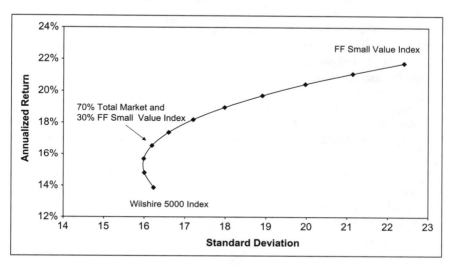

Figure 6-9 illustrates the theoretical diversification benefit that was achieved by adding 10 percent increments of the FF Small Value Index to the Dow Jones Wilshire 5000 Composite Index. The point on Figure 6-9 that is most interesting is a portfolio representing 70 percent in the broad market and 30 percent in the small value index. Over a 25-year period, a mix of 70 percent in the total market and 30 percent in the small value index would have increased U.S. equity returns by 2.7 percent with no increase in portfolio volatility.

The returns in Figure 6-9 are theoretical because there were no total market mutual funds or small-cap value index funds available in 1975. Thus, no investor held a portfolio of 70 percent in a broad market index and 30 percent in a small value index. That is not the case today. You can now purchase a wide assortment of total stock market index funds along with several competing low-cost small-cap value index funds. A few choice funds are listed at the end of this chapter.

T A B L E   6-9

Low-Cost U.S. Equity Funds

	Symbol	Benchmark
Total Stock Market Funds		
Vanguard Total U.S. Market Index	VTSMX	MSCI U.S. Broad Market Index
Schwab Total Stock Market	SWTIX	Dow Jones Wilshire 5000 Index
iShares S&P 1500 Index ETF	IVV	S&P 1500 Index
TIAA-CREF Equity Index Fund	TCEIX	Russell 3000 Index
iShares Russell 3000 Index ETF	IWV	Russell 3000 Index
iShares DJ US Total Market	IYY	Dow Jones U.S. Total Market Index
Small Value Funds		
Vanguard Small Value Index	VISVX	MSCI U.S. Small Cap Value Index
iShares S&P 600/BARRA Value	IJS	S&P 600/BARRA Value Index
iShares Morningstar Small Value	JKL	Morningstar Small Value Index
DFA Small Value Fund*	DFSVX	DFA Small Value Index
Micro Cap Funds		
Bridgeway Ultra Small Co. Mkt.	BRSIX	CRSP Decile 10 (smallest stocks)
DFA Micro Cap Fund*	DFSCX	CRSP Deciles 9 + 10 (small stocks)

*DFA funds are available through select investment advisors.

U.S. EQUITY INVESTMENT LIST

Table 6-9 gives a partial list of low-cost U.S. equity funds that are possible candidates for placing on your investment list. For more information on these and other low-cost no-load funds, go to the Web site of the fund provider. A list is given in Appendix A. In addition, read *All About Index Funds*, by Richard A. Ferri (McGraw-Hill, 2002).

CHAPTER SUMMARY

The cornerstone of any equity portfolio is a broadly diversified U.S. stock market index fund. There are several different total U.S. stock market indexes and index fund providers. The most complete U.S. stock market index is the Dow Jones Wilshire 5000 Composite Index. Other broad market indexes include the MSCI U.S. Broad

Market Index, Russell 3000, Dow Jones Total Market Index, Morningstar Total Market, and Standard & Poor's 1500. All of these indexes have low-cost index funds available.

Micro-cap stocks represent only 3 percent of the total U.S. stock market and can add diversification to a broad market index fund. The problem with micro-cap stocks is finding a fund to get into. Most funds are closed to new investors, and the ones that are still open either tend to be expensive or do not stick to a pure micro-cap strategy.

If you are going to add only one additional U.S. common stock mutual fund to a core position in a U.S. total stock market fund, I recommend placing about 30 percent in a small-cap value index fund. A small-cap value fund is a one-fund-fits-all method to add size and style premium exposure. There are many small-cap value indexes available to choose from. You will want to study the differences in those indexes before choosing one.

NOTES

[1]Rolf W. Banz, "The Relationship between Return and Market Value in Common Stocks," *Journal of Financial Economics*, vol. 9, 1981, pp. 3–18; Marc R. Reinganum, "Misspecification of Capital Asset Pricing: Empirical Anomalies Based on Earnings Yield and Market Values," *Journal of Financial Economics*, vol. 9, 1981, pp. 19–46.

[2]Benjamin F. Graham and David L. Dodd, *Security Analysis*, 4th revised ed., New York: McGraw-Hill, 1972 (originally published in 1934).

[3]Eugene F. Fama and Kenneth R. French, "The Cross-Section of Expected Stock Returns," *Journal of Financial Economics*, June 1992. The authors followed with a second paper, "Common Risk Factors in the Return of Stocks and Bonds," *Journal of Financial Economics*, February 1993, vol. 33, No. 1, pp. 3–57.

[4]Kenneth French Web site: http://mba.tuck.dartmouth.edu/pages/faculty/ken.french/index.html.

International Equity Investments

KEY CONCEPTS

- International equity increases portfolio diversification.
- Developed markets include advanced countries.
- Emerging markets expand a portfolio to new geographic areas.
- International equities exhibit size and style premiums.

The world is a very big place, and opportunities abound. There are many stock and bond markets around the globe offering U.S. investors substantial diversification benefits. Some opportunities can be found in developed markets, such as those in Japan, Australia, Germany, and the United Kingdom. Other opportunities are found in the emerging markets of less-developed countries, such as China, India, Turkey, and Eastern Europe. A well-diversified portfolio includes all regions of the world.

While investing internationally offers diversification benefits, it is not without added risk. Foreign stock prices tend to be more volatile than U.S. stock prices. The extra volatility is a product of many variables, including (1) foreign currency risk caused by a strengthening of the U.S. dollar, (2) political risk caused by government actions or inaction, (3) trading and custody risk caused by exchange restrictions on nondomestic investors, (4) regulatory risk caused by a lack of oversight and a weak judicial system, and (5) information risk caused by a lack of disclosure by foreign companies.

Because of all the extra risks involved, diversification is the key to international equity investing. No one knows which country will outperform the global markets in the near term, or whether the U.S. dollar will strengthen or weaken. Accordingly, investors would be wise to consider owning a small slice of every country and rebalancing their global exposures annually.

CURRENCY RISK

Currency fluctuations play an important role in the return on international investments. When U.S. investors buy foreign stocks and stock funds, they are also converting dollars into a foreign currency. Changes in the value of that currency relative to the dollar will affect the total loss or gain on the investment. Figure 7-1 illustrates the value of the U.S. dollar in relation to other major world currencies.

FIGURE 7-1

U.S. Dollar versus Other Major Currencies

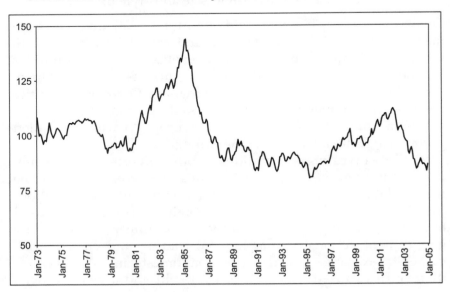

Assume that U.S. stocks and a composite index of international stocks have the same return in their native currency. If the value of the dollar rose during this period, then U.S. investors profited more from U.S. stocks than from international stocks. The opposite is true when the dollar falls in value. As it turned out, for the period 1995 to 2001, the dollar was strong against other major currencies and the U.S. stock market outperformed international stocks. When the dollar weakened between 2001 and 2004, U.S. stocks did not keep pace with the rest of the global marketplace.

GLOBAL MARKETS AND INTERNATIONAL INVESTING

International stocks are also called foreign stocks and overseas stocks. These companies have their corporate headquarters located outside the United States, and their primary accounting currency is the currency native to the country of their corporate headquarters. The media frequently refer to large companies with a worldwide presence as global or multinational firms. However, technically there is no such thing. For accounting purposes, a company is domiciled in only one country and reports in only one native currency.

All foreign companies list their shares on a local stock exchange. In addition, many larger companies list their shares on exchanges outside their native land to gain global exposure. When foreign companies list shares on a U.S. stock exchange, they do it through American Depositary Receipts (ADRs). ADRs represent shares of foreign stock held on deposit in a U.S. bank. The bank converts the shares into U.S. dollar-denominated ADRs, which trade alongside U.S. securities on the NYSE, AMEX, and Nasdaq. As an aside, many large U.S.-based corporations also list their shares on foreign exchanges, such as those in London and Tokyo.

Global equity mutual funds invest in both U.S. and foreign companies. Selecting a global fund is a good option if you have only a little money to invest and want to have some international exposure without having to buy a U.S. stock mutual fund and an international stock fund. However, while a global fund is convenient, you do not have control over the country or regional asset allocation within the fund. Depending on how the fund is being managed, an active global fund manager will decide which countries and regions he or she wants to bet on and which ones he or she does not. In the case of a global index fund, the amount owned in each country is based on the value of that country in relation to all others in the index. The country and regional mix can change substantially over the years, as we will see later in this chapter.

Building your own international stock allocation is a better method than using one all-encompassing international fund. There are greater diversification benefits achieved through using do-it-yourself asset allocation, although it does require more work. Holding different regional funds in a portfolio and rebalancing annually helps you control the amount of risk exposure to any particular region or currency.

CATEGORIZING GLOBAL MARKETS

Economists have traditionally divided the world into two distinct categories: developed markets and emerging markets. The difference between the two categories is based on both the size of the economy per capita and the level of development in the public stock and bond markets.

Developed markets are countries whose economy has advanced to the point where the per capita gross domestic product (GDP) exceeds $10,000 per year and that have deep and mature securities markets. Examples of developed markets include Australia, Germany, Japan, and the United Kingdom. Developed markets can be grouped into three regions: North America, Europe, and the Pacific Rim. North America includes U.S. and Canadian companies. Europe includes the United Kingdom and continental Europe. The Pacific Rim covers several major markets, including Japan, Australia, and Hong Kong.

Emerging markets are countries that do not meet the GDP requirement and have less-developed financial markets. They can be divided into early-stage and late-stage depending on the country's progress toward a free-market economy. Examples of early-stage emerging markets include Russia, Turkey, Poland, Indonesia, and China. Late-stage emerging markets are further along in their development of free markets and include Mexico,

Taiwan, South Africa, and South Korea. As a matter of interest, most emerging market mutual funds concentrate their holdings on late-stage emerging markets because those countries have the largest percentage of market capitalization.

Figure 7-2 illustrates the value of world markets based on their percentage of global market value. The chart is divided among four regions: North American developed markets, the Pacific Rim developed markets, European developed markets, and emerging markets.

Countries that are not categorized as either developed markets or emerging markets are generally not open to foreign investment. Examples of those countries include Saudi Arabia, Bahrain, and most African nations.

FIGURE 7-2

Global Equity Markets by Percent of Value

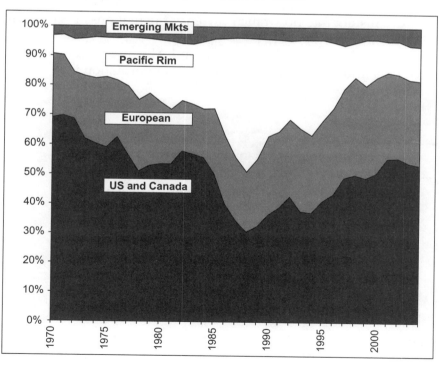

DEVELOPED-MARKET INDEXES

The most widely followed international index of developed-market countries is the Morgan Stanley Capital International Europe, Australasia, and the Far East Index, better known as the MSCI EAFE. The EAFE Index is composed of approximately 1,000 large-company stocks from 21 developed markets located in Europe and the Pacific Rim. The index is broadly diversified. It is designed to include at least 85 percent of the market value of each industry group within those 21 countries.

The best way to think of the EAFE Index is as a big international S&P 500 that covers all developed countries except the United States and Canada. The EAFE Index is a float-adjusted index and includes only tradable securities. Closely held blocks of stock and industry cross-holdings are not counted. Morgan Stanley does not attempt to control sector weights, country weights, or regional weights in the EAFE Index.

MSCI reports the EAFE Index performance in two ways; one is in local currency, and the other is in U.S. dollars. Table 7-1 provides insight into how much currency fluctuations affect return on a year-over-year basis.

MSCI has published the returns on EAFE and its components since 1970. Index methodology and return information is available for free on www.MSCI.com.

TABLE 7-1

Currency Effects on U.S. Investors in the EAFE Index

	EAFE Return in Local Currency	EAFE Return in U.S. Dollars	Effect on U.S. Investors
1997	13.5%	1.8%	−11.7%
1998	12.3%	20.0%	7.7%
1999	33.5%	26.9%	−6.6%
2000	−7.3%	−14.2%	−6.8%
2001	−16.3%	−21.5%	−5.2%
2002	−26.1%	−15.9%	10.1%
2003	20.3%	38.6%	18.3%
2004	12.7%	20.2%	7.5%

TABLE 7-2

Comparing Risk and Return from 1970 to 2004

	MSCI EAFE Net of Dividends ($)	Total U.S. Stock Market
Annualized return	10.4%	11.2%
Standard deviation	16.7%	16.0%

Table 7-2 compares the return on the EAFE Index net of dividends to the return on the total U.S. stock market. Net of dividends includes an adjustment for a foreign withholding tax that some countries place on dividends paid to outside investors.

The EAFE Index underperformed U.S. stocks between 1970 and 2004. Currency differences were near neutral over the complete 35-year period; therefore, they had little to do with the difference. In my view, the return on the EAFE Index was very good. The problem is, the return on the U.S. stock market was great. No one knows which region of the world will outperform in the future. As a result, it is better to have all regions in your portfolio at all times.

Some investors question the continued viability of holding international stocks because of the increase in correlation with U.S. stocks. Figure 7-3 illustrates that since 1998, the correlation of the EAFE Index and the U.S. total market has increased from about +0.5 to about +0.9.

We know that correlations can change abruptly. Therefore, the correlation between the EAFE Index and U.S. markets may change again in the future. As a result, an international equity allocation is still recommended by most financial advisors.

DECOMPOSING THE EAFE INDEX

To gain a better understanding of international investing, it helps to drill down to the performance and correlations of the underlying regions that make up the EAFE Index. The EAFE can be broken down into two separate geographical indexes, the MSCI Europe Index and the MSCI Pacific Rim Index. The MSCI Europe Index is

FIGURE 7-3

MSCI EAFE in U.S. Dollars and Total U.S. Market
Rolling 36-Month Correlation

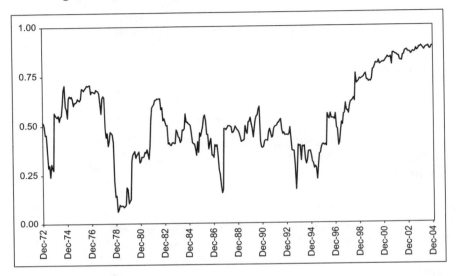

further divided into companies headquartered in the United
Kingdom (~35 percent) and MSCI Europe excluding the United
Kingdom (~65 percent). The Pacific Rim is divided into companies
headquartered in Japan (~75 percent) and those headquartered in
Australia, New Zealand, Hong Kong, and Singapore (~25 percent).

Figure 7-4 gives you a visual impression of how different the
returns for different geographical regions can be. As you see, at
times the returns of all regions can be similar, such as in 2004, and
at other times they can differ widely, such as in 1999.

Figure 7-5 illustrates the trends in exchange rates and local
market valuations that have caused the weight of the EAFE to
swing between Europe and the Pacific Rim over the years. In the
early 1970s, Europe dominated the EAFE Index, with a 78 percent
market share. By 1988, as a result of a huge run-up in Japanese
stocks, the Pacific Rim dominated the EAFE Index, with 70 percent.
In the 1990s, fortunes reversed again. A bear market in Japan and a
bull market in Europe pushed Europe back over 70 percent market
share.

FIGURE 7-4

Return Differences between U.S., European, and Pacific Rim Markets

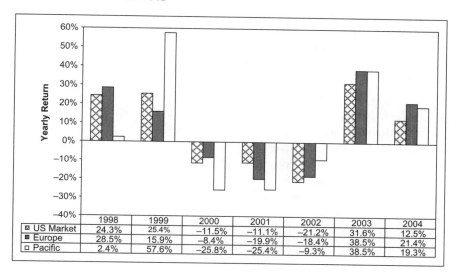

	1998	1999	2000	2001	2002	2003	2004
US Market	24.3%	25.4%	−11.5%	−11.1%	−21.2%	31.6%	12.5%
Europe	28.5%	15.9%	−8.4%	−19.9%	−18.4%	38.5%	21.4%
Pacific	2.4%	57.6%	−25.8%	−25.4%	−9.3%	38.5%	19.3%

FIGURE 7-5

Percentage of EAFE Index in European and Pacific Developed Markets

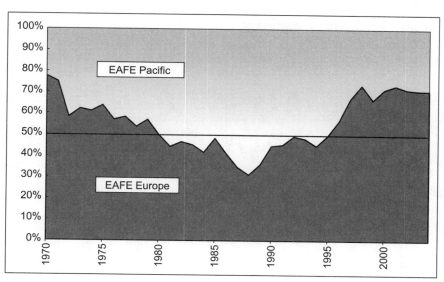

Splitting up these regions and analyzing individual correlations gives us more insight into the overall market. Figures 7-6 and 7-7 look at the rolling 36-month correlation between the U.S. equity market, the MSCI Europe Index, and the MSCI Pacific Rim Index. Recall that the correlation between the U.S. stock market and the EAFE Index has increased since 1998.

As Figure 7-6 illustrates, almost all of that increase in correlation was a result of the European markets. That increase in correlation between European stocks and U.S. stocks coincided with the introduction of the euro, a single currency that 11 European Union countries adopted in 1999. Perhaps the euro will lead to high correlations in the future; however, it is too early to draw that conclusion. There was also a brief increase in correlation between U.S. stocks and Pacific Rim stocks during the late 1990s; however, that correlation has since declined.

No one can be certain if the increase in correlation between European and U.S. equity markets is a short-term phenomenon or a long-term event. As a result, it is recommended that investors

FIGURE 7-6

EAFE European Indexes in U.S. Dollars and Total U.S. Market Rolling 36-Month Correlation

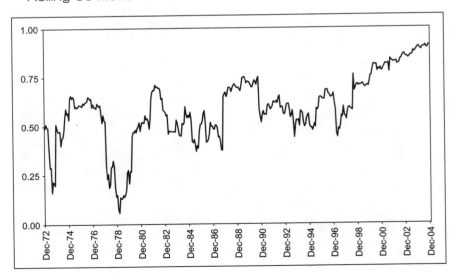

FIGURE 7-7

EAFE Pacific Indexes in U.S. Dollars and Total U.S. Market
Rolling 36-Month Correlation

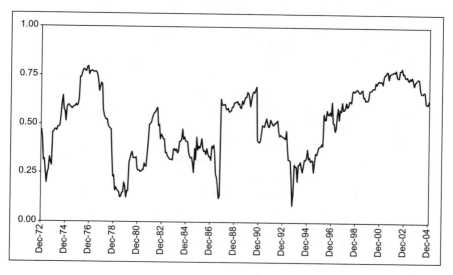

continue to invest in all regions of the world, including Europe.
Correlations between economic regions can change rapidly, and
your portfolio should be diversified accordingly.

A BETTER INTERNATIONAL ALLOCATION

Over the long term, the return on the EAFE Index should equal the
return on the U.S. market, plus or minus currency swings. We live
in a global economy. If there is an opportunity to profit from stocks
in one geographic region, then money will quickly flow across con-
tinents to bring that market up to its fair value. Since capital can
flow freely to most developed nations, there is no reason to believe
that one market or one industry within a market is going produce
higher returns for very long. For example, all developed countries
have large banks that make loans around the world. There is no
reason to believe that the banking industry in Europe or Japan is
going to outperform the banking industry in the United States for

very long. There are times when one region will outperform another, but they do not last.

Since all regions are expected to perform the same over the long term, why bother to invest internationally? You invest internationally to gain diversification benefits. However, you must remember to rebalance your portfolio annually.

Figure 7-5 clearly illustrates the flip-flop in value between the Pacific Rim and European indexes over the last 35 years. Table 7-3 shows that over the last 35 years, the EAFE Index has returned about 10.4 percent net of dividends. During the same period, a portfolio with 50 percent in the MSCI Europe Index and 50 percent in the MSCI Pacific Rim Index rebalanced annually has resulted in a 0.9 percent higher returning portfolio than the EAFE Index, and a constant portfolio of 25 percent in each of the four markets that make up the EAFE delivered 1.7 percent more than the EAFE.

The far right column in Table 7-3 takes international diversification down another level. The highest-performing combination of EAFE categories was a portfolio with 25 percent in the United Kingdom (FTSE All Shares Index), 25 percent MSCI Europe excluding U.K. stocks, 25 percent MSCI Japan, and 25 percent MSCI Pacific Rim excluding Japanese stocks. The "4 × 25" index combination gives more equal weight to multiple currencies, including the euro, Japanese yen, British pound, and a basket of Pacific Rim

TABLE 7-3

Various Mixes of MSCI Indexes, 1970–2004

	EAFE Index Net of Dividends in U.S. $	50% MSCI Europe, 50% MSCI Pacific	25% Each of United Kingdom, MSCI Europe x UK, Japan, and Pacific Rim x JPN
Annual return	10.4%	11.3%	12.1%
Standard deviation	22.3%	23.6%	22.3%
35-year high	69.4%	68.6%	66.2%
35-year low	−23.4%	−22.8%	−24.5%

Source: Morgan Stanley.

currencies including those of Australia, New Zealand, Hong Kong, and Singapore. The portfolio was rebalanced annually.

The increase in return on the two equal-weighted portfolios is due to the fact that Europe and Pacific Rim countries have a varying correlation with each other. That creates a diversification benefit. Figure 7-8 illustrates the rolling 36-month correlation between the MSCI Europe and MSCI Pacific Rim indexes.

Until recently, it was not possible to invest directly in the EAFE Index or regions of the EAFE independently. Thanks to the rapid growth of index mutual funds, it is now possible to put your money in a combination of investments that follow most of the indexes previously mentioned. As of this writing, the only exception to the 4 × 25 allocation is a MSCI Europe without U.K. index fund; however, new index funds are created every year. In the meantime, there are very close alternatives, such as a euro country index fund that tracks the performance of European countries that have adopted the euro (the United Kingdom has not done so). See the list of low-cost developed-market index funds at the end of this chapter.

FIGURE 7-8

EAFE European and Pacific Indexes in U.S. Dollars
Rolling 36-Month Correlation

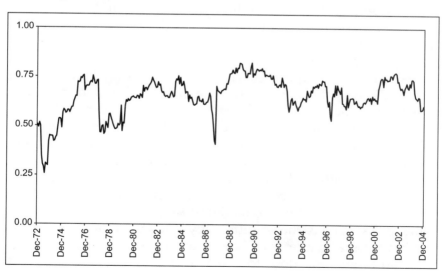

OH CANADA!

Our neighbor to the north should not be forgotten. Canadian stocks account for about 6 percent of the international equity market and about 3 percent of the global equity market. Adding a Canadian index fund to a well-diversified developed-market equity portfolio increases currency diversification. In addition, Canada's economy consists of three main industries: finance, energy (oil and gas), and basic materials (mining and lumber). An investment in a Canadian index fund increases the portfolio's allocation to natural resources, and that can act as a hedge against rising commodities prices. See the investment list at the end of this chapter for one index fund that follows the MSCI Canada Index.

EMERGING MARKETS

Broadly defined, an emerging market is a less-developed country that is improving its free-market economy and its standard of living. These countries are becoming more competitive in the global marketplace and opening their markets to more international investment. Emerging countries also have organized securities exchanges that trade stocks and bonds of large enterprises domiciled in that country. Foreigners are allowed to own those securities, either directly or indirectly through a fund.

An investable emerging market is defined by a number of factors, including gross domestic product per capita, local government regulations, perceived investment risk, foreign ownership limits, and capital controls. The MSCI Emerging Market Index covers 27 investable countries. It is a market-weighted index that uses the float-adjusted value of each company to reflect restrictions on foreign investment. Some countries have much larger stock markets than others. As a result, the MSCI Emerging Markets Index is dominated by a few countries; namely Taiwan (15 percent), South Korea (21 percent), and South Africa (20 percent) as of June 2003.

In an effort to reduce market dominance in the MSCI Emerging Market Index, the Dimensional Fund Advisors Emerging Market Index (DFA) is constructed differently. The DFA Emerging Market Index places a market-weight cap of 12.5 percent on countries to avoid large allocations to countries with large stock markets.

In addition, DFA has stricter criteria for inclusion in the index. Currently, DFA includes 16 emerging markets in its index. Yet to be included are three large markets with long-term potential: Russia, China, and India.

Table 7-4 compares the risk and return of the DFA Emerging Markets Index and the market-weighted MSCI Emerging Markets Index. During the 17-year period, the DFA fixed-weight methodology produced returns 4.2 percent higher than the market-weighted MSCI index. The return of the constrained DFA index is consistent with the previous section on the 4×25 EAFE strategy in Table 7-3. Controlled allocation to countries and regions with annual rebalancing generates a higher return without a meaningful change in risk.

Figure 7-9 illustrates the return differences between the U.S. stock index, the EAFE Index, and the MSCI Emerging Market stock index. Notice how much more volatile the emerging market index is than either the U.S. market index or the MSCI EAFE Index for developed markets. Volatility is a good trait for an investment to have, as long as the investor rebalances the portfolio annually.

The rolling 36-month correlation analysis in Figure 7-10 illustrates that since its inception in 1988, the MSCI Emerging Market Index has increased its correlation with U.S. stocks. However, it also important to remember that the correlation between markets can change very quickly.

Perhaps the increase in correlation is a short-term phenomenon, and perhaps it is permanent. It would not be surprising if the correlation between the U.S. stock market and emerging markets diverge

TABLE 7-4

Emerging Market Performance, 1988–2004

	DFA Emerging Market Index	MSCI Emerging Market Index
Annualized return	17.5%	13.2%
Standard deviation	23.3%	23.2%

Source: MSCI and Dimensional Fund Advisors.

FIGURE 7-9

Annual Return Differences between U.S. Stocks, EAFE, and
Emerging Markets

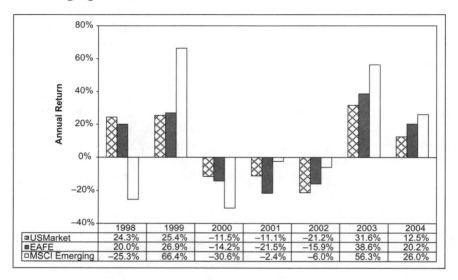

	1998	1999	2000	2001	2002	2003	2004
⊠ USMarket	24.3%	25.4%	−11.5%	−11.1%	−21.2%	31.6%	12.5%
■ EAFE	20.0%	26.9%	−14.2%	−21.5%	−15.9%	38.6%	20.2%
☐ MSCI Emerging	−25.3%	66.4%	−30.6%	−2.4%	−6.0%	56.3%	26.0%

FIGURE 7-10

Rolling 36-Month Correlation between the MSCI Emerging
Market Index and the Total U.S. Stock Market

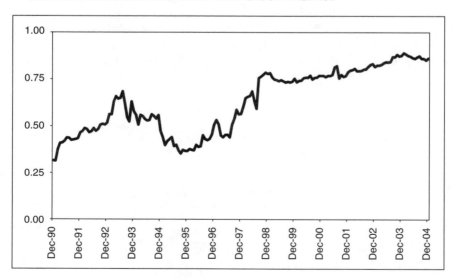

over the next decade as China, Russia, and India become more dominant. In any event, a fixed allocation to emerging market stocks is recommended for your potential investment list. A list of emerging market index funds can be found at the end of this chapter.

SIZE AND VALUE FACTORS IN INTERNATIONAL MARKETS

Chapter 6 explained three risk factors that have had a profound effect on the returns of U.S. stocks. According to researchers Gene Fama and Ken French, 95 percent of the return on a widely diversified U.S. stock portfolio can be explained by that portfolio's market risk (beta), percentage in small stocks (size risk), and percentage in high book-to-market stocks (value risk). Over the long-term, U.S. small-cap stocks have achieved a return premium over large-cap stocks, and value stocks have achieved a return premium over growth stocks.

Several independent studies have confirmed that the behavior of widely diversified international stock portfolios is consistent with the three factors found in U.S. stock portfolio returns.[1] Using MSCI and DFA data, Table 7-5 quantifies the historic premium paid to international small-cap stocks over international large-cap stocks and the premium paid to international value stocks over international growth stocks.

TABLE 7-5

International Size and Value Premiums, 1975–2004

Size Premium	DFA International Large-Company Index	DFA International Small-Company Index
Annualized return	15.0%	17.6%
Standard deviation	18.4%	17.7%
Value Premium	MSCI EAFE Net of Dividends	MSCI EAFE Value EAFEV Net of Dividends
Annualized return	12.1%	14.3%
Standard deviation	16.9%	16.8%

Between 1975 and 2004, the international markets exhibited both a size premium and a value premium. Based on the DFA indexes, the international size premium has annualized at about 2.5 percent over the period. Using MSCI EAFE indexes, a 2.2 percent premium for value stocks was evident.

The international size and value premiums have been documented in many countries during independent time periods. This leads researchers to believe that the two premiums are not an anomaly. Researchers are becoming more convinced that size and value premiums represent independent risks in the stock market that are not explained by beta, and as a result, a premium for taking size and value risk is expected in the future.

Figure 7-11 illustrates the 36-month rolling correlation between the DFA International Large Cap and DFA International Small Cap indexes. Figure 7-12 shows the 36-month rolling correlation between the MSCI EAFE and the MSCI EAFE Value indexes.

FIGURE 7-11

DFA International Large Cap Index and DFA International Small Cap Index in U.S. Dollars
Rolling 36-Month Correlation

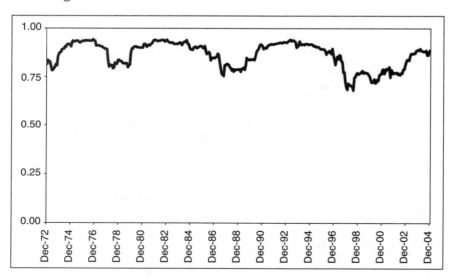

FIGURE 7-12

MSCI EAFE and EAFE Value Indexes in U.S. Dollars
Rolling 36-Month Correlation

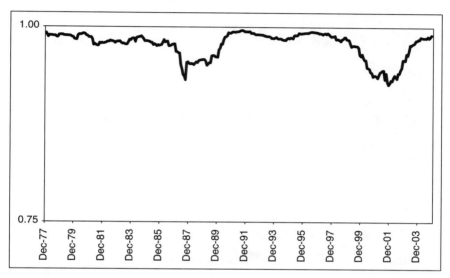

The charts provide an indication of the varying diversification benefits from small-cap and value stocks over different periods of time.

SAMPLE INTERNATIONAL ALLOCATION

Part 3 of this book includes several samples of portfolios that have international stocks in the asset allocation. Generally, the allocation to international stocks is about 30 percent of the equity portion of the portfolio. Within the allocation, a sample of international funds might be as follows:

20 percent Pacific Rim index fund

20 percent European index fund

20 percent international value fund

20 percent international small-cap fund

20 percent emerging markets index fund

This international portfolio is not a recommended portfolio—it is a sample of how a portfolio could be diversified internationally. There are many combinations of international funds that will provide adequate diversification with varying degrees of risk. Finding the one mix that is right for your unique situation is your mission. Whichever international mix you choose, maintaining that allocation through all market conditions is a key element of investment success.

INTERNATIONAL EQUITY INVESTMENT LIST

Table 7-6 gives a partial list of low-cost funds that are possible candidates for the international equity allocation. For more complete information on these and other low-cost no-load funds, read *All About Index Funds*, by Richard A. Ferri (McGraw-Hill, 2002).

CHAPTER SUMMARY

The international equity markets provide unique diversification opportunities for U.S. investors. The opportunities extend from established developed markets to emerging countries and from small-cap stocks to global giants. Unfortunately, excess return from international investing is not without risk. Foreign stocks are subject to currency risk, political risk, trading and custody risk, and regulatory risk, among others. An understanding of those risks is important during difficult market conditions.

The MSCI EAFE Index is a widely used benchmark for international investors. While the index is a convenient single measure by which to judge the level of all developed-market large-cap stocks, the shifting market weight of countries within the index does not make for a good investment. The problem is that there is no rebalancing in the index. Consequently, the weight of the index swings considerably among the geographic regions of the world.

Developed markets can be divided into two regions, Europe and the Pacific Rim. While buying an EAFE Index fund is a convenient way to invest in developed markets, the shifting allocation between Europe and the Pacific Rim is not the most desirable approach to asset allocation. Dividing developed markets into an equal portfolio of Europe and Pacific Rim and rebalancing

TABLE 7-6

Low-Cost International Mutual Funds

	Symbol	Benchmark
European Mutual Funds		
Vanguard European Index	VEURX	MSCI European Index
iShares Europe 350 Index	IEV	S&P Europe 350 Index
iShares MSCI UK Index	EWU	MSCI United Kingdom Index
iShares MSCI EMU Index	EZU	MSCI EMU Index
Pacific Rim Mutual Funds		
Vanguard Pacific Index	VPACX	MSCI Pacific Index
iShares MSCI Japan Index	EWJ	MSCI Japan Index
iShares MSCI Pacific ex-JPN	EPP	MSCI Pacific ex-Japan Index
Emerging Markets Funds		
Vanguard Emerging Markets	VEIEX	Select Emerging Markets Index
iShares Emerging Markets	EEM	MSCI Emerging Markets Free
DFA Emerging Markets*	DFEMX	DFA Emerging Markets Index
International Value Funds		
Vanguard International Value	VTRIX	Actively managed fund
DFA International Value*	DFIVX	DFA International Value
International Small Funds		
Vanguard International Explorer	VINEX	Actively managed fund
DFA Small International*	DFISX	DFA Small International
DFA Small International Value*	DISVX	DFA Small International Value
Single-Country Funds		
iShares MSCI Canada	EWC	MSCI Canada Index
iShares FTSE/Xinhua China 25	FXI	FTSE/Xinhua China 25 Index

*DFA funds are available only through select investment advisors.

annually is a better alternative than allowing your portfolio allocation to swing between the two regions.

Emerging markets have evolving economies, and that spells opportunity. However, those opportunities are not without added risk. Emerging markets are more volatile than developed markets, and there is the added risk of political uncertainty. As a result, a well-diversified emerging market fund is recommended.

Over the long term, international small-cap and value stocks have delivered higher returns than international large-cap and growth stocks. Adding a small-cap international fund and a value fund to your international portfolio may increase the return over time. Unfortunately, there is one disadvantage to this strategy: There is a genuine lack of available low-cost mutual funds that focus on small-cap international stocks.

NOTE

[1]For a summary of research on size and style premiums in international stocks, see Elroy Dimson, Paul Marsh, and Mike Staunton, *Triumph of the Optimists, 101 Years of Global Investment Returns*, Princeton, N.J.: Princeton University Press, 2002.

Fixed-Income Investments

KEY CONCEPTS

- There are many different categories of fixed-income investments.
- Different categories exhibit different risks and returns.
- Diversified fixed income enhances overall portfolio return.
- Low-cost bond mutual funds are an ideal way to invest.

There is no lack of diversification potential in the bond market. Fixed-income categories abound with unique investments, including government bonds, investment-grade and high-yield corporate bonds, mortgage-backed bonds, asset-backed securities, and foreign debt. Using a broad diversification strategy of fixed-income investments can increase portfolio returns without additional risk.

For reasons unknown to this author, fixed-income asset allocation is often overlooked in the investment advice industry. Other books on asset allocation tend to devote a significant amount of time to the benefits of equity asset diversification while largely ignoring the benefits of fixed-income diversification. It is also common for investment managers to place their clients' entire fixed-income allocation in government bonds and ignore all other fixed-income categories. Those advisors tell clients that they "prefer to take their risk on the stock side." I do not agree with that strategy. Using only government bonds may make the money manager's job easy, but it is not the most effective way to manage a portfolio.

The simplest way to gain instant fixed-income diversification is through a low-cost bond mutual fund. Investors should always use low-cost mutual funds in categories that would otherwise require significant analysis and expertise, such as high-yield corporate bonds and emerging market debt. In addition, there are several low-cost funds that follow popular investment-grade indexes, such as the Lehman Aggregate Bond Market Index. A partial list of mutual funds is provided at the end of the chapter.

Tax considerations may be an important element in fixed-income asset allocation. If you are investing a taxable account, such as a joint account or trust, tax-free bonds may be appropriate depending on your taxable income. Later in this chapter, there is a discussion of tax-free bond investing for investors who are in a high-tax situation.

The goal of this chapter is threefold. First, to help you appreciate the wide range of fixed-income categories that are available. Second, to show that those fixed-income investments can work with other investments in a portfolio to reduce risk and increase return. Third, to identify fixed-income categories that might be appropriate for your portfolio.

GLOBAL BOND MARKET STRUCTURE

The global bond market is as broad as it is deep. Investors have as much diversification potential on the fixed-income side of their portfolio as they do on the equity side. The range of bond opportunities stretches from governments to corporate to mortgages to foreign markets.

Index providers categorize bonds by different types and risk grades. The following is an example of how the bond market is generally segmented and categorized.

THE STRUCTURE OF THE FIXED-INCOME MARKET

    I. Federal, State, and Local Governments

         U.S. government backed

              Treasury-issued securities (bills, notes, bonds)

Government agency issues (FNMA, FHMLC)
FDIC-insured certificates of deposit
State and local government municipal bonds
General obligation backed by taxes
Revenue bonds backed by income other than tax
II. Corporate fixed income
Corporate bonds
Investment-grade corporate (BBB to AAA)
Non-investment-grade corporate (BB and lower)
Industrial revenue bonds (municipal bonds subject to AMT)
Preferred stocks and convertible preferred stocks
III. Mortgages
Government National Mortgage Association (GNMA)
Federal Home Loan Mortgage Corporation (FHLMC)
Federal National Mortgage Association (FNMA)
IV. Asset-Backed Securities
Pooled credit card receivables (Bank One, CitiGroup)
Pooled auto loans (Ford, GM)
Pooled home equity loans and other bank receivables
V. Foreign Bonds
Developed markets (sovereign and corporate)
Emerging markets debt (sovereign, Brady, and corporate)

FIXED-INCOME RISK AND RETURN

The expected risk and return of various U.S. fixed-income investments can be categorized on a two-axis grid, as illustrated in Figure 8-1. The horizontal axis of Figure 8-1 represents the maturity of a bond, and the vertical axis represents its creditworthiness.

The two-axis model of bond maturity and creditworthiness explains much of the risk and return associated with fixed-income investments. The more risk there is in a bond, the greater the expected return. Figure 8-2 illustrates this relationship.

FIGURE 8-1

Fixed-Income Maturity and Credit Risk Grid

Short-term 0–3 years	Intermediate 4–9 years	Long-term 10 years +	
SH	IH	LH	High yield corporate and some municipal bonds–Rating BB or lower
SI	II	LI	Investment grade corporate and most municipal bonds–Rating AA to BBB
SG	IG	LG	Government backed obligations and insured municipals–Rated AAA

FIGURE 8-2

Fixed-Income Risk-and-Return Comparison

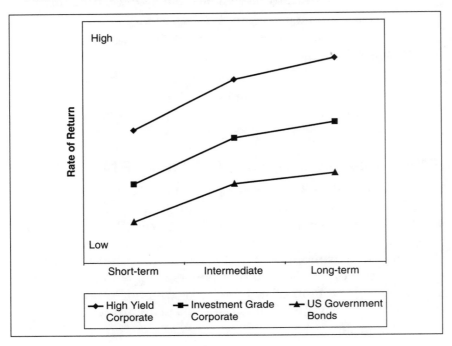

The two levers of interest-rate risk and credit risk determine how much a bond should pay in order to compensate investors for taking those risks. Higher potential returns are found in bonds with low credit quality and long-term maturities.

MATURITY STRUCTURE

Bonds are issued by governments and corporations using a variety of different maturities.

Figure 8-1 divides bond maturities into three ranges: short-term, intermediate-term, and long-term. Short-term bonds have an average maturity of three years or less, intermediate-term bonds have an average maturity of four to nine years, and long-term bonds have an average maturity of ten years or more. Under normal economic conditions, you should expect to get a higher return from long-term bonds because that segment of the market has more interest-rate risk. If a bond loses value when interest rates move higher, it has interest-rate risk. Long-term bonds have more interest-rate risk than short-term bonds because they have a longer time before maturing. Since long-term bonds have more risk, investors should get paid a higher interest rate for bearing that risk.

Economic factors cause interest rates for different bond maturities to change at different times and by different amounts. Those interest-rate shifts create changes in the "spreads" between different maturities. On average, the spread between the one-year and ten-year Treasuries is about 0.85 percent. As of January 2005, the spread was 1.6 percent. Figure 8-3 shows the changing interest-rate spread between one-year Treasury bills and ten-year Treasury notes since the early 1950s.

Most of the time a ten-year Treasury note has had a higher yield than the one-year T-bill. These are periods with a "normal" yield curve, so called because under normal conditions short-term T-bills are expected to yield less than intermediate-term Treasury notes. A "flat" yield curve occurs when the yield on T-bills and T-notes is the same. If T-bills have a higher yield than Treasury notes, this is known as an "inverted" yield curve.

CREDIT RISK

Credit risk is illustrated on the vertical axis in Figure 8-1. Bonds that have more credit risk should pay a higher interest rate than

FIGURE 8-3

Treasury Term Spread
1-Year T-Bills and 10-Year Treasury Notes

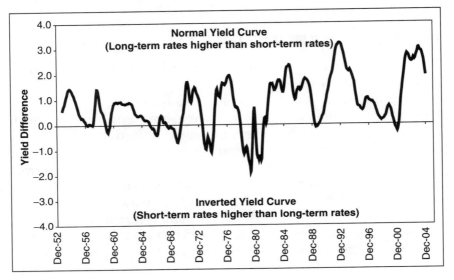

bonds with low credit risk. Table 8-1 shows how three different credit-rating agencies categorize bonds by creditworthiness.

Investment-grade bonds have an S&P and Fitch rating of BBB or higher and a Moody's rating of Baa or higher. Direct and indirect obligations of a government agency, such as Treasury bonds and federal agency bonds, have the least credit risk and yield the least. The middle investment-grade credit level includes investment-grade U.S. corporations and municipalities with sound fundamental characteristics. These bonds receive an investment-grade rating from credit-rating agencies such as Standard & Poor's. They pay more interest than government bonds.

At the bottom of the risk ladder are high-yield corporate bonds and non-investment-grade municipal bonds. Companies and municipal bond issuers with below investment-grade debt ratings have a questionable ability to repay their obligations. These bonds are also referred to as "junk" bonds because of their speculative nature. They will be discussed in more detail later in the chapter.

TABLE 8-1

Credit-Rating Agency Categories

	Moody's	Standard & Poor's	Fitch
Investment-Grade			
Prime	Aaa	AAA	AAA
Excellent	Aa	AA	AA
Upper medium	A	A	A
Lower medium	Baa	BBB	BBB
Non-Investment-Grade			
Speculative	Ba	BB	BB
Very speculative	B, Caa, Ca, C	B, CCC, CC, C	B, CCC, CC, C
Default		D	DDD, DD, D

Credit risk should be thought of as the amount that a bond will fall in value if the rating agencies cut the bond's rating. For example, if an AA-rated bond is cut to an A rating, the expected return to a new investor must go up to compensate for the lower credit quality, which means the price of the bond will go down. Thus, the amount that a bond will go down in value if the rating is cut is the bond's credit risk, which can also be thought of as its "downgrade" risk.

Figure 8-4 illustrates the historic spread between the highest-rated (AAA) corporate bonds and lower-medium-rated (BBB) corporate bonds. The credit spread appears to widen when the economy slumps and narrows when the economy recovers.

Some people believe that credit spreads widen and narrow for the same reasons that stocks go up and down. As a result, they say that using corporate bonds in a portfolio is nothing more than increasing the equity risk in a portfolio. While there are times when credit risk has a positive correlation with equity returns, the relationship is not consistent.

Figure 8-5 illustrates the correlation between excess return on investment-grade bonds and excess return on equities (credit risk premium to equity risk premium). The credit risk premium is calculated by subtracting the periodic return on the Lehman Brothers Intermediate-Term Treasury Index 1-10 Years from the return on

F I G U R E 8-4

Investment-Grade Spread
BBB Corporate Yield less AAA Corporate Yield

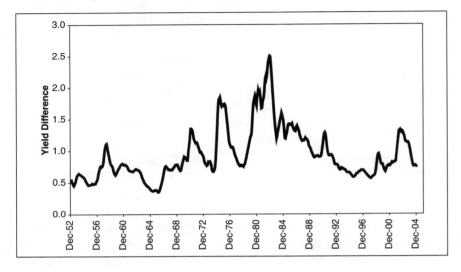

F I G U R E 8-5

Investment-Grade Credit Risk Premium to the Equity Risk Premium
36-Month Rolling Correlation

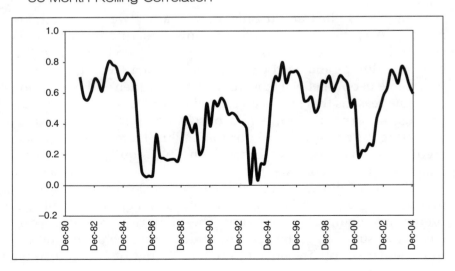

the Lehman Brothers Intermediate-Term Credit Index 1-10 Years. The equity risk premium is calculated by subtracting the return on Treasury bills from the return on the CRSP 1-10 total stock market index. Measuring the correlation between these two returns tells us if there is a relationship between them.

The average correlation between the credit risk premium and the equity risk premium suggests that about 25 percent of the credit risk premium is related to the same factors affecting equity returns. Adding investment-grade corporate bonds to a portfolio does slightly increase equity risk exposure in a portfolio, although the long-term effect is negligible.

INVESTING IN INVESTMENT-GRADE BONDS

Table 8-2 is an example of how the two risk factors of credit risk and maturity played out from 1973 to 2004. The higher interest-rate risk of intermediate-term Treasury bonds drove their return higher than the return on one-year Treasury bills. Also, the addition of credit risk increased the return of corporate bonds over Treasury bonds.

A well-diversified fixed-income portfolio includes a broad range of investment-grade bonds with different maturities, quality, and issuers. Most taxable investment-grade bonds issued in the United States are included in the Lehman Brothers U.S. Aggregate Bond Market Index. The Lehman Brothers U.S. Aggregate Bond Index tracks more than 6,600 U.S. Treasury, government agency, investment-grade corporate, and Yankee bonds. One exception is Treasury Inflation-Protected Securities (TIPS). Because of their unique characteristics, TIPS are placed in a separate index.

TABLE 8-2

Investment Returns from 1973 to 2004

1973 to 2004	One-Year T-Bill	LB Intermediate Treasury Index	LB Intermediate Credit Index
Annualized return	7.2%	8.2%	8.9%
Standard deviation	2.0%	4.4%	5.2%

The bonds in the LB U.S. Aggregate Index have an average maturity of about 7.5 years. Over 70 percent of the holdings are in U.S. Treasuries, government agency bonds, and government-backed mortgages. The remaining bonds are investment-grade corporate bonds and Yankee bonds. All of the bonds are investment grade. Table 8-3 is a breakdown of the index in early 2005.

Several index funds are available that track the Lehman Brothers U.S. Aggregate Bond Index. I recommend using one of those funds as the cornerstone of your fixed-income portfolio. A list of index funds can be found at the end of this chapter.

The LB U.S. Aggregate Bond Index has many subindexes. One way the indexes are categorized is by maturity. The category with the shortest average maturity is the LB 1-3 Year Short-Term Government/Credit Index, which includes government and corporate bonds but no mortgages. The next category of maturities is the LB Intermediate-Term Government/Credit Index. The category with the longest maturity is the LB Long-Term Government/Credit Index.

You can adjust the interest-rate risk in your portfolio by using a combination of a total bond market index fund and one of the three subindexes based on maturity. For example, investors with a short-term investment horizon of five years or less should probably have a generous portion in a short-term bond index fund benchmarked to the LB short-term index. Investors who are retired and are withdrawing money annually may want to have at least one year's worth of withdrawals in the short-term fund.

TABLE 8-3

Composition of the LB U.S. Aggregate Bond Index in 2005

Distribution by Issuer		Distribution by Quality	
Treasury securities	23%	AAA	77%
Government agency bonds	12%	AA	3%
Mortgage-backed securities	35%	A	10%
Corporate and asset-backed	26%	BBB	10%
Yankee bonds (foreign)	4%	BB or lower	~0%

ADDING OTHER FIXED-INCOME SECURITIES

A diversified fixed-income portfolio is not limited to the traditional bonds in the Lehman Brothers U.S. Aggregate Index. There are many diversification benefits to be gained from other fixed-income securities. Those categories include, but are not limited to, TIPS, high-yield corporate bonds, and foreign bonds, including emerging market debt.

Treasury Inflation-Protected Securities, or TIPS, were introduced in the late 1990s and are designed to protect against the damaging effects of inflation. Like traditional Treasury notes and bonds, TIPS pay semiannual interest and have a maturity date when the par value of the bond is returned. Unlike traditional Treasuries, the amount of the semiannual interest payments and the par value that is returned on TIPS are not fixed. Those items are linked to the rate of inflation during the issue period. If there was inflation during the time the bond was outstanding, the par value of the bond goes up with that rate of inflation. Since the par value of the bond goes up, the interest received is also higher. The inflation adjustment makes TIPS inflation risk–free, which is unique among all fixed-income investments.

Before investing in TIPS, there are a few things you need to know about the inflation adjustment. The fixed coupon rate is applied to the inflation-adjusted par price. If inflation occurs throughout the life of the security, the par value goes up consistently, and as a result every interest payment will be greater than the previous one. On the other hand, in the rather unusual event of deflation (lower prices), the par value of the bond goes down, and that means that your interest payments will decrease as well.

Before you get too excited about the inflation-adjustment feature of TIPS, you should understand that *all* bonds already have an inflation forecast built into their expected return. Assume that a traditional 10-year Treasury note is yielding 4.5 percent and a 10-year TIPS is yielding 2 percent. The 2.5 percent difference in yield is the expected inflation rate over the next 10 years. The inflation number is already worked into the traditional Treasury yield, whereas it is not in the TIPS.

Investors can gauge what the consensus believes the inflation rate will be in the future by subtracting the yield on a traditional Treasury bond from the yield on TIPS of the same maturity. Figure 8-6 depicts the historical values of the expected inflation rate as the difference in yield between a 2024 maturity TIPS bond and a traditional 2024 maturity Treasury bond. It is interesting to note that the expectation for inflation changes over time. Currently, investors expect inflation to average approximately 3.0 percent. That is up from 1.5 percent in 1998.

Since TIPS factor out inflation risk, the real return on Treasury bonds is evident from the yield on TIPS. Real return is the amount that investors earn after inflation. One would expect the real return on 10-year TIPS to be constant over time because there is no credit risk in the bond. However, that is not what happens. When inflation is high, the real return on TIPS tends to be higher than when inflation is low. One reason for the real-return volatility on all

FIGURE 8-6

Treasury Yield Spread
Traditional Treasury Bond Yield to Treasury Inflation-Protected Securities (20-Year Maturities)

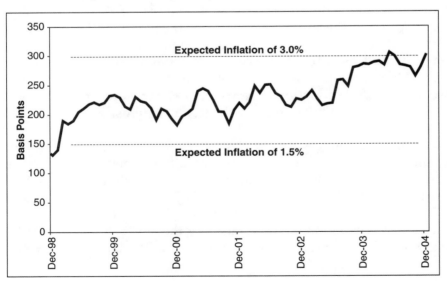

Treasury bonds has to do with taxes. Income tax must be paid on both the real return and the inflation portion of a Treasury bond return. Therefore, when inflation is high, investors need to make more money on the real-return portion of the return to pay the extra taxes on the inflation portion.

The U.S. Treasury issued the first inflation-protected securities in 1997. Consequently, there are not enough data to show you a rolling 36-month correlation. However, the annual return of TIPS is highlighted in Figure 8-7. That figure gives you a good idea of the difference in return between TIPS and the rest of the bond market.

There is one word of caution when analyzing Figure 8-7. When TIPS were first issued in 1997, investor demand was light because there were few securities available and little was known about inflation-adjusted bonds. Demand picked up considerably over the next few years as more bonds were issued by the Treasury and more information become available to investors. In addition, several mutual fund companies started TIPS funds. Prices went up

FIGURE 8-7

Total Return on the LB Aggregate Bond Index and LB TIPS Index

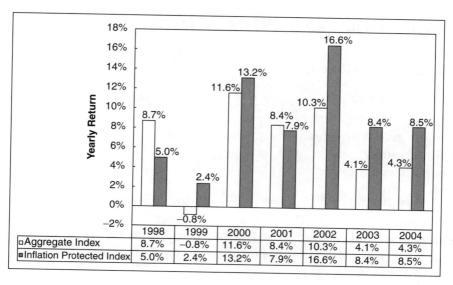

	1998	1999	2000	2001	2002	2003	2004
□Aggregate Index	8.7%	−0.8%	11.6%	8.4%	10.3%	4.1%	4.3%
■Inflation Protected Index	5.0%	2.4%	13.2%	7.9%	16.6%	8.4%	8.5%

as a result of the increase in demand, and some of the outstanding performance in Figure 8-7 can be attributed to that demand. However, this event will not be repeated, and investors should not expect superior performance to continue in the future.

U.S. Treasury iBonds are also a type of inflation-protected security that offers a way to save that protects the purchasing power of an investment. Like TIPS, the interest and inflation gain from iBonds are exempt from state and local income taxes. In addition, there are a few features that make iBonds more attractive than TIPS. First, they are sold at face value in small denominations of $50, $75, $100, $200, $500, $1,000, $5,000, and $10,000. Second, federal income tax on iBonds earnings can be deferred until the bonds are cashed or they stop earning interest after 30 years. Third, earnings may be withdrawn tax-free for certain educational purposes. Of course, there are also disadvantages to iBonds. First, investors are limited to $30,000 per year in purchases. Second, iBonds cashed before five years are subject to a three-month earnings penalty.

TIPS and iBonds are designed to protect investors from an unexpected jump in inflation. Since there are no inflation-adjusted bonds in the Lehman Aggregate Bond Index, TIPS and iBonds can be added to the list of potential fixed-income investments to place in your portfolio.

HIGH-YIELD CORPORATE BONDS

High-yield bonds are often referred to as non-investment-grade bonds, speculative-grade bonds, and junk bonds. Unlike investment-grade bonds, high-yield bonds have credit ratings that are in the lowest tier. They have S&P and Fitch ratings of BB or lower and Moody's ratings of Ba or lower.

Several entities issue high-yield bonds including corporations, municipalities, and foreign governments. As a group, these securities are expected to earn about the same return as the broad stock market.

High-yield bonds have a separate and distinct risk above and beyond credit risk. There is a real danger that the issuers will default on their obligations. Consequently, high-yield bonds have default risk in addition to credit risk. The added risk means that investors should get paid more.

Figure 8-8 compares the yearly returns on the Lehman U.S. High Yield Corporate Bond Index to the returns on the Lehman U.S. Aggregate Bond Index. Since the aggregate index includes most U.S. investment-grade bonds, the return difference between the two indexes is a result of changes in default risk. Default risk was increasing from 2000 to 2002 as several large telecommunications companies defaulted on their bonds. In 2003 and 2004, defaults on high-yield bonds fell sharply, and as a result the risk of default on existing bonds also decreased.

Some market researchers suggest that default risk is nothing more than a type of equity risk, and therefore that adding high-yield corporate bonds to a portfolio is the equivalent of adding more equity. That argument is not entirely correct. While there have been times when the correlation between default risk and equity risk was high, it has not been consistent, as Figure 8-9 illustrates.

FIGURE 8-8

Lehman U.S. Aggregate Bond Index and High Yield Corporate Index

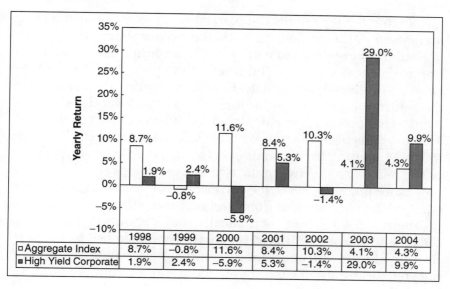

	1998	1999	2000	2001	2002	2003	2004
□ Aggregate Index	8.7%	−0.8%	11.6%	8.4%	10.3%	4.1%	4.3%
■ High Yield Corporate	1.9%	2.4%	−5.9%	5.3%	−1.4%	29.0%	9.9%

FIGURE 8-9

High-Yield Default Risk Premium to the Equity Risk Premium
36-Month Rolling Correlation

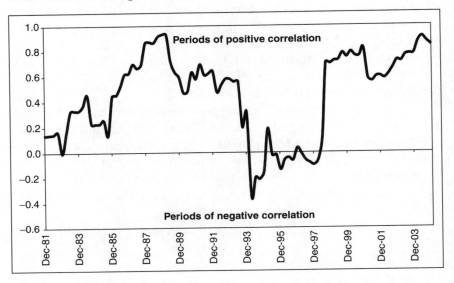

Figure 8-9 represents the correlation of excess return on U.S. high-yield corporate bonds with the excess return on equities (default risk premium to equity risk premium). The default risk premium is calculated by subtracting the periodic return on the Lehman Brothers Intermediate-Term Credit Index 1–10 Years from the return on the Lehman Brothers High Yield Bond Index. The equity risk premium is calculated by subtracting the return on Treasury bills from the return on the CRSP 1-10 total stock market index. Measuring the correlation between these two returns shows us the relationship between the two risk premiums.

Since the early 1980s, the correlation between default risk and equity risk has fluctuated from a high of about 0.9 percent to a low of about −0.4 percent. Statistically, only about 25 percent of the default risk in high-yield corporate bonds can be attributed to the same factors affecting equity returns; however, the results are not statistically significant. If you allocate 10 percent of your total portfolio to one of the BB–B-rated bond funds listed at the end of this chapter, at most perhaps 2 percent of that could be considered equity-related. The inconsistency of the correlation between default risk premiums and equity risk premiums provides the basis for adding BB–B high-yield corporate bonds to a well-diversified fixed-income portfolio.

That being said, very-low-quality bond funds (those with an average credit quality of CCC or less) do have a higher correlation with equity returns. Accordingly, an adjustment may need to be made in your overall stock and bond asset allocation. For example, if you place 10 percent of your overall portfolio in a very-low-quality junk bond fund, about 4 percent of that 10 percent should be considered as part of the equity allocation in your portfolio.

One note of caution: I do not recommend buying individual high-yield bonds because of their high trading costs and a genuine lack of investment information. A better approach is to purchase a low-cost mutual fund that concentrates holdings in high-yield bonds. Mutual funds provide instant access to a broadly diversified portfolio of high-yield bonds that have been selected by an experienced manager. A couple of low-cost BB–B-rated high-yield U.S. corporate bond funds are listed at the end of this chapter.

EMERGING MARKET DEBT

The global bond market is huge. At about $65 trillion, it has about the same market value as the global stock market. Half of the world's tradable fixed-income securities are denominated in U.S. dollars, and the other half are denominated in foreign currencies.

Countries are categorized into two broad types for investment purposes: developed markets and emerging markets. Developed markets are countries with advanced free-market economies and established financial markets. Emerging markets are less developed, with financial markets that may not be robust.

The political environment of some emerging markets can change rapidly, and that can create excess volatility. Accordingly, the expected return from emerging market bonds is higher than that in developed markets. The record on emerging market bonds is not long. The first emerging market bond mutual funds were established in 1993.

TABLE 8-4

Returns on Emerging Market Bond Funds

1993–2004	LB Aggregate Bond Index	Emerging Market Bond Funds
Annualized return	7.4	12.2
Standard deviation	6.3	18.5
Market correlation		+0.5

Source: Morningstar.

The results in Table 8-4 shows that since 1993, emerging market bond funds have had significantly higher compounded returns than the Lehman Aggregate Bond Index, with appropriately higher risk. I chose the returns of mutual funds for this study because this is the only practical way for individual investors to participate in emerging market debt. The return on the emerging market bond fund index is the median return on all emerging market funds each year over the past 12 years.

Emerging market bonds have had a high return, but that return is not without many risks. In addition to all the risks of high-yield corporate bonds, emerging market bonds have currency risk and political risk. Currency risk is inherent in international investments. Political risk is found mostly in emerging markets, where the political stability of a nation is never certain. These uniquely international risks were explained in detail in Chapter 7, "International Equity Investments." Figure 8-10 illustrates the difference in return that has occurred between the U.S. bond market index and emerging market bond funds.

Figure 8-10 includes the return of 1998, which was a very bad year for emerging market bond funds. This was the year when Russia defaulted on its foreign debt obligations. Russia's default sent tremors through all emerging markets, causing risk premiums to widen dramatically. However, as in all other financial panics, eventually the fear subsided and default risks moved back into a more normal range.

FIGURE 8-10

LB Aggregate Bond Market Index and Emerging Market Bond Mutual Funds

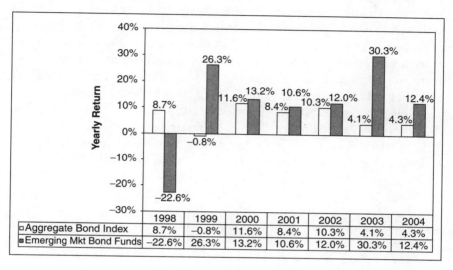

	1998	1999	2000	2001	2002	2003	2004
□Aggregate Bond Index	8.7%	−0.8%	11.6%	8.4%	10.3%	4.1%	4.3%
▪Emerging Mkt Bond Funds	−22.6%	26.3%	13.2%	10.6%	12.0%	30.3%	12.4%

PUTTING IT ALL TOGETHER

After completing your analysis of the fixed-income market, the next step is to select an asset allocation for your portfolio. Table 8-5 provides an example of a fixed-income asset allocation that my firm uses frequently. Please keep in mind that this is an example. Each investor should decide on his or her own how to allocation investments to meet his or her unique financial objectives and tax situation.

TABLE 8-5

Fixed-Income Allocation Using Taxable Bonds

Fixed-Income Allocation	Fixed-Income Category
50%	Lehman Aggregate Bond Index
20%	Treasury Inflation-Protected Bonds or iBonds
20%	High-Yield Corporate Bonds
10%	Emerging Market Debt

Figure 8-11 illustrates the benefits of a well-diversified fixed-income portfolio. The figure shows the returns on three portfolios with different allocations. One portfolio illustrates the growth of $1 invested in intermediate-term Treasury bonds only. The second portfolio illustrates the growth of $1 invested in a mix of investment-grade bonds that has an allocation of one-third in intermediate-term Treasuries, one-third in intermediate-term investment-grade corporate bonds, and one-third in GNMA mortgages (a mix similar to the LB Aggregate Bond Index).

The diversified portfolio is a mix very close to the one in Table 8-6, with the exception of TIPS. The return on TIPS was not available until 1998 and was included at that time. The diversified portfolio was rebalanced annually to the original target in Table 8-6.

FIGURE 8-11

Growth of $1

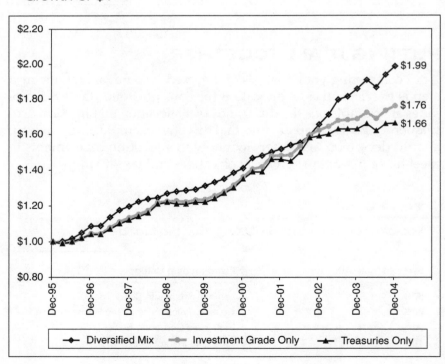

It is impossible to know that a multi-asset-class fixed-income portfolio will outperform Treasuries and investment-grade portfolios in the future. I believe it will, since investors should be rewarded for taking the added risks of high yield, default, and disinflation. Accordingly, investors who take the time to learn about fixed-income asset allocation will be happy that they did.

MUNICIPAL BONDS

Thus far, we have discussed only taxable bonds. Depending on the type of portfolio you are investing and your income tax bracket, tax-free municipal bonds may play an important role in your asset allocation. In a taxable account, the after-tax return on municipal bonds will be higher for those in upper income brackets.

Typically, the interest income from a municipal bond issued in the state in which you live is free from all federal, state, and city income taxes (there are exceptions). For that reason, municipal bonds have lower interest payments than taxable government bonds or corporate bonds. However, after tax, the net return is higher.

To compare the yield on taxable bonds to that on tax-free bonds, simply multiply the taxable yield by your tax rate and subtract the result from that yield. If you buy an intermediate-term taxable bond that pays 4 percent interest and your tax on that income is 30 percent, the after-tax return will be 2.8 percent. If the yield on a comparable maturity municipal bond were higher than 2.8 percent, then it would be to your advantage to invest in the tax-free bond. As a rough rule of thumb, if your combined state and federal income tax rate is 30 percent or more, municipal bonds may be an appropriate choice for taxable accounts.

Investors in a high income tax bracket should consider tax-free municipal bonds in place of investment-grade taxable bonds for their taxable accounts. A low-cost diversified tax-free fund is a good substitute for a total bond market index fund. Examples of municipal bond mutual funds are listed in the next section.

FIXED-INCOME INVESTMENT LIST

Table 8-6 gives a list of low-cost mutual funds that may be possible candidates for your fixed-income allocation. For more complete

TABLE 8-6

Low-Cost Fixed-Income Mutual Funds

	Symbol	Benchmark
Total Bond Market Funds		
Vanguard Total Bond Market	VBMFX	Lehman U.S. Aggregate Bond Index
iShares LB Aggregate	AGG	Lehman U.S. Aggregate Bond Index
Vanguard Short-Term Bond Index	VBISX	Lehman 1-5 Government/ Credit Index
Treasury Inflation-Protected		
Vanguard Inflation Protected Securities	VIPSX	Lehman Treasury Infl. Notes Index
iShares Lehman TIPS Bond	TIP	Lehman Treasury Infl. Notes Index
Individual iBonds	Purchase through banks or the U.S. Treasury	
High-Yield Corporate		
Vanguard High Yield Corporate	VWEHX	Actively managed B–BB grade
TIAA-CREF High Yield	TCHYX	Actively managed B–BB grade
Emerging Market Debt		
Payden Emerging Market Bond	PYEMX	Actively managed—partially hedged
Fidelity New Markets Income	FNMIX	Actively managed—partially hedged
Municipal Bond Funds		
Vanguard Inter-Term Tax-Exempt	VWITX	Actively managed, 6–12 years
Vanguard Limited-Term Tax-Exempt	VMLTX	Actively managed, 2–6 years

information on these and other low-cost no-load funds, read *All About Index Funds* by Richard A. Ferri (McGraw-Hill, 2002). In addition, go to www.Morningstar.com for a wide assortment of mutual fund tools and information.

CHAPTER SUMMARY

A well-diversified portfolio contains both fixed-income and equity investments. To obtain maximum benefit, the fixed-income portion of the portfolio should also be broadly diversified into several different fixed-income categories and rebalanced annually. Asset allocation of fixed-income investments leads to higher overall returns with little increase in portfolio risk.

There is no lack of diversification potential in the bond market. Fixed-income asset subclasses include government bonds, corporate bonds, home mortgage pools, asset-backed bonds such as those backed by credit card receivables, and foreign developed and emerging markets. A total bond market fund covers most investment-grade fixed-income securities. TIPS, high-yield bond funds, and emerging market categories can be purchased separately.

The best way to build the fixed-income portion of a portfolio is through low-cost bond mutual funds, particularly bond index funds. Index funds closely track many of the fixed-income indexes used in data analysis in this chapter. Some fixed-income asset classes cannot be purchased with in index fund. For those asset classes, a low-cost actively managed mutual fund is appropriate. Investors in a high tax bracket should consider municipal bond mutual funds as a substitute for taxable investment-grade bonds.

CHAPTER 9

Real Estate Investments

KEY CONCEPTS

- Real estate is a separate asset class from stocks and bonds.
- Real estate investment trusts (REITs) are a convenient way to invest in real estate.
- REITs have low correlation with common stocks and bonds.
- Home ownership provides both a place to live and earnings potential.

One of the great insights of modern portfolio theory is that holding low-correlated asset classes in a portfolio and rebalancing periodically reduces total portfolio risk and increases long-term return. Real estate is one of the few asset classes that have had a low correlation with stocks and bonds. A well-diversified portfolio that holds real estate investments alongside stock and bonds has proven to be a superior portfolio to one that does not include real estate.

The Brandes Investment Institute and Prudential Financial, in collaboration with Professor Elroy Dimson of the London Business School, conducted a study of the long-term returns on U.S. real estate investments.[1] Dimson found that the long-term return on U.S. real estate has been on a par with the return on the U.S. stock market since the 1930s (see Table 9-1).

TABLE 9-1

Long-Term Returns on U.S. Real Estate

	Real Estate Total Return	Total Stock Market	Inflation (CPI)
1930–2004	9.3%	9.7%	2.8%

Source: The Brandes Institute.

Further analysis of the Dimson data shows that income return from rent has been very consistent over the decades. Table 9-2 measures the average income return from real estate investments at about 7 percent, plus or minus 1 percent per decade. The 2000 to 2004 partial decade capital return was revised to reflect the full 2004 year.

Nearly all commercial lease contracts have a built-in inflation hedge. As the general level of prices increases, landlords pass through the increase to tenants. The ability of landlords to increase rent makes real estate investment particularly attractive as an inflation hedge in an investment portfolio.

In addition to rental properties, home ownership has been a reliable investment as well as providing a place to live. Over the

TABLE 9-2

U.S. Real Estate Returns by Decade

Decade	Total Return	Annual Income Return	Capital Return
1930–1939	8.1%	8.4%	−0.3%
1940–1949	13.7%	6.3%	7.0%
1950–1959	6.2%	6.1%	0.2%
1960–1969	6.5%	6.2%	0.3%
1970–1979	10.1%	6.3%	3.6%
1980–1989	11.1%	6.5%	4.3%
1990–1999	5.5%	6.6%	−1.1%
2000–2004	10.5%	7.5%	3.0%

Source: The Brandes Institute (2004 revised).

years, homeowners have enjoyed returns of about 5 percent per year, according to government housing data. Some areas of the country have seen housing prices appreciate at considerably higher rates than the national average, which has priced many new home buyers out of the market and is a cause for concern.

If possible, investors should consider both home ownership and commercial real estate investment opportunities as an integral part of their long-term investment plan. There is only a finite amount of land available for building, and resources for construction are limited. At the same time the population of the United States continues to increase. Those two facts should move prices higher in the long term.

COMMERCIAL REAL ESTATE INVESTMENT OPPORTUNITIES

Investments in commercial real estate can be acquired in three ways: direct investment in properties, indirect investment through limited partnerships (LPs), and indirect investment through publicly traded real estate investment trusts (REITs). Each approach has advantages and disadvantages.

Direct investment gives an investor full control over the property, including management of rents, costs, and selling decisions. A direct investment typically leads to the highest return for a real estate investor because it eliminates most intermediaries by relying on direct participation by the owner. The disadvantage of direct ownership is that it requires hands-on property management skills and knowledge of the real estate market. While a direct investor could hire a management company to handle the properties, that reduces the total return. In addition to management costs, prolonged vacancies and abusive or deadbeat tenants can also reduce returns. Finally, when an investor wants to sell, a poor resale market could make the sale of properties difficult or less profitable.

Investments in limited partnerships have the potential for attractive gains if you buy into the right one. Finding an honest and experienced general partner is the key. A competent and experienced general partner should handle everything, including the acquisition, management, and resale of the properties.

The disadvantage of owning an LP is that the limited partners must remain passive. They are not allowed to participate in any stage of the business. Limited partners have no say in decisions about which properties will be bought, how they will be managed, or when the properties will be sold. In addition, limited partnership shares are generally illiquid. Limited partners often have a very difficult time selling their shares because it is hard to find another investor who is willing to offer a fair and reasonable price.

REITs are the simplest way to participate in the real estate market. Property REITs are like baskets of real estate properties that trade on a stock exchange. The public market for REITs provides instant liquidity. The disadvantage of REITs is the cost of management and administration. If the current income from the underlying real estate is in the 8 percent range, the income to REIT investors is in the 6 percent range. In addition, REIT investors have no management say aside from voting annual proxies.

Over the past 10 years, the REIT market has grown significantly. As a result, REIT mutual funds have become very popular. An investor can own a small slice of thousand of properties in various market segments across the country with the purchase of a REIT index mutual fund. The disadvantage of REIT mutual funds is another layer of fund management on top of the management fees already in the REIT.

REITs AS AN ASSET CLASS

The investments recommended in this book are mainly low-cost mutual funds. Therefore, the only commercial real estate investment type analyzed in this book is equity REITs. However, the lessons learned in this section can be applied to other forms of commercial real estate holdings.

In 1960, Congress wrote legislation allowing the formation of pooled real estate trusts that could trade on a major stock exchange. Real estate investment trusts were designed as a tax-efficient vehicle through which investors could own a diversified real estate portfolio. Companies that manage REITs are generally exempt from federal and state income tax as long as the management company complies with certain Internal

Revenue Service code requirements. The most important of those requirements are:

1. Invest at least 75 percent of the total assets in real estate assets
2. Derive at least 75 percent of the gross income from real property rents
3. Pay dividends of at least 90 percent of the taxable income.

Though REITs were a novel concept in the 1960s, they did not catch on with investors. Institutions were not interested because the tax law prohibited five or fewer individuals from owning more than 50 percent of a REIT's shares. As a result, for the first 30 years, the market capitalization of the REIT industry grew to only $5.6 billion (including only equity REITs).

A tax law change in the early 1990s was the catalyst for an explosion in the REIT market. The change allowed pension trusts to take much larger positions in real estate investment without violating trust law. Because of the liquidity that REITs offered, institutions saw them as a perfect avenue for increasing their exposure to real estate.

According to the National Association of Real Estate Investment Trusts (NAREIT), between 1990 and 2004, the market grew from $5.5 billion in fewer than 60 small equity REITs to 150 issues with over $273 billion of market capitalization. Although those sound like impressive numbers, equity REITs still represent a relatively small part of the overall commercial real estate market and less than 2 percent of the capitalization of stock market.

The securitization of the real estate market still has a long way to go. The total value of the commercial real estate market is approximately $15 trillion, according to Federal Reserve data. But not all real estate is eligible for inclusion in REITs. Publicly traded corporations own a large amount of commercial real estate, which therefore is technically already included as part of their common stock price. After adjusting for corporate holdings, there is approximately $4 trillion in investable U.S. commercial real estate that is available, of which less than 7 percent is part of a publicly traded REIT.

EQUITY AND OTHER TYPES OF REITs

REITs are divided into three basic categories: equity, mortgage, and hybrid. Equity REITs are the only type that invest entirely in real estate properties. They are the purest form of real estate holding. Mortgage REITs do not own property directly. Instead, they finance properties through commercial loans. Mortgage REITs are basically a type of bond investment rather than a real estate investment. Hybrid REITs hold both properties and mortgages. As such, a hybrid REIT derives a portion of its return from the performance of properties and a portion from the performance of the mortgage portfolio.

The focus of this chapter on real estate is on isolating a unique asset class, i.e., commercial properties. Consequently, the data in this book reflect the risk and return of only equity REITs. Data on mortgage REITs and hybrids are not included.

There are close to 100 different equity REITs that trade on the U.S. stock market. Those companies invest in a wide variety of properties, including shopping malls, office complexes, apartment buildings, and hotels. Investors who wish to own it all can purchase an index mutual fund of equity REITs that gives them an equity stake in tens of thousands of properties across the country.

THE PERFORMANCE OF EQUITY REITs

The performance of equity REITs can be divided into two categories. The first is the performance of REIT share prices, and the second is the dividend payments and reinvestment return on the dividend. As long as REITs pay at least 90 percent of their taxable income out to shareholders in the form of a dividend, the company does not have to pay corporate tax on the earnings. For that reason, the majority of their performance comes from the dividend yield and reinvestment return on those dividends.

Figures 9-1 and 9-2 offer a graphic illustration on the importance of dividends to REIT investors. Figure 9-1 represents the growth of $1 invested in NAREIT equity shares only. The chart does not include dividends or the reinvestment return on the dividends. Figure 9-2 illustrates the total return with dividends paid and reinvested.

FIGURE 9-1

The Equity NAREIT Index (Price Only) Generally
Tracks Inflation
Starting Value of $1

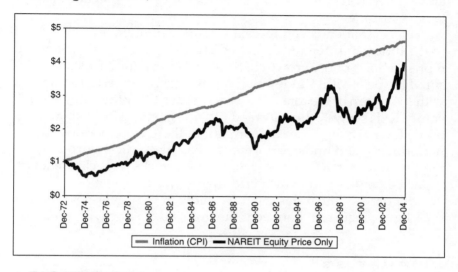

FIGURE 9-2

Equity NAREIT Total Return Index versus the CRSP Total
U.S. Stock Index
Growth of $1

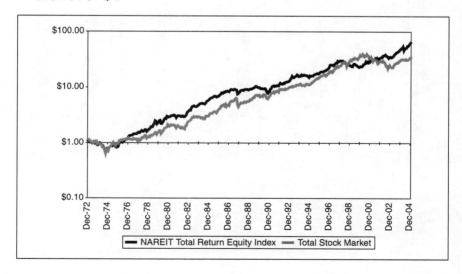

In general, the price of equity REITs has increased with the return of inflation as measured by the CPI. That is understandable, given the fact that rents typically increase with the rate of inflation and equity REITs are required to distribute 90 percent of their taxable income.

Once dividends and the reinvestment of dividends are added to the index, a different picture emerges. Figure 9-2 is a graphical representation of the growth of $1 invested in equity REITs as measured by the NAREIT Index with all dividends reinvested compared with the return of the total U.S. stock market. Over the entire period, equity REITs have outperformed other U.S. stocks by a small fraction. However, over the 33-year period, there were periods of outperformance and underperformance. For all practical purposes, the risk and return of REITs and U.S. common stocks were close enough to each other to say that the performance was the same.

Figure 9-3 illustrates the differences in year-over-year returns that have occurred between the total U.S. stock market, the

Annual Returns on CRSP Total U.S. Stocks, Intermediate Bonds, and REITs

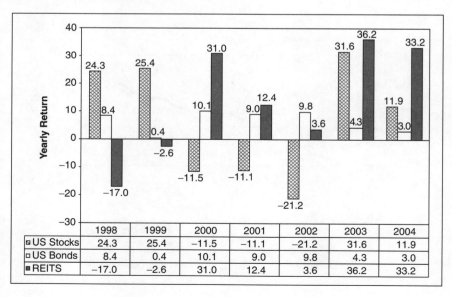

	1998	1999	2000	2001	2002	2003	2004
US Stocks	24.3	25.4	−11.5	−11.1	−21.2	31.6	11.9
US Bonds	8.4	0.4	10.1	9.0	9.8	4.3	3.0
REITS	−17.0	−2.6	31.0	12.4	3.6	36.2	33.2

Lehman Intermediate-Term Government/Credit Index, and the Wilshire REIT Index (an index of equity REITs). As you can see from the returns, there has been little consistency among the returns of the three asset classes.

CORRELATION ANALYSIS

Prior to the tax law changes concerning REITs in 1992, the risk and return characteristics of REITs were very similar to those of stocks. The high correlation between REITs and domestic stocks indicated that overall market movements affected real estate investment trusts. By the early 1990s, the market's perception of these securities began to shift. The REIT market was evolving, and investor understanding of the sector was increasing. In turn, shifts in the market began to alter the behavior patterns of this asset class. Over the next 10 years, correlations between REITs and the rest of the stock market declined and actually became negative for a brief period in 2001. Figure 9-4 documents this phenomenon.

FIGURE 9-4

Rolling 36-Month Correlation between the NAREIT Equity Index and the CRSP Total U.S. Stock Index

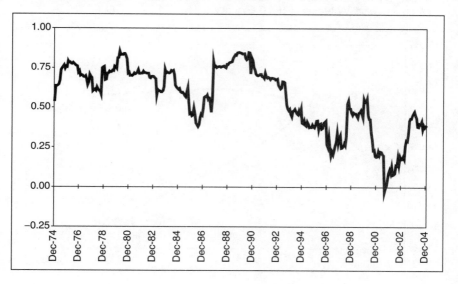

The varying correlation between REITs and the rest of the stock market has created a diversification opportunity for investors. Figure 9-5 represents the risk-and-return frontier that was created by adding REITs to all U.S. equity portfolio. Since the risk and return on REITs and the rest of the U.S. market is about the same and the correlation is low, there is a diversification benefit.

The Wilshire REIT Index is similar to the NAREIT Index in that it represents all publicly traded equity REITs. The difference between the two indexes is that Wilshire began its index in 1987, and it did not include hospital or health care facilities until 2002. The benefit of using the Wilshire REIT Index is that it is investable, meaning that there are index mutual funds that track the Wilshire REIT Index.

Real estate prices and interest rates are related. As interest rates fall, real estate prices rise as demand increases. Therefore, many people assume that there must be a high correlation between the return on bonds and the return on REITs. However, that does

FIGURE 9-5

Risk-and-Return Chart between the CRSP Total Stock Market and Wilshire REIT Equity Index, 1978–2004

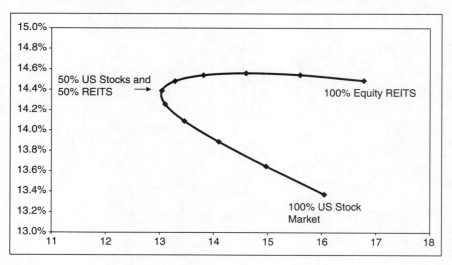

not show up in the data. Figure 9-6 illustrates the rolling 36-month correlation between REIT returns and the returns from the Lehman Intermediate-Term Index. Over the years, any degree of positive correlation has been inconsistent at best.

Figure 9-7 puts an investment in REITs into perspective. It illustrates the benefit of a multi-asset-class portfolio. The risk-and-return chart is based on a portfolio of intermediate-term bonds and an equity allocation of 20 percent REITs and 80 percent in the total stock market. At every point, an allocation to REITs lowered the risk of the portfolio, which in turn increased the long-term return.

Equity REITs are a low-correlation asset class that should be included in your list of potential investments. There are several low-cost REIT index funds that mirror the return on REIT indexes. See Table 9-3 at the end of this chapter for a partial list.

FIGURE 9-6

Rolling 36-Month Correlation between the NAREIT Equity Index and the Lehman Intermediate Government/Credit Index

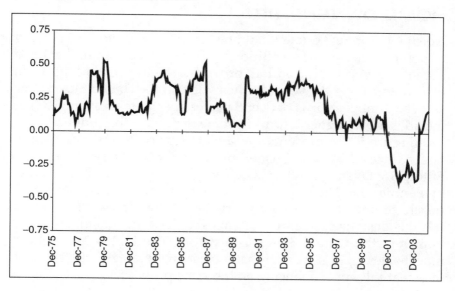

FIGURE 9-7

Frontier Comparison of Portfolios with and without REITs, 1978–2004

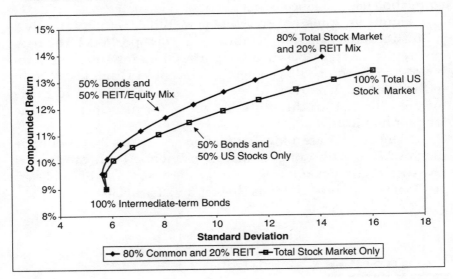

HOME OWNERSHIP

No chapter on real estate would be complete without a discussion of home ownership. In addition to living quarters, purchasing a home in a good location has proved to be a reliable long-term investment. Over the years, homeowners in the United States have enjoyed annual returns of over 5 percent per year on average. That includes much higher returns in some regions of the country.

Figure 9-8 represents the average price of a single-family home since 1975, as published by the Office of Federal Housing Enterprise Oversight (OFHEO). The data are provided to OFHEO by Fannie Mae and Freddie Mac, two government agencies that purchase and insure home mortgages. The House Price Index (HPI) is designed to capture changes in the value of single-family homes in the United States as a whole. The HPI is a weighted repeat-sales index, meaning that it measures average price changes in repeat sales or refinancing on the same properties.

For 1975 through 1996, the HPI basically kept pace with the inflation rate. Then in the mid-1990s, housing prices experienced a steady increase in real returns. Some people claim that this run-up in prices is an indication of a bubble in home prices created by very low mortgage rates. It is likely that housing prices are in a bubble in some parts of the country. However, it is not correct to state that the entire country is in a housing bubble because some regions of the country have had very limited price appreciation.

Figure 9-9 represents the year-over-year increase in the HPI, and there are several points of interest on the chart. The high-inflation years of the late 1970s and early 1980s drove housing prices up at double-digit rates. In the early 1990s, a recession and the Gulf War caused prices to flatten. Since about 1995, housing prices have been climbing steadily upward.

I find home values during the 2000 to 2003 period to be of particular interest. Housing prices continued upward during a difficult period in the U.S. economy, gaining between 4 and 7 percent

FIGURE 9-8

House Price Index versus the Consumer Price Index

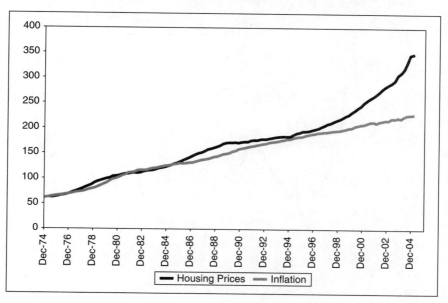

per year. This advance occurred despite a collapse in the stock market, an economic recession, the tragic events of September 11, and two wars. One obvious reason for the increase in housing prices during the 2000 to 2003 period was historically low mortgage rates. Figure 9-10 reflects 30-year mortgage prices as reported by the Federal Home Loan Mortgage Corporation.

The 30-year mortgage rate hit a 50-year low in June 2003, thereby making home ownership affordable for a greater number of people, which in turn kept demand high. Logically, interest rates cannot go to 0 percent. If fact, because of various investment risks and administrative costs, there is not a large chance that the 30-year mortgage rates will go below the 5 percent mark in the future. Consequently, the excess gains in home prices may be close to peaking. Perhaps there may even be a gradual decline in housing prices for some areas of the country. That could occur in areas that have experienced abnormally large price gains relative to the rest of the country.

FIGURE 9-9

OFHEO House Price Index
Year-over-Year National Price Change, 1974–2004

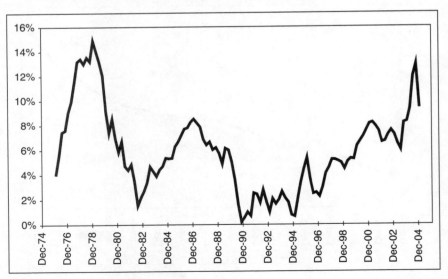

FIGURE 9-10

30-Year Mortgage Rates as Reported by the Federal Home Loan Mortgage Corporation

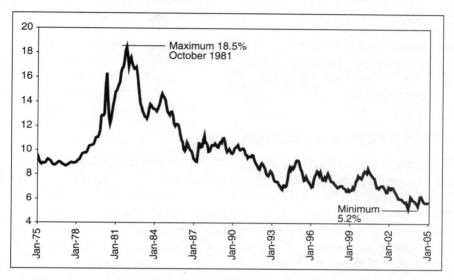

For practical reasons, home equity should be left outside of the asset allocation of your investment portfolio. The primary purpose for buying a home is as a place to live. Any appreciation of that property after taxes, interest expense, and inflation is purely incidental to its function as shelter. Trying to include your home as part of your asset allocation to real estate in an investment portfolio creates a number of problems because you can never be sure of the true market value, and you cannot rebalance your home equity against other assets. For example, you cannot buy or sell a percentage of your home equity to rebalance it against other asset classes.

REIT INVESTMENT LIST

Table 9-3 is a partial list of low-cost funds that are candidates for your REIT allocation. For more information on these and other low-cost no-load funds and the indexes they follow, read *All About Index Funds* by Richard A. Ferri (McGraw-Hill, 2002).

TABLE 9-3

Low-Cost REIT Mutual Funds

Equity REIT Index Funds	Symbol	Benchmark
Vanguard REIT Index Fund	VGSIX	Morgan Stanley REIT Index
iShares Dow Jones U.S. REIT	IYR	Dow Jones U.S. REIT Index
StreetTRACKS Wilshire REIT	RWR	Wilshire REIT Index

CHAPTER SUMMARY

Adding low-correlation asset classes to a portfolio reduces total portfolio risk and increases long-term return. Real estate is one of the few asset classes that has had a low correlation with both stock and bond markets. A well-diversified portfolio that holds real estate investments alongside stock and bond investments has proved to be a more efficient portfolio than one that does not include real estate investment.

There are many ways to invest in the commercial real estate market; however, equity REITs are the most liquid and convenient way. Equity REITs are portfolios of apartments, hotels, malls, industrial buildings, and other rental property that trade on a stock exchange. Several low-cost REIT index funds that give you instant diversification across the entire REIT market are available.

In addition to commercial real estate, make your home an investment. Traditionally, home prices have kept pace with the inflation rate and have outpaced inflation during a falling interest rate environment. Pick your location carefully. Every town and city has areas that have appreciated more than others, and there are some areas of the country where home prices have appreciated so much that further gains in the near term are doubtful.

NOTE

[1]Brandes Institute, *A Perspective on Long-Term Real Estate Returns: United States*, San Diego, CA, April 2004.

CHAPTER 10

Alternative Investments

KEY CONCEPTS

- Alternative asset classes extend beyond traditional stocks and bonds.
- Many alternative asset classes are difficult to invest in.
- Illiquidity and high costs overshadow most of the advantages.
- Some mutual funds are available at a moderate fee.

Modern portfolio theory is not limited to stocks, bonds, and real estate. Over the years, alternative asset classes have been playing a larger role in portfolio design. Alternative asset classes include investments in commodities, currencies, and collectibles such as artwork, rare coins, and wine.

The advantage of adding alternative assets to a portfolio is that they tend to exhibit low correlation with traditional stock and bond investments. For that reason, including alternative asset classes in a portfolio has the potential to lower overall portfolio risk and increase long-term returns.

Although the allure of a diversification benefit is enticing, there are some major obstacles to adding alternative asset classes to a portfolio. The biggest obstacle is the cost. Whether you are building a portfolio of collectibles or investing in a pooled commodities account, the cost of adding alternative asset classes can far exceed the diversification benefit.

No chapter on alternative investing would be complete without a discussion of hedge funds. Over the last decade, investors have become obsessed with the mystique of hedge funds. This is especially true in the high-net-worth marketplace, where investors clamor for access to some hedge fund opportunities. What makes a hedge fund uniquely different from a typical mutual fund is the manager's freedom to invest. Hedge funds are not regulated by the Securities and Exchange Commission (although that is slowly changing), so the managers can do an assortment of things that mutual funds cannot. A hedge fund may hold a large, concentrated stock position; employ a liberal use of leverage; use futures, options, swaps, and other derivatives; or sell investments short (sell investments that the fund does not own).

The manager's freedom comes at a price to investors in the fund. The management fees for hedge funds can be very high compared to those for mutual funds. In addition, investors incur trading costs, administrative fees, and incentive fees if the fund makes money after all the other costs. Isn't it strange that despite the fact that the fund managers are paid a high management fee, they also keep part of the profit as an incentive fee just because they did what they were paid to do? Of course, if they do a poor job and lose money, the managers still are paid the higher-than-average management fee.

In addition to high costs, hedge funds lack liquidity. Investors may have to wait a long time before being allowed to take money out. Some hedge funds require a 5- or 10-year commitment before you are allowed to invest.

Many people incorrectly believe that hedge funds are an alternative asset class. Hedge funds themselves are not an alternative investment. They are merely a private pool of capital formed by a limited number of qualified investors. Hedge funds are entities that hold investments. Perhaps a hedge fund manager will place the money from a fund in alternative assets, but that alone does not make the hedge fund an alternative asset class.

Should you consider hedge funds or alternative asset classes in your portfolio? If you have expertise in a certain area of collectibles and know that you can make money with low costs involved, then you may want to try. Or, you may find a low-cost managed fund that provides adequate diversification in the area you are interested in investing in. In either case, the alternative investments are appropriate for only a small portion of your equity allocation.

Be careful not to pay too much for access to alternative asset classes. The costs of acquiring direct investments in alternative assets can quickly outweigh the diversification benefits. A good rule of thumb for all alternative investments is, when in doubt, stay out.

INVESTING IN COMMODITIES

Commodities are common products that are used every day, such as food, basic materials, and energy-related items. Food products include items such as sugar, corn, and oats; basic materials include items such as steel and aluminum; energy is traded in the form of crude oil, natural gas, and electricity. Another category is precious metals such as gold and silver. All together, these resources make up the global commodities market.

The global market for commodities is as wide as it is deep. Since commodities are dug up, manufactured, or grown in almost every nation in the world, there are hundreds of global commodities markets. There is trading going on some place 24 hours a day, 7 days a week. If you want to buy an ounce of gold at 10:00 p.m., it can be arranged through any large commodities broker. If you want to sell oil at 3:00 a.m., that can also be arranged.

Pick up any *Wall Street Journal* and turn to the Money and Investing section to find a partial list of commodities that trade on U.S. exchanges. The *Wall Street Journal* gives both *spot* and *futures* prices. The spot price is what a physical commodity is changing hands for today, while a futures price is a contract for delivery of a set amount of the physical commodity some time in the future.

By definition, commodities mean abundance. There are a lot of them around. Although there are occasional shortages that create a temporary jump in prices, the shortage tends to fix itself. If wheat prices rise because of greater demand, farmers will grow more wheat next season. If a shortage of steel causes prices to rise, producers will dig more ore. If oil is scarce, companies will explore for more oil. Whenever a commodity is priced high enough to make a profit, more is produced by current suppliers and more competitors come into the market.

In addition, if the price of a commodity stays high for an extended period of time, there are substitutes. For example, if the price of gasoline remains high for many years, auto companies will make a major effort to convert cars to hydrogen, natural gas, or some other alternative fuel. It may take a few years for users and producers to figure out how to get around high energy prices, but eventually supply catches up with demand and the price of energy drops.

The supply-and-demand cycle is true even for precious metals such as gold. Although it is not always possible to locate more ore and dig it out, new techniques for extracting gold from the current production can also increase supply. In addition, if prices are high enough, increased selling by governments and large institutions can dump a large supply on the market and quickly bring prices down. Finally, when the supply of gold is greater than the demand, the price falls back to its true economic value.

Figure 10-1 illustrates the price of gold since 1925, adjusted for the rate of inflation. There have been a few spikes in the price of gold over the years, but in the aggregate the price has not changed much. If you take storage costs into consideration, in the long run gold investors have earned the inflation rate.

Oil prices are always in flux based on changes in global supply and demand. The price we pay for gasoline reflects that volatility. In recent years, the price volatility has been heightened as a result of increasing demand for oil from emerging markets such as China and India. Nonetheless, like the price of gold, the price of oil has a cycle of boom and bust. Figure 10-2 illustrates the biggest run-up in price occurred in 1981. During that year, the price of oil hit an inflation-adjusted high. Another run-up in prices occurred during 2004. During the 2004 run-up the inflation-adjusted price of oil did not reach its 1981 peak. Over the long term, the inflation-adjusted spot price of oil has been relatively consistent for 50 years. According to Figure 10-2, the price of oil basically keeps pace with the inflation rate.

The commodities markets are older than the stock markets. As a result, there are some commodities price series that go back hundreds of years. The data used in this chapter go back about 50 years, which covers a period of moderate inflation.

FIGURE 10-1

Gold Prices Adjusted to 2004 Dollars
Gold Prices = Inflation

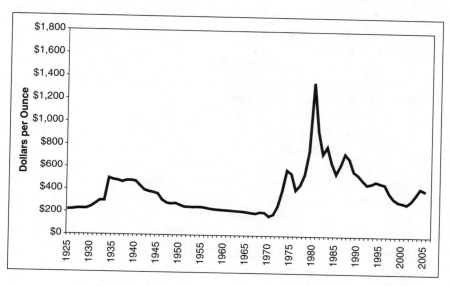

FIGURE 10-2

Crude Oil Prices Adjusted to 2004 Prices
A Couple of Spikes—Little Change

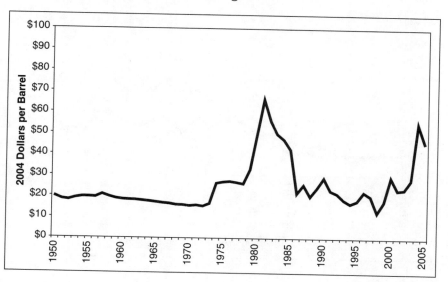

The Commodity Research Bureau (CRB) Spot Market Price Index is the most comprehensive measure of the price movements of 22 actively traded commodities: cocoa beans, corn, steers, sugar, wheat, burlap, copper scrap, cotton, lead scrap, print cloth (spot), rubber, steel scrap, wool tops, butter, hides, hogs, lard, rosin, tallow, tin zinc, and the basic energy-related items. The prices on these commodities are obtained from trade publications or from other government agencies. Figure 10-3 is a graphical history of the CRB Spot Index since 1956. For free information and charts on Reuters–CRB indexes, visit www.CRBtrader.com.

Between 1956 and 1980, commodities prices more or less kept pace with the rate of inflation. Then prices trended sideways in a fairly tight range for the next 25 years. That meant that the real price of commodities was falling in relation to inflation. There are many explanations for the general decline in real commodities prices over the last couple of decades. Those reasons include an increase in foreign competition, new technologies and innovations, and failed

FIGURE 10-3

CRB Commodities Spot Prices versus Inflation (CPI)
Base of 100 in 1956

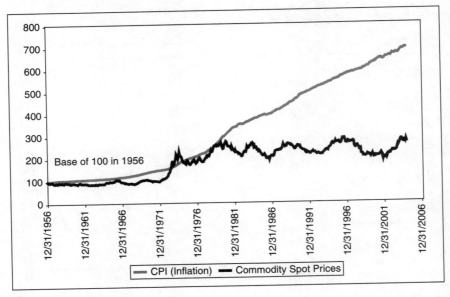

government policies on price controls and tariffs. Some people believe that the world is destined for an extended boom in commodities prices. However, there is no knowing whether the long-awaited boom in commodities prices will occur or when it will occur.

During the 2003 and 2004 time period, U.S. commodities indexes jumped, and some people called that the beginning of a long-term trend. However, much of the gain can be attributed to a decline in the value of the dollar rather than a global shortage.

COMMODITIES FUTURES

The trading of physical commodities is not an option for most individuals. Unless you own a silo to store 10,000 bushels of corn or a tank to store 1,000 gallons of crude oil, a direct investment in most commodities is not practical. To make investing in commodities easy, most people invest in commodities futures contracts.

A futures contract is an agreement to buy or sell a set amount of a commodity at a designated date in the future and at an agreed-upon price. Futures are part of a class of securities called derivatives, so named because they derive their value from the worth of an underlying asset. In the case of commodities futures, a contract is priced in part on today's spot price for that commodity and in part on the anticipated spot price on the future delivery date.

Think of a futures contract as nothing more than buying a commodity on layaway. As a buyer, you agree on the price of a standardized commodity contract and put down a deposit. The balance on the contract is due on the delivery date of the commodity. A contract is an obligation, so it must be honored by both the buyer and the seller. However, you do not need to take delivery of the commodity. You are allowed to sell the contract anytime before the delivery date and close out your position.

A standardized futures contract for a commodity has a preestablished size and settles on a preestablished date. It is traded on one of the established futures exchanges and confirmed with a standard down payment known as *margin*. Margin is typically 2 percent to 7 percent of the value of the contract. That money is placed in escrow until the contract expires.

Here is an example of how a commodities futures contract may be used. Assume that an oil refinery wants to lock in the price it pays for crude oil three months in advance. The refinery simply buys crude oil futures for delivery in three months and puts up a small amount of margin. Now the refinery knows the price that it will pay for crude in three months in advance and can budget for it. In the same way, oil producers can sell oil futures to be delivered in three months, even though they do not have the oil on hand today. That allows the oil producers to know what price they will receive for the oil they sell three months from now and know how much they will need to produce.

The price of a futures contract depends on many factors. The most important factor is the spot price of the commodity today. Typically, a near-term futures contract will be priced very close to the spot price. Other factors that influence price include the outlook for supply and demand, the cost of storage until delivery, and the level of interest rates between now and the delivery date. At times the futures price of a commodity contract may be higher than the spot price, and at other times it may be lower. That depends on the consensus price forecast. Figure 10-4 illustrates the historical

FIGURE 10-4

CRB Commodities Spot versus Near Contract Futures Prices
Base of 100 in 1956

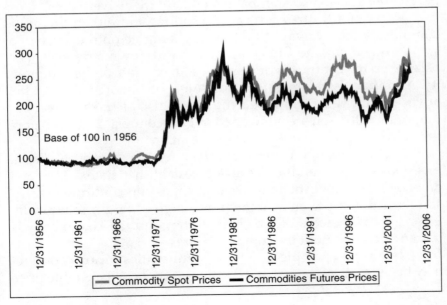

difference in price between CRB spot prices and one-month CRB futures prices.

It is interesting to note that during the 1990s, near-term delivery futures prices lagged spot commodity prices by a considerable amount. During the decade, futures buyers were anticipating lower raw material costs as productivity gains and foreign competition drove prices down. The low point for commodities futures prices was February 1999. Between 2000 and 2004, commodities prices rallied. That caused the spread between spot prices and futures prices to tighten, which created one-time excess gains for futures market investors.

COMMODITIES TOTAL RETURN INDEXES

The CRB Commodity Total Return Index in Figure 10-5 takes some explaining. The index is designed to replicate the return on an investable basket of commodities, which cannot be invested in directly. Therefore, the way the index is calculated uses a

FIGURE 10-5

CRB Futures Total Return Index Assuming a T-Bill Return on the Cash Portion

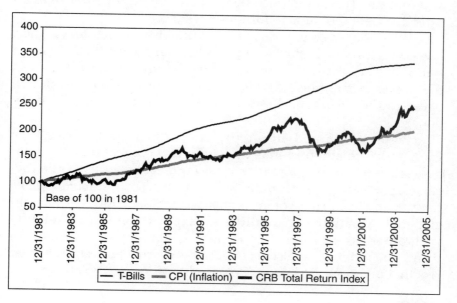

combination of the price movement of commodities and the difference in price between old futures contracts near expiration and
new futures prices on the day contracts are rolled to the next
month, plus the income from Treasury bills.

As you recall, a down payment or margin is required to buy a
futures contract. Typically, the margin is about 5 percent of the
value of the commodities that the futures contract represents. For
example, a futures contract for $4,000 worth of gold for delivery in
one month may require a 5 percent margin of $200, which gains
money market interest. That means that the other $3,800 is still
sitting in your account and can be invested in something else while
you wait for delivery. The total return on your investment for the
month equals the price change on the gold futures contract plus
the interest on the other 95 percent that is sitting in your account. If
you roll the contract to the next month, there will be another gain
or loss based on the difference between near-term futures prices
and one-month futures prices.

For the sake of calculating total return indexes, it is assumed
that the 95 percent cash is invested in Treasury bills. A total return
commodities index includes the price change of the commodity,
the price difference between near-term and one-month futures
contracts, and the interest income earned overall on the cash
and margin. The one-month returns are linked together over an
extended period of time to form Figure 10-5.

What makes commodity funds attractive to investors is their
low correlation with stocks and bonds. That means that when the
traditional securities markets are going down, this does not affect
the prices of commodities. Figure 10-6 illustrates the correlation
between the CRB Total Return Index, U.S. stocks, and Treasury
bonds.

Figures 10-5 and 10-6 represent a dilemma for investors.
Commodity total return indexes have a low correlation with other
asset classes, *but they also have historically low returns.* While low
correlation is a great attribute for an asset class, *you cannot eat low
correlation.* The purpose of investing is to achieve a long-term financial goal. Although commodities indexes exhibit low correlation
with other asset classes, that in itself is not a reason to invest in
them. The index must also be expected to earn a fair return for the
risk that investors are taking. Commodity prices are volatile, and if

FIGURE 10-6

Rolling 36-Month Correlation of the CRB Total Return Index to U.S. Stocks and Intermediate-Term Treasury Bonds

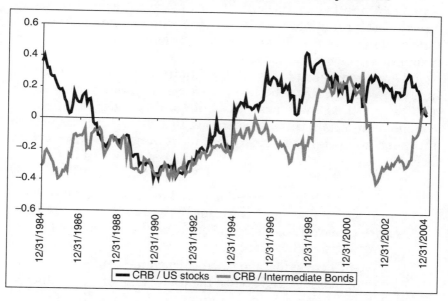

an investment in the asset class is expected to achieve T-bill rates of return at best, then you are better off skipping this asset class and putting your money in something that rewards you for the risk.

IF YOU MUST OWN COMMODITIES

If you insist on owning commodities, then be sensible about how you invest. Buying individual commodity futures contracts is not a good idea. Individual contracts are very risky because of their high degree of leverage. You would need to invest in several different contracts on several different commodities to gain proper diversification. A better alternative is to get commodity exposure through a broadly diversified mutual fund. Another different approach is to invest through an industry-sector mutual fund that holds commodity-producing companies. A few reasonably priced mutual funds are listed in Table 10-4 at the end of this chapter.

Commodities mutual funds invest in derivatives of commodity total return indexes. Therefore, investors in those funds should understand how commodity indexes are constructed. There are several competing commodity total return indexes. Like stock indexes, each commodity index provider has its own methodology for calculating returns and its reasons for believing that its system is superior to everyone else's.

Three popular indexes are the Commodity Research Bureau Index (Reuters-CRB), the Goldman Sachs Commodity Index (GSCI), and the Dow Jones–AIG Commodity Index (DJ-AIGCI). The most important difference among these three indexes is their approach to weighting the different commodity groups they include.

- Reuters-CRB is an equal-weighted index of 22 commodity prices. Equal weighting means that a 1 percent rise in the price of nickel has the same effect on the index as a 1 percent rise in the price of crude oil.
- The GSCI considers the price of 24 commodities based on overall market value. Since the total value of oil produced globally dominates the commodities markets, the GSCI methodology generates an excessively heavy energy weighting. In other words, a 1 percent rise in the price of crude oil has a significantly larger effect on the GSCI than a 1 percent rise in the price of nickel.
- The DJ-AIGCI is derived from the value of 19 commodities. The DJ-AIGCI is also a market-weighted index, but with a twist: no commodity group in the index starts at over 33 percent (energy), and no single group component may be more than 15 percent (crude oil). The DJ-AIGCI is reweighted and rebalanced annually with restrictions.

The difference in the three approaches to commodities indexes can be understood by referring to Table 10-1. It indicates the relative importance of different commodity groups in each of the three indexes.

Despite the differences in the group weights, the returns on the three commodity indexes have high correlation with one

TABLE 10-1

Commodity Index Weights in 2005

Commodity Group	Reuters-CRB Weight	GSCI Weight	DJ-AIGCI Weight
Energy	18%	73%	33%
Grains	17%	8%	21%
Softs (sugar, cocoa)	23%	3%	9%
Base metals	12%	7%	18%
Precious metals	18%	2%	8%
Livestock	12%	7%	11%

another and low correlations with U.S. equities and bonds. The risk of owning this volatile asset class should compensate investors with appropriate returns. Table 10-2 highlights the performance and risk of the three methodologies since 1991.

From 2001 to 2004, the rise in the prices of oil and gas boosted the GSCI and DJ-AIGCI total return indexes because of their greater energy and metals exposure. Heavy agricultural and livestock weightings hurt the Reuters-CRB total return index during the same period.

The GSCI and DJ-AIGCI are relatively young compared to the Reuters-CRB, which has been around since 1940. In the long term, I anticipate that all the total return indexes are likely to result in similar performance, which should be something close to the return of Treasury bills.

Now that we have looked at the major commodity total return indexes, let us examine the feasibility of investing in those indexes.

TABLE 10-2

Commodity Total Return Index Statistics

1991–2004	Reuters-CRB	GSCI	DJ-AIGCI	T-Bills
Annualized return	3.6%	5.7%	6.8%	3.9%
Standard deviation	15.9%	17.2%	17.5%	0.5%

The published returns of the indexes do not reflect the return to investors in those indexes. Every managed fund of commodities and futures has annual management fees, and possibly a sales commission to buy in. The costs can be high. Some commodity mutual funds fees reach 2 percent per year in addition to a sales charge reaching 5.75 percent. Hopefully, more competition will enter the marketplace and drive costs lower. There are a couple of reasonably priced commodity mutual funds listed in Table 10-4 at the end of this chapter.

A second downside of commodity funds is that they are extremely tax-inefficient. The amount of turnover in these funds generates a lot of distributable income. Investors in a high income tax bracket should hold these funds only in a tax-deferred retirement account.

There is an alternative to a direct investment in commodities mutual funds. Several low-cost industry-specific index funds concentrate their holdings in companies that are in a commodities business. Those funds specialize in mining, energy, and other natural resources stocks. A partial list of commodity industry mutual funds is provided in Table 10-4 at the end of this chapter.

INVESTING IN HEDGE FUNDS

A hedge fund is a pooled investment vehicle that is privately organized and administered by professional investment managers. The hedge fund industry is not highly regulated, and that allows managers to skirt many regulatory requirements that mutual funds must follow. Limited disclosure has a couple of advantages for hedge fund managers. First, they are not required to disclose fund holdings to the public. Second, the secrecy is great for marketing. Fund managers tend to whisper loudly about their super-duper top-secret proprietary investment methods. But that is just marketing hoopla. There are over 8,000 hedge funds in existence. It is inconceivable that more than a few hundred are really good at what they do.

Only recently has the Securities and Exchange Commission started to demand more disclosure from hedge funds about their trading practices, and that includes conflicts of interest between fund managers and investors. Since hedge funds have assets of over $1 trillion and leverage that extends well beyond that amount, the sheer size and power of the hedge fund industry warrants a closer look by regulators.

HEDGE FUND STRATEGIES

There is a wide range of hedge fund strategies. Depending on the investment style of a hedge fund, the managers may buy, or "go long," securities to take advantage of rising prices, and may "short" securities, or sell them without owning them, to take advantage of falling prices. Some hedge fund trading strategies are designed to earn a profit regardless of the direction of the financial markets. These include a market-neutral strategy, in which the managers go long and short in equal amounts, thus negating the effect of the overall market movement. The idea of market-neutral strategies is to capture value from underpriced and overpriced securities.

There are a few advantages and many disadvantages to hedge funds. Low correlation is one advantage. Several styles of hedge funds exhibit low correlation with major asset classes such as stocks and bonds. That makes these funds an attractive investment for diversification. In addition, several hedge fund managers have produced higher returns than the stock markets with less risk. On the negative side, hedge funds are very expensive. The average management fee for a single fund is 1.5 percent per year, plus there is a profit incentive averaging 20 percent. In addition, hedge fund performance is notoriously inconsistent. Good performance by a fund one year does not ensure or even predict good performance the next. Finally, there are high barriers to entry. Hedge funds are available only to high-net-worth investors. The minimum investment of some funds is $1,000,000 or more.

There are three broad categories of hedge funds and several subcategories.

- *Arbitrage strategies.* Arbitrage is the practice of exploiting price inefficiencies in the marketplace. Pure arbitrage has no risk. The trades guarantee a return. Consider this very simple example. Assume XYZ stock is trading for $42 per share on the New York Stock Exchange and $41.90 on the London Stock Exchange. An investor can buy 1,000 shares in London for $41,900 and simultaneously sell 1,000 shares in New York for $42,000. The net gain to the investor is $100 risk free. There are hundreds of arbitrage opportunities that present themselves on a daily basis if you have access to the information and can trade very inexpensively.

- *Event-driven strategies.* Event-driven strategies take advantage of corporate transaction announcements and other one-time events. An example would be "distressed securities," which involves investing in companies that are in or near bankruptcy. Another type of event-driven strategy is an activist fund, which is predatory in nature. The managers of an activist fund take sizable positions in small, flawed companies, then use their influence to force management changes and restructuring. A third type of event-driven fund is venture capital. Venture funds invest in start-up companies.
- *Directional or tactical strategies.* The largest group of hedge funds uses directional or tactical strategies. An example of a directional fund is a commodities trading advisor (CTA). CTAs use charts and mathematical models to identify trends in global futures markets. CTAs may go long or short a market to profit from both rising and falling futures prices. A second example of a tactical fund is a macro fund. These are fundamentally driven "top-down," big-picture bets on currencies, interest rates, commodities, and global stock markets.

Table 10-3 lists the three major categories of hedge funds and the major strategies within each category. Table 10-3 represents

TABLE 10-3

Hedge Fund Categories and Strategies

Arbitrage Strategies	Event-Driven	Directional/Tactical
Fixed-income arbitrage	Mergers and acquisitions	Equity long/short
Convertible arbitrage	Distressed securities	Managed futures (CTA)
Special situations	Venture capital	Macro strategies

only a sample of hedge fund types and strategies. The number of strategies is limited only by the imagination of people in the investment industry.

THE PROBLEM WITH HEDGE FUNDS

Hedge funds have a certain sex appeal. The secretive nature of the business, the allure of high potential returns, and the low correlation with stocks and bonds—it is all very enticing. However, in this author's opinion, much of the hype surrounding the role of hedge funds in a portfolio is misplaced. For most individual investors, the disadvantages of high cost, low disclosure, lack of diversification, illiquidity of some funds, and poor consistency of performance far outweigh the benefits.

Since hedge funds are largely unregulated, the managers are not required to report their holdings or performance to the public. There are several companies that monitor the performance of hedge funds, although those published numbers are often biased. Some monitoring companies are paid by the hedge funds to promote the funds they report on. Other monitoring companies use flawed data collection methodologies. For instance, they do not include the performance of funds that have closed or merged. That produces an upward *survivorship bias* in the hedge fund indexes. When a hedge fund has a bad quarter, the managers may simply choose not to report the results. That leads to a *selection bias* in the index performance. Most monitoring companies allow a newly reporting fund to "back fill" performance with simulated historic returns that no investor actually earned. That creates a *backfill bias* in the indexes. Finally, most monitoring companies allow the hedge fund managers to price their own illiquid securities, thus introducing a *pricing bias* into the indexes.

When all the inconsistencies of the published hedge fund indexes are eliminated from the data, the total return of the indexes drops dramatically. Wholesalers of hedge funds claim that the returns on these funds are equal to the long-term return on the stock market, with less risk. However, after factoring out all inconsistencies in the indexes, the returns on hedge funds fall more in line with the return of intermediate-term government bonds, albeit with much greater risk than bonds.

If the flaws in the hedge fund index performance do not stop you from investing in this investment vehicle, the lack of consistency of performance should. The funds that performed well one year cannot be relied upon to deliver top returns in the following year, or in any year thereafter. In fact, after one good year, the probability of having a below-average second year is higher than that of having an above-average one.

Vikas Agarwal of Georgia State University and Narayan Naik of the London Business School wrote one of many published research reports documenting the erratic and unpredictable returns from hedge funds.[1] Agarwal and Naik found that persistence of return among hedge fund managers is short-term in nature, and that what little persistence there is disappears over a multiyear period. Thus, it is very unlikely anyone can predict which hedge funds will perform well in the future and which ones will perform poorly.

In 1990, there were fewer than 300 hedge funds with assets totaling less than $30 billion. Today there are over 8,000 hedge funds with total assets over $1 trillion. It is illogical to assume that the opportunities for gains have grown at the same rate. More than likely, the opportunity for gain has been severely diluted by an abundance of cash chasing fewer opportunities.

A statistical analysis of the data from the 2003 edition of the U.S. Offshore Funds Directory shows that the closure rate of hedge funds has increased from roughly 2 percent per year for funds outstanding during the early 1990s to more than 12 percent of funds outstanding today. Many funds have already failed, and many, many more will fail. Consequently, many of the funds that exist today will not be around 10 years from now.

IF YOU MUST INVEST IN HEDGE FUNDS

If you still believe hedge funds are a good idea, and you feel compelled to invest in one, here are some ideas. Investing in just one hedge fund can be a gamble. You simply cannot predict when a hedge fund's glory days are coming to an end. Investors who are attracted to hedge funds need to diversify among many of them. The problem is that many funds have high minimums, so it is not possible for small investors to buy several funds at one time. A simple way to solve the diversification problem is with a fund of funds. A fund of funds is a limited partnership that invests in several hedge funds. Typically a fund of funds is diversified across multiple manager styles for added diversification.

The diversification benefit of a fund of funds is a plus, but the major disadvantage is that it adds another layer of annual management fees to the already high cost of the individual funds within the investment. In addition to another layer of management fees, some funds of funds collect a profit incentive on top of the management fee. After adding up all the fees and incentives paid to the individual fund managers and the fees and incentive fees paid to the fund of funds manager, the cost of owning one of these investments can easily eat up 50 percent of the profits—assuming there are profits.

The high cost of hedge fund participation, the lack of diversification ability, and poor performance consistency puts hedge funds in an investment category that this author does not consider appropriate for most individual investors. If you are interested in hedge funds, there are several easy-to-understand books available that will help, including *All About Hedge Funds,* written by veteran hedge fund manager Robert A. Jaeger (McGraw-Hill, 2002).

INVESTING IN COLLECTIBLES

Investing in collectibles can be financially rewarding and an enjoyable hobby. Traditional collectibles include fine art, coins, stamps, gems, documents, antiques, and other such objects. However, profitability is not limited to traditional collectibles. Any rare or unusual item can be a better investment than a fine oil painting by a well-known artist.

There are a few disadvantages to investing in collectibles. The cost of acquiring, storing, and insuring the items can be high, and that takes away from long-term returns. In addition, collectibles do not qualify for lower long-term capital gains rates. The long-term capital gains rate on stocks is 15 percent; however, on collectibles, it is 28 percent.

There are also limitations to investing in collectibles. Expertise is required in the items being collected, as well as a passion for details. If you do not have expertise, you would need to hire a professional consultant, which can add considerable cost. Another disadvantage of collectibles is they can be illiquid assets. When you want to sell, there is not always a willing buyer at a fair price. You need to find a liquid market for buying and selling. Online auction companies such as eBay have helped tremendously in the search for liquidity and fair pricing.

On the positive side, the aesthetic value of collectibles may make up for most of the disadvantages. You can admire your collection with friends, relatives, and other collectors. In many cases, the social benefits of collecting outweigh the monetary benefits.

COLLECTIBLES PERFORMANCE

Tracking the performance of collectibles is difficult at best. Most transactions are between private parties, and prices either are not disclosed or are not compiled in a single database. There are limited indexes that track collectibles.

New York University professors Jianping Mei and Michael Moses have created an index of the long-term return on fine art. The Mei Moses Fine Art Index tracks the sale prices of paintings, drawings, and sculpture auctioned in New York since 1875. Figure 10-7 illustrates the 50-year compounded return of the Mei Moses Fine Art Index versus the U.S. stock market.

FIGURE 10-7

Mei Moses All Art Index versus CRSP Total U.S. Stock Market

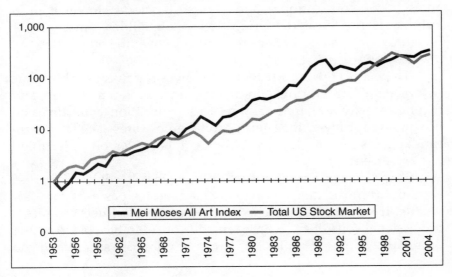

From 1954 to 2004, the Mei Moses Fine Art Index return was slightly higher than the return from U.S. stocks. The art index was slightly riskier than stocks during the period, with an annual standard deviation of 23 percent versus 18 percent for stocks.

Jianping Mei and Michael Moses have a free Web site with interesting research and periodic updates of their index. The Web site address is www.meimosesfineartindex.org. Registration is required; however, there is no cost to view the index and read the online research of Mei and Moses.

Another interesting collectibles benchmark is the PCGS Coin Universe 3000 Index (CU3000). The Professional Coin Grading Service (PCGS) in Newport Beach, California, is a division of Collectors Universe, Inc. The CU3000 is an index that represents a broad list of 3,000 graded coins chosen by Coin Universe to represent the overall U.S. coin market. PCGS has several indexes on its Web site at www.pcgs.com. The data are free of charge.

Figure 10-8 compares the return on the CU3000 Index to the return on the total U.S. stock market since 1970. Between 1970 and 1989, the price of the index jumped by an amazing 181-fold, from

FIGURE 10-8

PCGS Coin Universe 3000 Index versus the
CRSP Total U.S. Stock Market

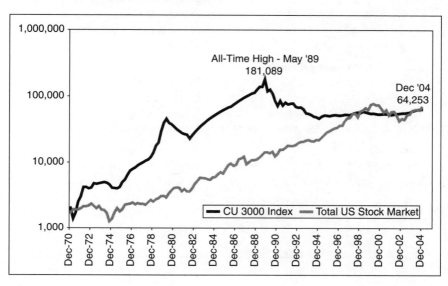

1,000 to 181,089. This dramatic rise was unsustainable. Over the next five years, coin prices tumbled by nearly 75 percent. Ironically, in spite of the huge surge and ultimate collapse of the CU3000 Index, over the complete 25-year period, the total return has been in line with the return on the stock market.

ALTERNATIVE ASSET INVESTMENT LIST

Table 10-4 gives a partial list of mutual funds that invest in the alternative asset classes discussed in this chapter. Some funds invest in commodities using derivatives, and others invest in companies that are in the commodities business. The mutual funds

TABLE 10-4

Low-Cost Alternative Asset Mutual Funds

	Symbol	Benchmark
Commodities Funds		
Oppenheimer Real Asset	QRAAX	Goldman Sachs Commodity Index
PIMCO Commodity Real Return	PCRAX	Dow Jones-AIG Commodity Index
Energy Mutual Funds		
iShares DJ Energy ETF	IYE	Dow Jones U.S. Energy Sector Index
iShares SP Global Energy ETF	IXC	S&P Global Energy Sector Index
Energy SPDR ETF	XLE	S&P U.S. Energy Select Sector Index
Vanguard Energy Fund	VGENX	Actively managed fund
Gold and Precious Metal Funds		
iShares COMEX Gold Trust	IAU	Gold and gold futures contracts
streetTRACKS Gold Shares	GLD	Direct investment in gold bullion
Vanguard Precious Metals Mining	VGMPX	Actively managed fund
American Century Global Gold	BGEIX	Actively managed fund
Basic Materials		
iShares Basic Materials	IYM	Dow Jones U.S. Basic Materials
Vanguard Materials VIPERS	VAW	MSCI U.S. Investable Market Materials
Combined Natural Resources		
iShare Natural Resources	IGE	Goldman Sachs Natural Resources Index

listed in the table are presented as examples of alternative investments rather than investment recommendations.

CHAPTER SUMMARY

Do commodities and hedge funds make sense in your portfolio? My belief is that they are not needed. The expenses associated with those alternative investments are high, and those costs outweigh the benefit of an increase in portfolio diversification. Nonetheless, I am not giving up hope. Money management companies are always seeking new ideas, and it would be a good idea for one or more of the low-cost index fund providers to develop products that are affordable and offer low correlation with stocks and bonds. Those index funds may include low-cost commodities funds, and possibly low-cost arbitrage and market-neutral indexed hedge funds.

Collectibles offer a unique investment opportunity. The monetary rewards of collecting can be large, and the aesthetic value is an added benefit. Collect what you like, enjoy what you collect, and maybe you will even make money at it.

NOTE

[1]Vikas Agarwal and Naranyan Y. Naik, "Multi-Period Performance Persistence Analysis of Hedge Funds," *Journal of Financial and Quantitative Analysis*, Vol. 35, No. 3, September 2000.

Managing Your Portfolio

Realistic Market Expectations

KEY CONCEPTS

- Realistic market expectations are important to investment planning.
- Market risks are more stable than market returns.
- The relationship between market risk and expected return is an essential one.
- Market forecasts are useful in the long term, but not in the short term.

Several tools are used in the design, implementation, and maintenance of an asset allocation strategy. Part 3 provides you with those tools so that you can design an asset allocation that fits your financial needs.

One important element in the asset allocation process is for the investor to have realistic market expectations. An investment plan works only if an investor's expectations for market returns are in line with economic reality. In passing, some investors may say that market returns cannot be predicted. While that may be true in the short term, it is not true in the long term. The long-term return on markets can be predicted with a reasonable degree of accuracy, and those expectations should be used to assist in the investment planning process.

There are several methods used by investment analysts to forecast market returns. Some of those methods rely on a "top-down" picture of economic variables, which filter down into the expected returns on various asset classes. Other methods rely on a "bottom-up" strategy, building from individual securities forecasts that cumulate in asset-class expected returns. Most analysts and economists agree to disagree on every element of market forecasting, from the methodology used to the modeling techniques to the inputs into those equations. Interestingly, despite differences of opinion, most long-term market forecasts tend to fall within a narrow range of returns. At the end of the chapter is a composite of forecast market risks and returns.

FORECASTING MARKET RETURNS

Two market forecasting methodologies are discussed in this chapter. The first method is a risk-adjusted return model that relies on historical market volatilities to forecast the future performance of various asset classes relative to one another. The second method is an economic top-down model that relies on a long-term forecast of gross domestic product (GDP) to forecast various asset-class returns.

Forecasting a market's future return always involves the analysis of historical risk and return. While history does not repeat itself exactly, it casts a long shadow. There are important lessons to be learned from a study of economic history. Forecasting requires the confidence to extend some of those past characteristics into the future.

Analysis of market returns requires a long-term perspective. The past 25 years ending in 2004 have been unusually generous to U.S. stock and bond investors. The annualized return from stocks was over 13 percent, despite a bear market in stocks from 2000 to 2002. During the same period the compounded return on the five-year Treasury bond was over 9 percent. Inflation was less than 4 percent during the period, meaning that the real return from stocks was over 9 percent and the real return from intermediate bonds was over 5 percent.

Although the last 25-year period was one of the most profitable in history for stock and bond investors, there is almost no chance of those returns happening again over the next 25 years. In fact, based on current economic conditions, the returns on U.S. stocks and bonds are likely to be about half those produced in the previous 25-year period. Nevertheless, those returns are still attractive relative to the return from money market funds.

MODEL 1: RISK-ADJUSTED RETURNS

The risk-adjusted return model relies on historical market volatilities to forecast the relative future performance for various asset classes. Market returns can vary considerably over different periods of time, although the volatility of those returns is more consistent. In the long term, the volatility of a market can be used to forecast its returns relative to those of other markets with different risks.

Depending on economic conditions, market returns can differ significantly from period to period. Table 11-1 lists the difference in return during five independent 10-year periods starting in 1955.

While the returns during different 10-year periods can vary considerably, the standard deviations of those returns during these independent 10-year periods tend to be more stable than the returns themselves. Table 11-2 highlights the standard deviation of market returns over the same five independent 10-year periods starting in 1955.

The standard deviation during these independent 10-year periods is very close for the S&P 500 and for Treasury bills. There was some extra volatility in bond returns during the high

TABLE 11-1

Independent 10-Year Period Compounded Returns

	S&P 500	5-Year T-Notes	T-Bills
1955–1964	12.8%	2.9%	2.6%
1965–1974	1.2%	5.1%	5.4%
1975–1984	14.8%	9.1%	8.8%
1985–1994	14.4%	9.4%	5.8%
1995–2004	12.1%	7.2%	3.9%

TABLE 11-2

Standard Deviation of Market Returns

	S&P 500	5-Year T-Notes	T-Bills
1955–1964	12.0%	3.0%	0.2%
1965–1974	14.6%	4.6%	0.4%
1975–1984	14.8%	7.6%	0.9%
1985–1994	15.3%	5.0%	0.5%
1995–2004	15.7%	4.6%	0.5%

FIGURE 11-1

The Relationship between Risk and Return
CRSP Total U.S. Stock Market Index

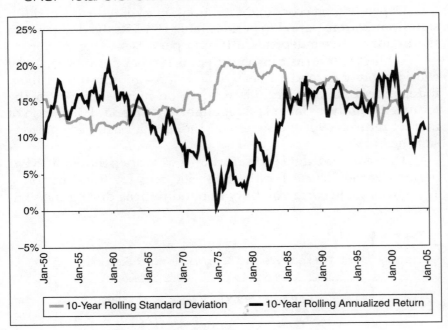

inflationary period from 1975 to 1984; however, the volatility has since fallen back to pre-1975 periods.

Figure 11-1 compares the rolling 10-year annualized return of U.S. stocks to the rolling 10-year standard deviation of those returns. Notice that the volatility of the stock market is more consistent than the return on the market. Also note that the periods of highest volatility were also the periods of lowest return.

Bond market volatility has not been as consistent as stock volatility over the last 50 years. During the late 1970s and early 1980s, unusually high inflation caused an aberration in fixed-income prices. Interest rates surged with inflation to historic levels, and that caused an increased volatility of bond prices. By the late 1990s, bond market volatility had subsided to more moderate levels. Figure 11-2 illustrates the rolling 10-year standard deviation of various fixed-income investments.

Volatility is not risk in itself; rather, is it an indication of some economic risk. When prices swing in one direction or the other, it signifies rapid change in the attitude of investors toward that asset. Each asset class has its own unique financial risks that generate the price swings. For example, stock market volatility is an indication of a widespread change in corporate earnings estimates. Bond

FIGURE 11-2

10-Year Rolling Standard Deviation of U.S. Fixed-Income Securities

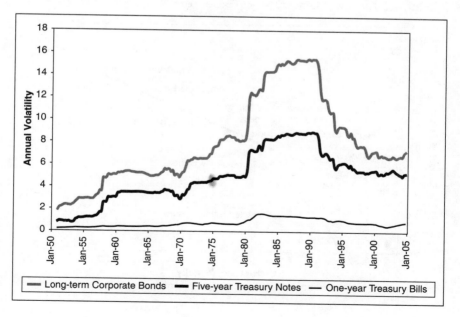

market volatility is an indication of a widespread change in expected inflation.

Although there are spikes in volatility during uncertain and changing economic conditions, in general asset-class return volatility remains relatively constant across major asset classes. Therefore, an investor can develop a model that predicts future expected returns using past volatility as a proxy. In the long run, the volatility of a market explains a large amount of that market's return relative to other markets. Investments that have higher volatility have higher expected returns, and investments that have lower volatility have lower expected returns. Accordingly, if you know the historical volatility of an investment, you can forecast its expected long-term return relative to all other asset classes.

Figure 11-3 illustrates the theoretical relationship between the known price volatility of several asset classes discussed in previous chapters, including the relationship of inflation to all investment returns. As the risk in an asset class increases, so does the expected return.

FIGURE 11-3

Historic Market Volatility and Expected Return

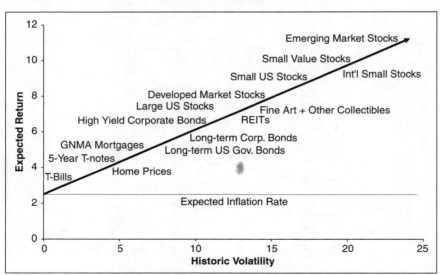

THE EFFECT OF INFLATION

One problem with the volatility model is that it can be biased by inflation. The inflation rate is an inherent part of all market returns, although the returns from inflation are not profits. The inflation part of investment return does not buy any extra goods and services, although it is taxed as though it did. Thus, volatility-based models should factor out inflation expectations to derive a real return component.

Figure 11-4 illustrates the effect that inflation has on annual Treasury bill returns. The top line is the nominal return on Treasury bills for a one-year period, and the darker line below is the after-inflation return (real return). Over the long term, the inflation-adjusted rate of return on T-bills has averaged about 1.3 percent.

FIGURE 11-4

One-Year Treasury Bill Returns, 1955–2004

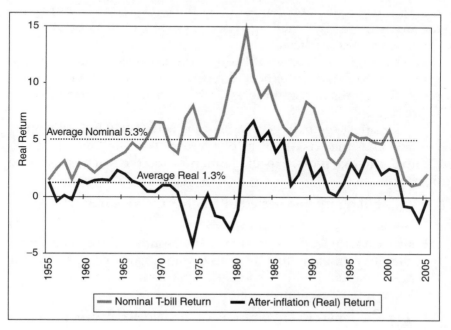

Taxes are also an issue. Over the last 50 years, the one-year Treasury bill earned 5.3 percent interest; the real gain was about 1.3 percent, reflecting a 4.0 percent inflation rate over the period. However, income taxes are still due on the entire 5.3 percent. The IRS does not factor out inflation when calculating how much money you earned. Consequently, an investor in the 25 percent income tax bracket lost 1.3 percent to taxes. Add a 4.0 percent inflation loss to a 1.3 percent tax loss and the real after-tax and after inflation return to the investor was 0 percent.

T-bills are supposed to be risk-free, and in an efficient market that means they should also be return-free. No risk means no return. For all practical purposes, assume that going forward, the after-tax real rate of return on T-bills will be 0 percent.

STACKING RISK PREMIUMS

All investments have risk. Risk-free Treasury bills have inflation risk and taxes. Every other asset class has risks in addition to the risks inherent in T-bills. By analyzing the different risks inherent in an investment and summing the expected return premiums for taking those risks, you can estimate the expected total return on the investment. By stacking risks, expected returns of all asset classes can be constructed.

This section steps you through the process of stacking risk premiums to derive an expected return. It starts with the risk and return for T-bills and completes with the risk and return of small value stocks.

The safest security you can own is a Treasury bill. It is often referred to as the "risk-free" rate of return. The T-bill return can be divided into two parts, expected inflation and the real risk-free rate of return.

T-bill return = expected inflation + real risk-free rate

Since Treasury bills are the safest investment available, all other investments must earn at least the T-bill's return. In addition, all other investments must have an extra return to compensate for the risks inherent in the particular investment. The extra return is known as a risk premium.

Expected investment return = T-bill yield + risk premium

Every investment other than T-bills has an expected risk premium that is based on the investment's unique greater risk than T-bills. For example, Treasury bonds have term risk. That is the price risk that results from interest-rate changes. Bonds with longer maturities have greater term risk. The greater the term risk of a bond, the higher the expected return.

Figure 11-5 highlights the term risk derived from Treasury Inflation-Protected Securities (TIPS) based on different maturities. Since the inflation rate is already factored out of TIPS yields, the curve shown in Figure 11-5 represents pure term risk, known as duration (see Chapter 8 for more information on TIPS).

Figure 11-5 shows the premium that investors will earn by increasing the maturities of their fixed-income investments. By moving fixed-income maturities from short-term bonds to inter-mediate-term bonds, investors can increase their returns by about 0.5 percent, while also increasing their term risk.

Treasury bonds = T-bill return + term risk premium

FIGURE 11-5

TIPS Duration and Real Yield Spreads
Premiums for Taking Term Risk Assuming 2.5 Percent Inflation

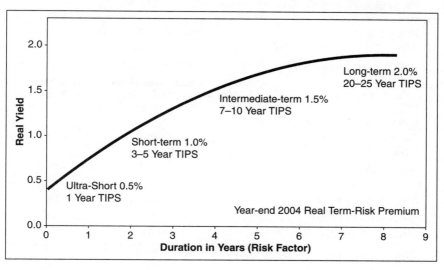

Corporate bonds, municipal bonds, and foreign bonds also have term risk, which will be reflected in their expected returns. In addition, unlike U.S. Treasury bonds, those issues also have the risk of credit downgrade, and the lower-quality bonds have the risk of default. Both of those risks will cause bond prices to fluctuate.

If investors purchase a bond with credit risk, they should expect to receive a premium for taking that risk. Table 11-3 represents the credit "spreads," or expected premiums across different maturities and credit quality. AAA to BBB rated bonds are investment-grade, and BB to C rated bonds are non-investment-grade, also known as high-yield bonds or junk bonds.

It is interesting that there is some extra term risk in addition to credit risk in corporate bonds. As investors move further out in maturity, they expect to be paid extra credit risk for the extra years they hold the bonds.

Investment-grade corporate bonds = Treasury bonds
+ credit risk premium

High-yield corporate bonds = Treasury bonds + credit risk
premium + default risk premium

TABLE 11-3

Average Spreads for U.S. Corporate Bonds over U.S. Treasury Securities

Credit Rating	Short-Term (1–5 Years)	Intermediate-Term (6–10 Years)	Long-Term (11–30 Years)
High Quality (AAA–AA)			
Minor credit risk premium	0.4%	0.6%	0.7%
Good Quality (A–BBB)			
Higher credit risk	0.8%	1.0%	1.1%
Fair Quality (BB–B)			
Credit risk and some default risk	2.4%	2.6%	2.7%
Poor Quality (CCC–C)			
Credit risk and high default risk	6–15%	6–20%	10–20%

Source: Bloomberg, Federal Reserve, Wall Street Journal.

Let's turn our attention to the equity market. Stocks have more risk than corporate bonds in a variety of ways. The owners of common stock experience more price volatility, the board of directors can cut common stock dividends without shareholder approval, and shareholders are the last people to be paid in the event of a corporate bankruptcy.

Figure 11-6 illustrates the rolling 10-year equity risk premium based on the returns on stocks over the returns on long-term corporate bonds. The equity risk premium is far from consistent. The difference between the 10-year annualized returns from stocks and bonds has varied from minus 10 percent ending in 1938 to over 17 percent ending in 1958. Given the risk of stocks and the current valuation of the market, a good prediction for the long-term equity risk premium going forward is about 3 percent annualized.

U.S. equity market returns = expected corporate bond returns
+ equity risk premium

FIGURE 11-6

Rolling 10-Year Equity Risk Premium
Total Stock Market Return Less Long-Term Corporate
Bond Return

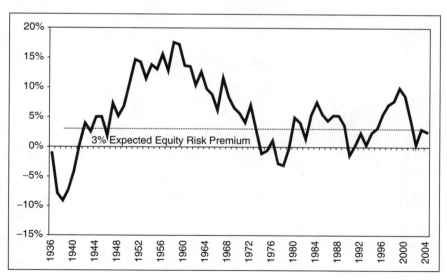

There are other risk premiums that can be applied to the expected return on a portfolio in addition to the inherent risk of the equity market. For example, small-cap value stocks have a distinctive risk premium over large-cap stocks. Figure 11-7 illustrates the rolling 10-year equity risk premium that small-cap value stocks earned over the return on the total U.S. stock market.

The return premium for taking small-cap value risk has been quite large and consistent over the years. There have been only a few 10-year rolling periods when small-cap value stocks have not performed better than the total stock market. A conservative long-term prediction for the long-term small-cap value premium over the total stock market is 3 percent annualized.

Small-cap value stocks = expected U.S. market returns
+ small cap premium + value premium

FIGURE   11-7

Rolling 10-Year Small-Cap Value Premium
FF Small-Cap Value Stock Return Less the
Total Stock Market Return

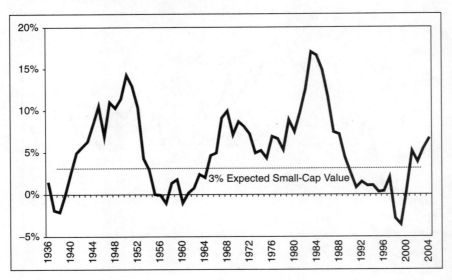

AN ILLUSTRATION OF STACKING RISK PREMIUMS

Table 11-4 puts the entire stacking process into perspective. It is an example of layering risks to derive the expected long-term return for an asset class. The expected risk premiums in this chapter are the author's own estimates, which may or may not agree with other sources.

Table 11-4 does not include all expected risk premiums for all the varied risks known in the markets. There are many other risks that are unique to individual investments that also deserve a return premium. Some of those risk premiums are used to calculate the long-term market return estimates at the end of this chapter.

MODEL 2: FORECASTING RETURNS USING ECONOMIC FACTORS

A second method for calculating expected market returns is through a "top-down" approach using an economic growth assumption. Gross domestic product (GDP) is the sum of all goods

TABLE 11-4

Examples of Expected Returns Derived by Layering Risk Premiums

	Inflation	T-Bills	Government Bonds	Corporate Bonds	Large-Cap Stocks	Small-Cap Stocks
Inflation	3.0%	3.0%	3.0%	3.0%	3.0%	3.0%
Real risk-free rate		0.5%	0.5%	0.5%	0.5%	0.5%
Term risk (intermediate)			1.5%	1.5%	1.5%	1.5%
Credit risk				0.8%	0.8%	0.8%
Equity risk					2.0%	2.0%
Small-cap value risk						2.0%
Total expected return	3.0%	3.5%	5.0%	5.8%	7.8%	9.8%

and services produced or sold in the United States. The Federal Reserve has a target for overall GDP growth, and it attempts to control that growth through changes in monetary policy. That growth number is about 3.0 percent after inflation.

About 10 percent of corporate-generated GDP eventually flows through to corporations as earnings. That number has been fairly consistent over time. Since corporate earnings are ultimately reflected in stock prices, economic growth forecasts can be used to forecast stock returns.

A simple formula for expected stock market returns using the earnings growth method is as follows:

$$\text{Equity return} = \text{earnings per share growth} \\ + \text{cash dividends} + \text{valuation change}$$

To better understand this model, each variable needs to be explained:

1. *Earnings growth.* The primary driver of long-term stock market gains is corporate earnings. The more money companies earn, the higher the stock market goes relative to inflation. Earnings are a derivative of GDP growth.

2. *Cash dividends.* Many U.S. corporations pay out a portion of their earnings in the form of cash dividends. At the end of 2004, the dividend on the total U.S. stock market was about 1.6 percent. The growth of dividend payments has been about 3 percent per year, although it varies. Because of tax law changes, the growth in dividends is expected to increase over the next decade. While dividends increases sound attractive, there is no free lunch. Higher dividend payout means less cash for corporations to invest, and therefore the expected growth rate of earnings will be lower.

3. *Valuation change.* The valuation is the price that investors are willing to pay for $1 worth of earnings. If investors believe that the growth in real corporate earnings will increase, they will pay more for the anticipated earnings stream. Thus, the ratio of price to earnings (P/E) increases. If economic conditions decline, the P/E of

stocks typically falls as prices fall. The changing valuation affects overall investment return, but it does not have any effect on dividend payments.

Forecasting earnings growth can be accomplished using GDP per capita data. GDP per capita is the sum total of all goods and services produced in the United States during the year divided by the population. There is a direct and consistent relationship between GDP per capita growth and corporate earnings growth. Figure 11-8 clearly illustrates this relationship.

The long-term correlation between annual GDP per capita growth and S&P 500 earnings growth has been over +0.9. The correlation is higher if earnings are smoothed over a five-year period to reduce the effect of recessionary earnings lulls.

FIGURE 11-8

Per Capita GDP Compared to S&P 500 Earnings
The Growth Rate Is Nearly Identical

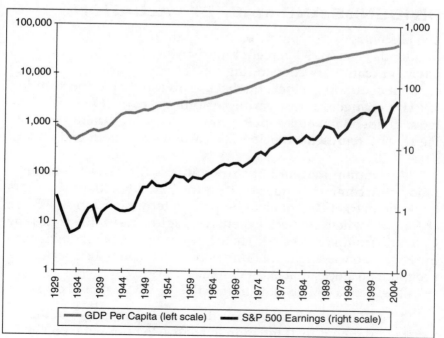

THE FEDERAL RESERVE AND GDP GROWTH

The Federal Reserve has two primary mandates: first, to foster full employment by promoting controlled GDP growth, and second, to keep inflation in check. Basically, the Federal Reserve targets the economy to grow at about 3 percent per year (after inflation). That encourages steady job creation and holds inflation at a reasonable level. If the economy grows faster than the target, it can cause a supply and demand mismatch, which can lead to higher inflation.

The Federal Reserve controls economic growth with monetary policy decisions, mostly through the adjustment of the short-term interest rates that banks charge each other for overnight loans. Short-term rates can affect interest rates on mortgages and other lending rates. Those rates, in turn, have a direct impact on consumer and corporate borrowing behavior, which has a direct effect on economic activity. In a sense, the Federal Reserve is the tail that wags the dog.

DIVIDENDS AND MARKET VALUATION

The percentage of corporate earnings paid out in the form of cash dividends is about 30 percent and rising slightly. Cash dividend payment can vary depending on current earnings, general economic outlook, stock buybacks, investment opportunities, tax law changes, and a variety of other factors. Over the long term, dividend payouts should grow in line with earnings growth. Figure 11-9 represents the S&P 500 earnings and dividend growth since 1950.

A common measure of stock value is the price-to-earnings ratio, more commonly referred to as the P/E ratio. Many investors track the market P/E in an attempt to determine when stocks are cheap and when they are expensive. Figure 11-10 illustrates the P/E ratio from 1950 to 2004. There have been several periods when the P/E ratio was high, although none quite match the speculative premium on stocks that existed in the late 1990s.

There are a couple of items that P/E watchers should consider:

1. P/E multiples increase or decrease with changes in the inflation rate. If inflation increases, the present value of

FIGURE 11-9

S&P 500 Earnings and Dividend Growth

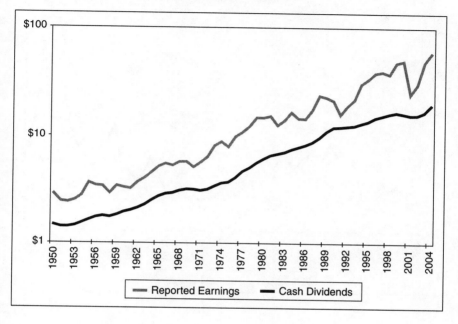

future earnings diminishes, and that causes the stock market to go down and the P/E ratio to go down. A decrease in inflation causes higher stock prices because of the increase in the purchasing power of future earnings.

2. If most investors believe that corporate earnings will increase faster and at a greater rate than the average, then the prices of stocks will increase in anticipation of the higher earnings forecast. The run-up in prices causes the P/E of the market to expand. This is the reason the market kept going higher in the late 1990s. Earnings growth was robust in the late 1990s, and investors believed that this growth would continue as a result of rapid technological advances. When earnings growth did not materialize, the value of the stocks fell to a more normal level.

FIGURE 11-10

U.S. Stock Market Price-to-Earnings Ratio (P/E), 1950–2004

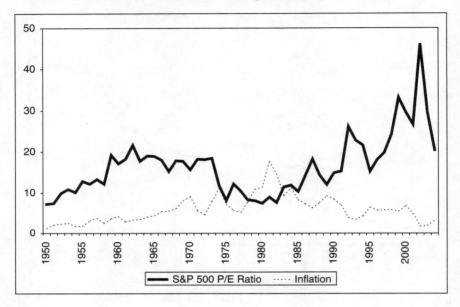

P/E ratios tend to be volatile because corporate earnings rise and fall with the economic cycle. To get a smoother representation of market valuation, Figure 11-11 illustrates the price of the S&P 500 as a percentage of actual GDP (in billions). Using P/GDP eliminates a lot of noise that market P/E ratios create.

In September 1981, the price of the S&P 500 was about 4 percent of GDP in billions. By the end of 1999, it was about 16 percent, or four times the 1981 level. You can see how stock speculation radically changed the value of the market in the late 1990s, even though the level of economic activity in the United States remained historically stable during the period. In a good economy and low inflation, the P/GDP percentage should be around 10 percent, which is close to where it was in January 2005.

In the short run, speculation may drive stock prices, but in the long term, earnings growth is the real driver. Speculative moves are not predictable, so there no sense trying to put a speculation

FIGURE 11-11

S&P Price Only as a Percent of GDP (in Billions of Dollars), 1950–2004

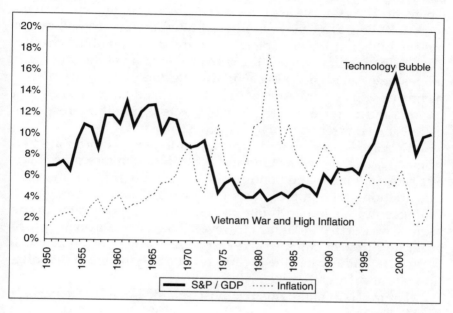

variable into a long-term forecast. Rather, for the forecasts that follow, it is assumed that the price-to-GDP ratio is held constant at the 10 percent level, thereby eliminating speculative noise.

FORECASTING FIXED INCOME

Forecasting bond returns is simpler than forecasting stock returns. In the very long run, stock returns are driven by corporate earnings growth and the cash paid out as stock dividends. The only factor that affects future bond returns is interest rates. The formula for calculating the expected long-term return of bonds is

Fixed-income return = yield at purchase + change in yield

Change in yield = changes in the inflation rate,
                                the real risk-free rate, and credit spreads

If you buy a five-year corporate bond that has a 6 percent yield to maturity and interest rates do not change before the bond matures, then your annualized return after five years will be 6 percent. The example assumes that all interest payments are reinvested. If there is a change in interest rates, then your total return may be higher or lower depending on the direction of the change. That is due to differences in the reinvestment rate of the interest. If interest rates go higher while you own the bond, then your interest payments will be reinvested at higher rates, and you will achieve a higher return than 6 percent. The opposite is true if interest rates go lower—your return will be less than 6 percent.

Reported inflation and future inflation expectations are two primary drivers of interest rates. If actual inflation increases, interests rates go higher and bond prices fall. If there is lower inflation (disinflation), then interest rates go down and bond prices go up. Changes in anticipated inflation also move interest rates in the same way as actual inflation. However, if the forecasts do not prove accurate, interest rates will revert back to their original level. Figure 11-12 illustrates the inverse relationship between the inflation rate and Treasury note yields.

Figure 11-12 highlights the most volatile interest-rate periods in U.S. economic history. From the early 1960s to the early 1980s, inflation soared to 15 percent. That created a huge sell-off in the bond markets. By 1982, inflation had dropped as fast as it accelerated, setting the stage for a historic rally in bonds. However, the rally was slow in developing because investors *anticipated* that the inflation rate would move higher again. But those fears were not justified. Since the early 1980s, inflation has averaged about 3 percent. As a result, by 2003 the yields on Treasury bonds hit their lowest level in 50 years.

A third driver of interest rates is a change in the real risk-free rate. The real return is the after-inflation yield of a bond. The easiest way to understand changes in the real risk-free rate is by observing changes in the Treasury Inflation-Protected Securities (TIPS). One reason that the spreads on TIPS change is taxes. As inflation forces interest rates higher, it is also adds to the principal value of TIPS. Since more taxes are due in high-inflation periods, the real yield on the bonds must be higher to pay the extra taxes. As we learned in Chapter 8, taxes are due on the total

FIGURE 11-12

Interest Rates Track Inflation over Time

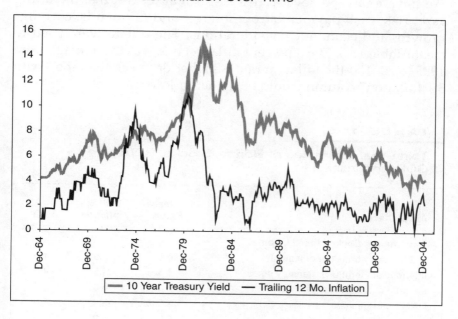

return of Treasury bonds, whether is it from inflation gains or interest.

There are several other drivers of interest rates that are specific to particular types of bond. Corporate bonds have a risk premium for credit risk. The spread between Treasury bonds and corporate bonds will increase or decrease with changes in economic conditions. Mortgages have prepayment risk. The yield of a mortgage fund will vary with the amount of prepayments that occur in the mortgage market.

One problem in forecasting interest rates is that it is nearly impossible to predict changes in inflation or changes in credit spreads. That is where the Federal Reserve can help. The Federal Reserve tends to have an acceptable range for inflation of between 1.5 and 3.5 percent. An amount over 4 percent causes concern among the Federal Reserve Board members, and that generally leads to monetary action.

CREATING A FORECAST

We have analyzed several drivers of market returns, including asset risk, cash payments from interest and dividends, earnings growth, and economic considerations. These data were used to create Table 11-5. The 3 percent inflation rate was the average from 1985 to 2004. If the inflation rate is higher or lower, then the "With 3% Inflation" column would be higher or lower as well.

TABLE 11-5

Thirty-Year Estimates of Bonds, Stocks, REITs, GDP, and Inflation

Asset Classes	Real Return	With 3% Inflation	Risk*
Government-Backed Fixed Income			
U.S. Treasury bills (1-year maturity)	0.5	3.5	1.5
Intermediate-term U.S. Treasury notes	1.5	4.5	4.8
Long-term U.S. Treasury bonds	2.0	5.0	5.3
GNMA mortgages	2.0	5.0	8.0
Intermediate tax-free (AA rated)	1.0	4.0	5.0
Corporate and Emerging Market Fixed Income			
Intermediate high-grade corporate	2.0	5.0	5.5
Long-term investment-grade bonds	2.8	5.8	8.5
Preferred stocks (rated A or better)	3.5	6.5	9.0
High-yield corporate (B to BB)	4.0	7.0	15.0
Emerging market bonds	4.0	7.0	15.0
U.S. Equity			
U.S. large-cap stocks	5.0	8.0	15.0
U.S. micro-cap stocks	7.0	10.0	25.0
U.S. small value stocks	7.0	10.0	22.0
REITs (real estate investment trusts)	5.0	8.0	14.0
International Equity			
International developed country stocks	5.0	8.0	17.0
International small country stocks	6.0	9.0	22.0
International emerging country stocks	7.0	10.0	25.0
Gross Domestic Product Growth	3.0	6.0	2.0

*The estimate of risk is the estimated standard deviation of annual returns.

Table 11-5 represents this author's best estimate of market returns over the next 30 years. There are no guarantees that any of these forecasts will be accurate; however, they are as good as any forecast made in a logical manner.

CHAPTER SUMMARY

The acceptance of a market forecast is an important step in creating a proper asset allocation. No one knows exactly what the returns on the markets or the results of economic indicators will be over the next 30 years. However, there are stable factors that contribute to those market returns, and those factors are likely to persist into the future.

A forecast should always try to err on the conservative side. It is wiser to expect and plan for lower returns and then be pleasantly surprised if the forecast is too low than to rely on a rosy forecast and possibly run out of money later in life. As the saying goes, it is better to be safe than sorry.

While the actual 30-year return on the markets cannot be known, the relationship between risk and return is predictable. Small stocks have more risk than large stocks and should outperform large stocks in the future. Corporate bonds have more risk than Treasury bonds and should outperform Treasury bonds in the future. With the order of investment risks and comparable returns in hand, you can move on to the next step to create an asset allocation that is right for your needs.

Building Your Portfolio

KEY CONCEPTS

- A proper asset allocation is designed to match an investor's needs.
- The portfolio should be broadly diversified.
- The overall risk cannot be above one's tolerance for risk.
- Life-cycle investing is one place to start.

A successful investment plan is one that is designed specifically for the person who intends to use it. While people's asset allocations will be broadly similar in some ways, each person's allocation will be uniquely different in others. The next three chapters offer guidance on designing an investment plan that is right for your needs.

Asset allocation books tend to have several examples of portfolios, and this one is no exception. The portfolios in this chapter are categorized into four generic groups based on different stages of life. The sample portfolios provided are generic in nature and should be considered only a guide.

LIFE-CYCLE INVESTING

People of different ages have different financial needs and different perceptions on investing. My previous book, *Protecting Your Wealth in Good Times and Bad* (McGraw-Hill, 2003), classifies investors into four general groups based on age. Those groups are Early Savers, Mid-Life Accumulators, Preretirees and Active Retirees, and Mature Retirees. The material in this chapter is a synopsis of the four stages and how each would approach the management of an investment portfolio.

The four life phases of investing are

- *Early Savers.* These are investors who are in the beginning stages of their careers and families. They start with few assets and a lot of ambition. This group generally spans ages 20 to 39.
- *Mid-Life Accumulators.* These are investors who are established in their careers and family life. They are accumulators of many things, from cars to homes to appliances to children. Between ages 40 and 59, accumulators know where they stand on career and family, and they have a good idea about what to expect in the future.
- *Preretirees and Active Retirees.* This stage covers people who are near retirement, the transition into retirement, and Active Retirees who are enjoying the fruits of their labors. The stage generally covers people from ages 60 to 79.
- *Mature Retirees.* These fully retired investors are not as active as they used to be. They have different needs, ranging from long-term care to estate planning issues. At this stage, financial matters are often jointly decided with children and/or other family members.

Investors in all stages have some similar financial goals and similar concerns. Similar goals include a desire for financial security and the desire to pay less income tax. Similar concerns include the fear of running out of money and the fear of not having adequate health-care coverage when needed. These common goals and concerns are considered in every asset allocation regardless of stage.

In addition to these similarities, investors have a range of differences. These include personal investment experiences, career challenges, health issues, family situations, risk tolerance differences, and personality strengths and weaknesses.

When all the pieces of the puzzle are put together, portfolio design is a balance between a technical solution and a behavioral solution. The right asset allocation should have a high mathematical probability of achieving your financial goal while at the same time being compatible with your emotional makeup. The goal of this chapter is to address the issues that drive the technical asset allocation decisions. Behavioral issues are discussed in Chapter 13.

TWO PORTFOLIOS FOR EACH STAGE

The remainder of the chapter is devoted to discussing the four stages of life-cycle investing. At the end of each stage, two sample portfolios are offered. Both portfolios offer broad diversification across several global asset classes. The first portfolio is a simple allocation utilizing four or five low-cost mutual funds. The second portfolio is a more advanced multi-asset-class portfolio utilizing between nine and twelve low-cost mutual funds.

Either portfolio offers a good base from which to build. Start with one of the portfolios and add or take away mutual funds to suit your particular needs. You probably want to limit the number of funds you have in your portfolio. Twelve funds should be more than adequate to achieve broad diversification. More than that can reduce the effectiveness of the portfolio because it becomes too cumbersome to manage.

The mutual funds recommended in this chapter are samples. Substitutes are available in many investment categories from many difference mutual fund companies. Under some circumstances, you may not have access to any of the mutual funds mentioned. Many self-directed employer retirement plans restrict participants to a narrow set of investment options. In that case, you will have to make the best of the funds that are available.

The sample portfolios provided should help you narrow your asset allocation decision, but they cannot solve the puzzle completely. Other issues need to be considered in an investment plan, including taxes, fees, and your tolerance for investment risk. Several of those topics are addressed in later chapters.

STAGE 1: EARLY SAVERS

Three key components for accumulating wealth are consistency, time, and cost control. For Early Savers, the rate of return on the mutual funds selected is important, but it is not nearly as important as a consistent savings plan. Saving and investing regularly in a prudently selected mix of mutual funds will build wealth faster than any other strategy. Young investors certainly have the advantage of time, so they can make some investment mistakes. However, the biggest mistake they can make is not to save. Ideally, a young person will start saving at the same time he or she lands the first full-time job. If people make a habit of saving a portion of their income from the very beginning, they should not have to worry about financial security later in life. The amount of saving does not need to be excessive. A rate of 10 percent of annual earnings per year will work fine.

Time is on the side of younger investors. However, developing a consistent saving plan is often difficult. Incomes are low and expenses are mounting. Housing costs in some parts of the country are almost unbearable, demanding a growing allocation of income. In addition, the arrival of children adds considerably to current living expenses, not to mention the new need to save for college.

Career uncertainty is another distraction for Early Savers. Many young adults do not know the direction in which their career will take them, or what their true earnings potential will be. People change careers more often than in past generations, and that can result in the interruption of a savings plan.

With increasingly limited free cash and career uncertainty, what can a young person do to formulate a plan for the future? First, many employers have a company retirement plan that employees can contribute to on a pretax basis. Young investors should take full advantage of that opportunity, especially if the employer offers to match the amount contributed. Second, young people should develop an asset allocation that is within their tolerance for investment risk. Do not try to time the markets or chase last year's winners. Third, young people need to realize early that investment costs matter. Every dollar wasted on exorbitant mutual fund fees and high brokerage commissions is money down the drain. A consistent pretax savings plan that is invested in a sensible asset allocation of low-cost mutual funds is an excellent way to begin accumulating wealth for the future.

EARLY SAVERS—STOCK AND BOND ALLOCATION

Ironically, designing an asset allocation for young investors is more difficult than designing one at any other time in life. On the one hand, young investors have many years ahead of them, so they should choose an aggressive allocation. On the other hand, they have the least amount of investment experience and do not know their personal tolerance for financial risk. Consequently, while an aggressive asset allocation may be appropriate from a time perspective, Early Savers need to ensure that they are selecting an asset allocation that is within their personal tolerance for investment risk.

Most young investors should be aggressive because they have a lot of time to benefit from the allocation. However, investing 100 percent in stocks is too aggressive. There are two reasons for not having an all-stock portfolio:

1. Most investors cannot handle 100 percent in stocks 100 percent of the time. The volatility of a fully invested stock portfolio is too much to stomach in a bear market (that is true for all phases, not just Early Savers). When a bear market takes a portfolio down, a person's true risk tolerance becomes evident, and overly aggressive investors will abandon their strategy. That allocation change is an emotional decision, not a rational decision, and it is not in the best interest of the investor. There are two recent examples when that occurred. The first was after the "crash" of 1987, and the second was during the bear market of 2000 to 2003. During both of those periods, many investors who thought they had the tolerance to handle 100 percent in stocks did not finish with 100 percent in stocks. They reduced their position after sustaining a large loss, which made the loss permanent.

2. Another reason not to have 100 percent in stocks is that it precludes rebalancing. When stocks fall in value,

investors should take that opportunity to move more
into stocks. The opposite is true when stocks go up in
value; rebalancing forces investors to sell at higher prices.
There is a diversification bonus available to investors who
rebalance between stocks and bonds on an annual basis.
The bonus is a reduction in portfolio risk that leads to an
increase in long-term returns.

It is interesting to note that a misunderstanding of risk causes
many Early Savers not to have enough equity in their portfolio,
and as a result they give up the potential for higher return.
According to data available from the TIAA-CREF Institute, a surprising number of young people invest a portion of their employer
pension funds in the low-interest-bearing fixed accounts.[1] As those
people move into mid-life, they seem to have a better understanding of their tolerance for risk and increase their equity exposure.

There is no one-size-fits-all asset allocation that Early Savers
should use. Figure 12-1 highlights appropriate allocations for

FIGURE 12-1

Early Savers Allocation Range

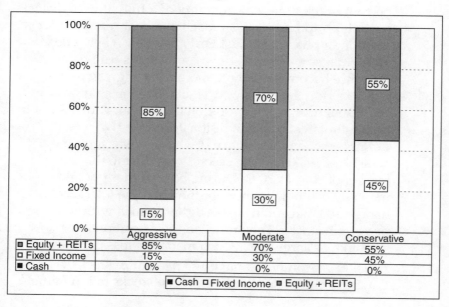

	Aggressive	Moderate	Conservative
▣ Equity + REITs	85%	70%	55%
▢ Fixed Income	15%	30%	45%
▪ Cash	0%	0%	0%

▪ Cash ▢ Fixed Income ▣ Equity + REITs

young investors who have some understanding of financial risk. Figure 12-1 represents an "either-or" allocation, not a "to-from" allocation. In other words, an investor chooses a fixed allocation of between 55 and 85 percent in stocks and stays with that fixed target. Investors should not be moving from 55 percent to 85 percent and back again based on their perception of market risk.

An appropriate median asset allocation for young people is about 70 percent in stocks and 30 percent in fixed income. The 70 percent stock and 30 percent fixed-income allocation provides significant risk reduction over a 100 percent stock portfolio and allows room for rebalancing. The result is a portfolio with acceptable risk that has the potential for gratifying long-term returns.

EARLY SAVERS—ASSET-CLASS CATEGORIES

Once a strategic asset allocation between stocks and bonds has been decided on, the next step is category allocation. The two portfolios shown in Tables 12-1 and 12-2 highlight a basic asset allocation and a multi-asset-class allocation. All of the investments listed are no-load low-cost mutual funds.

All asset allocations recommended in this chapter should be adjusted to match an investor's needs, tax situation, and risk tolerance.

TABLE 12-1

Early Savers—Basic Portfolio

Asset Class	Percent	Sample Low-Cost Funds and Symbols
U.S. equity	40%	Vanguard Total US Stock Market Index (VTSMX)
International equity	20%	Vanguard Total International Portfolio (VGTSX)
Real estate	10%	Vanguard REIT Index Fund (VGSIX)
Fixed income	30%	iShares Lehman Aggregate Bond Fund (AGG)

TABLE 12-2

Early Savers—Multiple-Asset-Class Portfolio

Asset Class	Percent	Sample Low-Cost Funds and Symbols
U.S. Equity		
Core U.S. equity	25%	Vanguard Total U.S. Stock Market Index (VTSMX)
Small value	10%	iShare S&P 600 Barra Value (IJS)
Micro cap	5%	Bridgeway Ultra Small Company Market (BRSIX)
Real estate	10%	Vanguard REIT Index Fund (VGSIX)
International Equity		
Pacific Rim—large	5%	Vanguard Pacific Stock Index (VPACX)
Europe—large	5%	Vanguard European Stock Index (VEURX)
Small cap	5%	Vanguard International Explorer Fund (VINEX)
Emerging markets	5%	DFA Emerging Markets* (DFEMX)
Fixed Income		
Investment-grade	10%	iShares Lehman Aggregate Bond Fund (AGG)
High-yield	10%	Vanguard High Yield Corporate Bond (VWEHX)
Inflation-protected	5%	Vanguard Inflation-Protected Securities (VIPSX)
Emerging markets	5%	Payden Emerging Markets Bond (PYEMX)

*DFA funds are available only through select investment advisors. Alternative funds are available to all investors.

GROUP 2: MID-LIFE ACCUMULATORS

As we progress through life, most people mature physically, emotionally, professionally, and financially. Accordingly, during mid-life, people develop a different attitude about their money and, accordingly, need different financial tools to help them tailor an asset allocation that is correct for them.

Some time during mid-life, most people concede that they are mortal, that there are ceilings to their careers, and that a conservative lifestyle is probably more rewarding than an extravagant one. In addition, people in mid-life have seen a recession or two, they have jumped out of good investments and held onto bad ones, and they have watched consumer prices and interest rates flip-flop over the years. As a result of these experiences, Mid-life Accumulators are better equipped to design a portfolio that best fits their long-term needs.

By mid-life, investors are forming a vision of what retirement will look like for them and are beginning to calculate how much they will need in order to get there. Once those estimates are made, it is time for the Mid-life Accumulator to refine the investment allocation so that the portfolio is in line with that vision of retirement.

There are two important realizations that mid-life investors have that trigger a need for a portfolio adjustment. First, they realize that their productive working years are about half over. Second, they realize that for the remainder of their working years, a viable savings and investment plan is critical.

At mid-life, not only do savings have to be consistent, but the investment return on those savings will have a large impact on a person's lifestyle in retirement. Therefore, investing experimentation is over. It is time to treat retirement savings as serious business. Sound asset allocation principles must be understood and applied with discipline. A sound and stable plan will help ensure that Mid-life Accumulators make their retirement goals.

MID-LIFE ACCUMULATORS—AN INVESTMENT FRAMEWORK

During mid-life, people begin to estimate how much money they will need in order to sustain their standard of living in retirement. Granted, the estimate will be in rough form at best; however, it is a useful exercise.

Liability matching is a method of investing by which a person's asset allocation is matched to that person's future cash-flow needs. In other words, your portfolio is structured so that your investments match your retirement income needs. There are five basic steps in liability matching:

1. Estimate future living expenses. An estimate of future living expenses can be made by tracking current living expenses and making adjustments for expected changes to those expenses in the future. There are many different budgeting tools that can be found on the Internet and in books that can help you with a personal cash-flow analysis. You could also hire a professional financial planner to help you put those estimates together.

2. Estimate sources of noninvestment income during retirement. Sources of noninvestment income include social security and pension income. They do not include income from retirement accounts or personal savings.

3. Compare your noninvestment income to your expected living expenses during retirement. If there is an income gap, it will need to be filled with investment income.

4. Determine how much you need to accumulate to fill the annual income gap. Expect that you can withdraw a maximum of 5 percent from your investments, which means that you will need about 20 times the annual amount of income. For example, if you need an extra $12,000 per year in income, your portfolio at retirement should be at least $240,000.

5. Design, implement, and maintain a savings and investment plan that has the highest probability of growing your portfolio to the amount needed at retirement with minimum risk. Asset allocation is a major part of that investment plan.

These steps are a synopsis of the liability-matching process. To gain a more detailed understanding, acquire a copy of my previous book, *Protecting Your Wealth in Good Times and Bad.* There is also an explanation in my free online book, *Serious Money, Straight Talk about Investing for Retirement*, which is available as a download at www.PortfolioSolutions.com.

MID-LIFE ACCUMULATORS—ASSET ALLOCATION

During mid-life, investors reach the halfway mark in their careers. It is a period when salaries are increasing, and that that means the amount allocated to savings should also be increasing. It is a point in life where investors can see the future with more clarity and can use that vision to develop a strategic asset allocation that matches future retirement needs.

During mid-life, retirement accounts are growing larger and working years are growing shorter. A balanced asset allocation is appropriate. Figure 12-2 highlights the range of asset allocation

Mid-Life Allocation Range

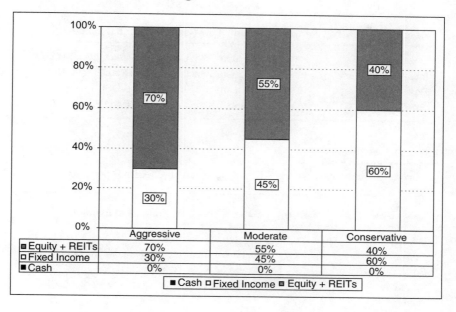

	Aggressive	Moderate	Conservative
■ Equity + REITs	70%	55%	40%
□ Fixed Income	30%	45%	60%
■ Cash	0%	0%	0%

■ Cash □ Fixed Income ■ Equity + REITs

that is typical for Mid-life Accumulators. Like asset allocations for all groups, Figure 12-2 represents an either-or allocation, not a to-from allocation. Do not try to shift between stocks and bonds at what seem like appropriate times. No one can time the markets.

The median asset allocation for people in mid-life is 60 percent in stocks and 40 percent in fixed income. There is no need for a cash allocation, since investors are still putting money into their accounts, not taking it out.

Tables 12-3 and 12-4 give basic and multi-asset-class portfolios for Mid-Life Accumulators.

During mid-life, people begin to reach higher levels of earnings, which may affect their investment choices. Taxes can play a considerable roll in asset allocation. If a person's income places him or her in an income tax bracket of 30 percent or more, that person should consider municipal bonds rather than taxable bonds for a taxable fixed-income account. More information on how taxes affect asset allocation can be found in Chapter 14.

TABLE 12-3

Mid-Life Accumulators—Basic Portfolio

Asset Class	Percent	Sample Low-Cost Funds and Symbols
U.S. equity	30%	Vanguard Total U.S. Stock Market Index (VTSMX)
International equity	15%	Vanguard Total International Portfolio (VGTSX)
Real estate	10%	Vanguard REIT Index Fund (VGSIX)
Fixed income	45%	iShares Lehman Aggregate Bond Fund (AGG)

TABLE 12-4

Mid-Life Accumulators—Multiple-Asset-Class Portfolio

Asset Class	Percent	Sample Low-Cost Funds and Symbols
U.S. Equity		
Core U.S. equity	23%	Vanguard Total U.S. Stock Market Index (VTSMX)
Small value	5%	iShare S&P 600 Barra Value (IJS)
Micro cap	2%	Bridgeway Ultra Small Company Market (BRSIX)
Real estate	10%	Vanguard REIT Index Fund (VGSIX)
International Equity		
Pacific Rim—large	4%	Vanguard Pacific Stock Index (VPACX)
Europe—large	4%	Vanguard European Stock Index (VEURX)
Small cap	3%	Vanguard International Explorer Fund (VINEX)
Emerging markets	4%	DFA Emerging Markets* (DFEMX)
Fixed Income		
Investment-grade	20%	iShares Lehman Aggregate Bond Fund (AGG)
High-yield	10%	Vanguard High Yield Corporate Bond (VWEHX)
Inflation-protected	10%	Vanguard Inflation-Protected Securities (VIPSX)
Emerging markets	5%	Payden Emerging Markets Bond (PYEMX)

*DFA funds are available only through select investment advisors. Alternatives are available to all investors.

GROUP 3: PRERETIREES AND ACTIVE RETIREES

A person typically enters the preretirement phase about five years before leaving full-time employment. Preretirement is not a formal announcement of impending retirement; rather, it is a thought process. During this period, many people become perplexed about questions such as when to retire, whether they have enough money to retire, and what amount of money they can safely withdraw from savings so that they do not run out of money in retirement. It is probably the most conservative period in a person's life.

Most people who are nearing retirement are also in their peak career earning years. They are at or very close to their highest level of advancement. On the home front, household expenses have stabilized and are possibly going down. Children are either self-sufficient or only a few years away from becoming self-sufficient. Because of peak earnings and lower living expenses, the preretirement years also tend to be the greatest savings years.

As investors close in on a retirement date, they should shift their portfolios to the asset allocation that they will use during retirement. The shift does not need to be made all at once. The change in allocation can take place gradually during the transition.

People tend to think and act in a most conservative manner during the transition years. They are not yet completely comfortable with how their cash flow is going to work, or whether they have a good retirement plan. That causes some people to be very defensive with their asset allocation, reducing risky investments to a small percentage of their portfolio. Sometimes people want to go too far and eliminate all risks from their portfolio.

There is little reason to be overly conservative in a portfolio during the transition phase. The risk of eliminating all risky assets from a portfolio prior to retirement is that some very attractive returns could be forgone, and those returns cannot be made up. While some extra cash may be appropriate, I have yet to see a well-thought-out retirement asset allocation that did not work. Normally, the cash-flow jitters go away after about a year or two, and people become very comfortable with that allocation.

ISSUES TO CONSIDER WHEN MOVING TOWARD RETIREMENT

Expenses will vary during retirement, but over time they will not be as high as they are when you are working. Early on, you will be traveling more, eating out more, fixing up the house, spending more time shopping, possibly joining a gym, and taking care of small medical concerns that you didn't have time for while you were working full time. As time passes and you grow accustomed to being retired, you'll spend less on clothes, less on travel, less on food, and less on housing, and you'll stop spending so much for automobiles. If you have two automobiles, you may decide to reduce to one.

Your home may become a source of cash if needed. The house you own may become too big, so you will downsize. That will release equity from your house, which can be used to generate more income. If you keep your house, you can always tap into the equity in your home by using a mortgage, a home equity loan, or a reverse mortgage that pays monthly income.

Social security is another source of revenue, and the system will not be disappearing any time soon. All those who are eligible to receive payments will get something, even if the benefits are reduced. Changes in payout amounts and retirement ages will undoubtedly be made for younger people, but not for those already collecting benefits.

If you have living parents who have an estate, or other persons who have named you as a beneficiary of an estate, your net worth will increase upon their passing. No one likes to talk about or count on the money he or she will eventually get from an inheritance. Nonetheless, it is a fact that the money will eventually come to you.

All of these items plus more are important when forecasting cash flow in retirement. If you need help figuring all of this out, it would help to contact a reputable fee-only financial planner. To find a financial planner located in your area, contact the Garrett Planning Network at (866) 260-8400. Two other sources of financial planner referrals are the Financial Planner Association at (800) 322-4237 and the National Association of Personal Financial Advisors at (800) 366-2732.

WITHDRAWAL RATES IN RETIREMENT

One question asked by most people in preretirement is how much they can safely withdraw from their portfolios without touching the principal. There have been several in-depth studies on this question, and they all point to about a 4 percent withdrawal rate.

However, there are many factors that need to be considered before you limit your rate to 4 percent or less:

- At what age are you retiring? Younger retirees should probably limit their withdrawal rate to 4 percent or less because they have a long time horizon. Older retirees can afford to have a higher withdrawal rate because their time horizon is shorter.
- How much do you want to leave behind when you are gone? Retirees who want to leave their children or other heirs as much as possible should withdraw less than those who do not wish to leave so much behind.
- How long do you believe you will be an "active" retiree? Everyone eventually slows down as a result of age or health. Spending during the mature retirement years is typically less than in the active retirement years. That means it is okay if you spend a little more in your active years.

Cash for withdrawals can be produced in a portfolio in many ways. Interest and dividend income are two sources. There is also annual rebalancing in a portfolio. You can easily calculate the amount of income your investments will give you, then take any shortfall during a rebalancing.

PRERETIREES AND ACTIVE RETIREES—ASSET ALLOCATION

The transition from full-time work to retirement signals a new investment phase in a portfolio. The portfolio will convert from accumulation to distribution. That means that investors will soon stop putting money in and start taking some out. Accordingly, new retirees will probably want to play it safe, at least at first. Figure 12-3 highlights an appropriate asset allocation for people entering retirement and in early retirement.

The transition from working to retirement is an uncertain time. Accordingly, a retiree's portfolio should be managed with stability and safety of principal as its primary objectives. However, a retirement portfolio still needs growth. The average lifespan of a

FIGURE 12-3

Preretirees and Active Retiree Allocation Range

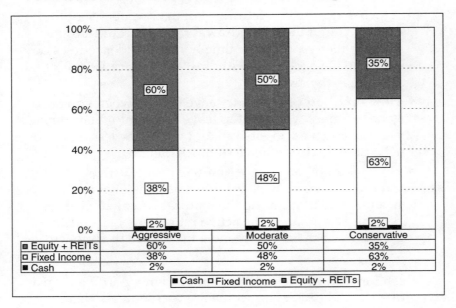

	Aggressive	Moderate	Conservative
■ Equity + REITs	60%	50%	35%
□ Fixed Income	38%	48%	63%
■ Cash	2%	2%	2%

■ Cash □ Fixed Income ■ Equity + REITs

65-year-old is over 20 years, according to data from IRS Publication 590. Therefore, the median asset allocation for people in early retirement is 50 percent in stocks, 48 percent in fixed income, and 2 percent in cash-type investments such as a money market fund. The 2 percent in cash is to cover monthly distributions.

Tables 12-5 and 12-6 give basic and multi-asset-class portfolios for investors in this stage.

The 13 percent short-term bond allocation has two functions for early retirees. First, it lowers the overall volatility of the portfolio, which is appropriate in an account that is distributing cash. Second, it provides a high-yield cash substitute. If unexpected cash distributions over 2 percent are needed from the portfolio, they will come from the short-term bond fund. One disadvantage of the short-term bond allocation is that it tends to have a lower yield than a total bond market fund; thus, the total return on the portfolio is lower.

TABLE 12-5

Preretirees and Active Retirees—Basic Portfolio

Asset Class	Percent	Sample Low-Cost Funds and Symbols
U.S. equity	35%	Vanguard Total U.S. Stock Market Index (VTSMX)
International equity	10%	Vanguard Total International Portfolio (VGTSX)
Real estate	5%	Vanguard REIT Index Fund (VGSIX)
Fixed income	35%	iShares Lehman Aggregate Bond Fund (AGG)
Short-term bonds	13%	Vanguard Investment Grade Short-Term (VFSTX)
Money markets	2%	Low-cost money market fund with checking

TABLE 12-6

Preretirees and Active Retirees—Multiple-Asset-Class Portfolio

Asset Class	Percent	Sample Low-Cost Funds and Symbols
U.S. Equity		
Core U.S. Equity	25%	Vanguard Total U.S. Stock Market Index (VTSMX)
Small value	8%	iShares S&P 600 Barra Value (IJS)
Micro cap	2%	Bridgeway Ultra Small Company Market (BRSIX)
Real estate	5%	Vanguard REIT Index Fund (VGSIX)
International Equity		
Pacific Rim—large	3%	Vanguard Pacific Stock Index (VPACX)
Europe—large	3%	Vanguard European Stock Index (VEURX)
Small cap	2%	Vanguard International Explorer Fund (VINEX)
Emerging markets	2%	DFA Emerging Markets* (DFEMX)
Fixed Income		
Investment-grade	10%	iShares Lehman Aggregate Bond Fund (AGG)
Short-term bonds	13%	Vanguard Investment Grade Short-term (VFSTX)
High-yield Corporate	10%	Vanguard High Yield Corporate Bond (VWEHX)
Inflation-protected	10%	Vanguard Inflation-Protected Securities (VIPSX)
Emerging markets	5%	Payden Emerging Markets Bond (PYEMX)
Cash		
Money markets	2%	Low-cost money market fund with checking

*DFA funds are available only through select investment advisors. Alternatives are available to all investors.

Preretirees can ease into an income-producing portfolio during the remainder of their working years by placing new retirement investments into a fixed-income fund. Dividends from stock funds can also be diverted to fixed-income investments. Shortly after retirement, a new retiree can use the rollover from a former employer's retirement account to restructure the portfolio based on the current needs.

GROUP 4: MATURE RETIREES

The good news is that Americans are living longer; the bad news is that we do not live forever. According to the Department of the Treasury, the average life expectancy of a 65-year-old is 86, which is about 10 years longer than it was in 1940. In addition, today's seniors are healthier and more active. They eat better, get more exercise, and smoke less than prior generations. Longevity trends are so strong that new life insurance tables recently introduced by the Society of Actuaries go out to age 120.

Alas, the Fountain of Youth has still not been discovered. Consequently, no one lives forever. At some point, we all need to get our financial house in order and prepare for the afterlife. It is inevitable that at some point in time, someone else will be handling our financial affairs. That may occur while we are still alive, and it will definitely occur after we are gone.

Besides maintaining good health, the most common concern for Mature Retirees is estate planning. One of the decisions we all need to make is who will manage our affairs when we are no longer able too. If both husband and wife are still living, this chore is normally taken over by the healthy spouse. In other cases, when there is only one spouse living the job is typically taken on by a sibling, a relative, or a professional representative.

I highly recommend that if you choose a son or daughter to handle your finances, you do it far in advance, while you're still capable of managing your own affairs. Once a helper has been chosen, that person will need to become fully informed of your financial situation, and the earlier the better. That includes an understanding of your estate plan, your investment accounts, and your insurance documents, and knowing where everything is.

Any financial planner will tell you that the transition of financial responsibility from parents to children can work out either very well or very poorly. To ensure that the transition occurs smoothly, there are steps you can take to avoid cost and confusion. The following list pertains to your investment accounts, and steps you can take to ensure a smooth transition.

1. Consolidate all of your investment accounts at one or two custodians, such as Charles Schwab, Vanguard, or Fidelity. This will make management of the investments easier, and will help your heirs settle the estate when you pass away.

2. Write a detailed statement, in your own words, describing how your portfolio is being managed and how you expect it to be managed in the future. The document should include a general investment strategy as well as points of contact.

3. Insist that the child or representative you choose to manage your investments understand basic principles, including asset allocation, taxation, and the use of low-cost mutual funds.

MATURE RETIREES—ASSET ALLOCATION

The asset allocation of a Mature Retiree's portfolio can vary depending on who is going to use the money. On the one hand, a portfolio should be conservatively managed to carry a retiree through the remainder of his or her life. On the other hand, if a retiree is not going to need all of his or her money, the allocation could favor the needs and ages of the beneficiaries. Generally, a portfolio is managed based on a combination of both scenarios. Figure 12-4 highlights suggested asset allocation for Mature Retirees.

As in the other stages, the range of allocations presented in Figure 12-4 is three separate portfolios. Trying to time markets by moving between allocations is not a prudent strategy.

Tables 12-7 and 12-8 give sample portfolios for investors in this stage.

Many people in the Mature Retiree stage of life make annual gifts to charities and family members. An increase in the cash allocation is recommended if a person is inclined to gift.

FIGURE 12-4

Mature Retiree Allocation Range

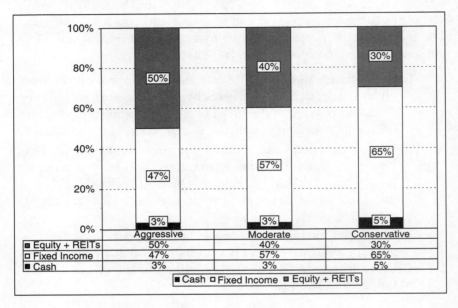

	Aggressive	Moderate	Conservative
■ Equity + REITs	50%	40%	30%
□ Fixed Income	47%	57%	65%
■ Cash	3%	3%	5%

■ Cash □ Fixed Income ■ Equity + REITs

The asset allocation recommendations outlined in Tables 12-7 and 12-8 represent that portion of the portfolio that will be used by a Mature Retiree during his or her lifetime. More than likely, a majority of the assets are not going to be used by the retiree. Rather,

TABLE 12-7

Mature Retirees—Basic Portfolio

Asset Class	Percent	Sample Low-Cost Funds and Symbols
U.S. equity	25%	Vanguard Total U.S. Stock Market Index (VTSMX)
International equity	10%	Vanguard Total International Portfolio (VGTSX)
Real estate	5%	Vanguard REIT Index Fund (VGSIX)
Fixed income	35%	iShares Lehman Aggregate Bond Fund (AGG)
Short-term bonds	22%	Vanguard Investment Grade Short-Term (VFSTX)
Money markets	3%	Low-cost money market fund with checking

TABLE 12-8

Mature Retirees—Multiple-Asset-Class Portfolio

Asset Class	Percent	Sample Low-Cost Funds and Symbols
U.S. Equity		
Core U.S. equity	20%	Vanguard Total U.S. Stock Market Index (VTSMX)
Small value	5%	iShares S&P 600 Barra Value (IJS)
Real estate	5%	Vanguard REIT Index Fund (VGSIX)
International Equity		
Pacific Rim—large	4%	Vanguard Pacific Stock Index (VPACX)
Europe—large	4%	Vanguard European Stock Index (VEURX)
Small cap	2%	Vanguard International Explorer Fund (VINEX)
Fixed Income		
Investment-grade	25%	iShares Lehman Aggregate Bond Fund (AGG)
Short-term bonds	22%	Vanguard Investment Grade Short-term (VFSTX)
Inflation-protected	10%	Vanguard Inflation-Protected Securities (VIPSX)
Cash		
Money markets	3%	Low-cost money market fund with checking

they will be passed on to heirs. Therefore, a portion of the portfolio should be allocated based on the needs of those inheriting the assets.

The appropriate portfolio asset allocation for a Mature Retiree may well be a combination of two asset allocations. One portion of the portfolio should be based on the income needs of the retiree, and the other portion based on the financial needs of the heirs. For example, assume that an 85-year-old woman may have an appropriate asset allocation of 30 percent in stocks and 70 percent in bonds and cash, and assume that she does not take any money from the portfolio. The woman has named her two grandchildren as heirs. Their ages are 30 and 34. In this situation, an appropriate asset allocation may be 50 percent in stocks and 50 percent in bonds. That is a good balance between the potential needs of the woman retiree and the long-term growth needs of her two grandchildren.

CHAPTER SUMMARY

Selecting an appropriate asset allocation during all phases of life is essential to your long-term investment plan. A successful investment plan incorporates the basic necessities of broad diversification, stability, tax management, and growth, while also including special styling that makes a portfolio unique to the person who intends to use it.

While all investors are alike in some ways, we are different in many others. Accordingly, most investment portfolios will be broadly similar in some ways and unique in others. If you manage your portfolio well over the years, and do not become emotional about investment decisions, then it should pay dividends to you through retirement, and eventually be passed on your heirs.

A life-cycle methodology is one strategy for beginning your quest to discover an appropriate asset allocation. The asset allocation and investment selections for the four stages provided here are only guides. You will need to adjust the portfolios to fit your specific situation.

NOTE

[1]Jacob S. Rugh, "Premium and Asset Allocations of Premium-Paying TIAA-CREF Participants as of March 31, 2004," TIAA-CREF Institute, www.tiaa-crefinstitute.org.

CHAPTER 13

How Behavior Affects
Asset Allocation Decisions

KEY CONCEPTS

- Behavioral finance is the study of investor decision making.
- Knowing your tolerance for risk is critical to investment success.
- Risk questionnaires are a start in assessing investor risk tolerance.
- Asset allocation stress testing helps refine investor risk tolerance.

Asset allocation theory assumes that investors will act rationally and with discipline when managing their portfolios. It presupposes that investors understand the nature of various markets and the correlations between markets before deciding on an allocation. Once an asset allocation plan has been designed and implemented, the theory expects that rebalancing will occur on a regular basis to capture diversification benefits and control risk.

Unfortunately, theory and reality seldom coincide. Although all investors have good intentions, typically they are not entirely rational in their decision-making process or disciplined in the maintenance of their plan. As a result, the performance of most individual investment portfolios is rarely as good as that of the markets people are investing in.

Researchers have uncovered a surprisingly large amount of evidence showing that irrational behavior and repeated errors in judgment explain a significant portion of the shortfall in personal investment performance. The researchers found that these human flaws are consistent, predictable, and widespread.

The studies of investment behavior show that the financial markets are not the cause of investment plan failure; rather, it is the investors themselves who cause the failures. I have about 20 years' experience working with individual investors, and I would agree with that conclusion. If an investor has a plan (which is rather rare), the plan does not fail the investor, the investor abandons the plan. The abandonment usually occurs either during difficult market conditions or when a segment of the market makes large gains and an investor starts chasing high returns. A successful asset allocation strategy demands that individuals understand the dynamics behind diversification and reallocation, as well being watchful for potential errors in human judgment that can cause the plan to collapse.

Underestimating market risk is a major culprit in behavioral errors. If an investor adds too much risk to the portfolio without knowing the downside, that investor runs the risk of becoming emotional when cyclical losses occur. If an investor becomes anxious about the asset allocation, that investor tends to act on impulse and abandon a long-term investment plan for the safety of low returning short-term investments. To avoid this type of behavior, it is critical that each investor know how much risk there is in an asset allocation and ensure that is below the investor's true tolerance for risk *before* implementing that plan.

BEHAVIORAL FINANCE

Behavioral finance is an academic field that attempts to understand and explain how psychology influences an investor's decision-making process. A fledging field of study in the early 1960s, behavioral finance has grown to be an important area of research at several influential institutions. Professors recognized as experts in the field include Daniel Kahneman (Princeton), Meir Statman (Santa Clara), Richard Thaler (University of Chicago), Robert J. Shiller (Yale), and

Amos Tversky. Tversky is frequently cited as the forefather of the field. He passed away in 1996.

The following list touches on a few observations made by behavioral finance researchers. Unfortunately, the list only scratches the surface. Much more information about this fascinating field is available on the Internet and in your local library.

- People tend to be more optimistic about stocks after the market goes up and more pessimistic after it goes down.
- Investors give too much weight to recent information, such as one quarter's earnings, and too little weight to long-term fundamentals.
- People tend to buy investments that have recently had a large run-up in performance. Over 80 percent of new mutual fund purchases go into the funds that have the best one-year return.
- Investors label investments as "good" or "bad" based on where the current price is relative to the price they paid rather than on the underlying fundamentals of the investment.
- People are reluctant to admit an error in judgment. Consequently, many people pay high commissions and fees to brokers and advisors so that they have someone to blame.
- The confidence investors have in the future earnings of high-priced companies is often too high, and the confidence they have in the earnings growth of low-priced companies is often too low.
- Overconfident investors generally believe that they have more knowledge and information than they actually have. As a result, they tend to trade too much and underperform the market.
- The profile of an overconfident investor is male, professional, with at least one advanced academic degree.
- Women tend to have a longer-term view of the markets than men. They maintain an investment plan longer, and as a result they generally perform better.

Asset allocation strategies are based on rational decisions and the discipline to maintain those decisions. Unfortunately, individual investors can become quite irrational when it comes to investment decisions, especially during large swings in the markets. Successful investors understand the limitations of the markets as well as their own limitations, and develop a proper asset allocation that accommodates both.

MORE INTERESTING INFORMATION

One surprising aspect of behavioral finance research is that a majority of individual investors surveyed know that they don't invest well. According to a Vanguard Group survey of 401(k) participants, a sizable 85 percent of employees consider themselves unskilled investors and would rather hire a professional manager.

Interestingly, the Vanguard Group found that the poorest-performing investment accounts in 401(k) plans belong to those participants who have the most education, have the highest incomes, and consider themselves skilled investors. Researchers Olivia Mitchell and Stephen Utkus at the University of Pennsylvania's Wharton Pension Research Council studied why a high-paid professional might have low returns.[1] They found that individuals who earn more are likely to be higher up the management hierarchy, making them feel more in control of their destiny. Utkus found that the overconfidence of higher-income participants caused them to trade more often, which was a factor leading to lower investment performance.

Professor Meir Statman (Santa Clara) is an expert in a behavior known as the *fear of regret*. People tend to feel sorrow and grief after having made an error in judgment. Investors are typically emotionally affected when a security was bought for more than the current price. Some psychologists have concluded that investors typically consider the loss of $1 twice as painful as the pleasure from a $1 gain.

Statman's findings have a direct impact on investors using asset allocation strategies. Rebalancing a portfolio requires that investors sell part of a winning investment and buy more of a losing one. It is hard for investors to sell what makes them happy and buy more of what makes them sad, especially during a deep bear market when everyone is gloomy.

The research on behavioral finance is wide and deep. In recent years there have been dozens of books published on the subject. Most of those books can be checked out from your local library. There is also a significant amount of information available on the Internet for free. A virtual clearinghouse of behavioral finance studies can be found at www.behaviouralfinance.net.

DISCOVERING YOUR RISK TOLERANCE

After formulating an appropriate asset allocation based on your assets and your future liabilities, the other side of the coin is your tolerance for investment risk. Risk tolerance is a measure of the amount of price volatility and investment loss you can withstand before changing your behavior. The ideal portfolio may give you concern during a bear market, but it does not have enough volatility to lead you to change your investment strategy. A portfolio with too much risk will cause a change in behavior during a volatile period, which results in a change or abandonment of an investment plan.

An emotional decision to change or abandon an investment plan as a result of market risk ultimately *increases* portfolio risk and reduces return. People become emotional only after they lose money. If an investor has been in a bad market long enough to lose money, that investor doesn't want to be out of the market when it turns around. That becomes a strategy of all risk and no return.

An emotional decision does not necessarily mean the sale of risky investments. It could simply mean not investing new money in the markets at the time when you intended to, or delaying portfolio rebalancing into stocks while you "wait and see" what happens to the market.

If by chance an investor happens to time the market correctly in the short term, it may lead to large losses in the long run. Investors who guess correctly one time tend to attribute their good fortune to their investment skill rather than to luck. Once people believe that they are able to "read" the markets, they set themselves up for bigger and more costly mistakes in the future.

HOW BEHAVIORAL FINANCE AFFECTS YOU

Finding your personal risk tolerance can be a tricky business. People understand that investing requires risk; however, it is common for people to overestimate the amount of risk they can handle. This is especially true during a prolonged bull market in stocks.

During the late 1990s, almost every investor was making money in the stock market. Investing seemed like a one-way street of high returns with little risk. Every time stock prices hiccuped, all that was said was, "Buy the dips." It was difficult to find an active investor who didn't think he or she was smart. The television media reinforced that belief by keeping investors informed through continuous "live" market broadcasts. Stock chat rooms on the Internet were filled with homespun stock analysts who had no formal training. Favorite clichés of the period were "This time it's different" and "We are in a new paradigm of stock valuation."

Opportunistic authors were not going to miss out on the action. In early 1999, James Glassman and Kevin Hassett published their highly acclaimed bestseller *Dow 36,000*. The two used historical data to show that there was no risk in the stock market over long periods. They argued that when the world understood this fact the Dow Jones Industrial Average (DJIA) would triple in value. Not to be outdone, in September of 1999, Charles W. Kadlec published *Dow 100,000: Fact or Fiction*. He predicted that the DJIA would increase 10 times in value by the year 2020.

Time proved painful to those who chose to ignore risk or rationalize it away. Between March 2000 and March 2003, the DJIA fell by 40 percent and the tech-heavy Nasdaq index fell by 80 percent. There was blood in the streets as investors slashed their stock holdings and tried to preserve what little they had left. Needless to say, both *Dow 36,000* and *Dow 100,000* can now be found at most flea markets priced at less than $1.

When a person overestimates his or her tolerance for risk, a prolonged bear market will expose the misjudgment. It will be an expensive and painful lesson that will not be forgotten for a long time. The bear market that occurred between 2000 and 2002 cleared out overextended investors and left only those who had an asset allocation at or below their tolerance for risk. Finding and maintaining an investment plan that will last through all market cycles is not easy, but it is worth the effort.

RISK TOLERANCE QUESTIONNAIRES

Risk tolerance questionnaires are common in the investment industry. Questionnaires are available through all mutual fund companies, brokerage firms, and private investment advisors. In addition, you can find them in financial planning books and in some investment-related magazines.

The goal of risk tolerance questionnaires is to find the maximum level of risk that an investor is capable of handling. In doing so, they ask various questions about your investment experience and try to model your risk-and-return profile. Some go as far as recommending an appropriate mix of investments based on the answers. If you are curious, there are sample questions from one questionnaire at the end of this chapter.

Questionnaires are one place to start your inquiry into your risk tolerance; however, they are not the final say. One problem with this approach is that most questionnaires are too vague, and people interpret the questions and answers differently. Since each answer is important to the numeral risk score, a misunderstanding of the questions or answers could change the entire result. In addition, if the same questionnaire were given to a person several times over a one-year period, the results would be different each time the questions were asked, depending on the investor's mood and recent experience.

Another concern with questionnaires is that sellers of investment products and services often misuse the results. The purpose of a questionnaire is to determine your *maximum* level of risk. They are not designed to determine the *appropriate* level of risk to have in a portfolio based on the circumstances. Nevertheless, sellers of investment products tend to use the results of the questionnaires to guide people into portfolios that have the maximum level of risk, whether they need it or not. Risky investments tend to generate higher commissions and fees to the sellers of investment products, and thus a greater allocation to risky assets increases the cash revenue to the firms pushing those products.

Despite the problems surrounding investment questionnaires, the questions do get people thinking about the maximum level of risk they can handle, and that is important. They are just one more tool that can help guide you into an appropriate portfolio.

THE ASSET ALLOCATION STRESS TEST

Once you believe you have an asset allocation that is appropriate for your needs, there is another tool that can help you determine if it is at or below your risk tolerance level. The Asset Allocation Stress Test is a simple form of market simulation that will help you understand how you might react during the next downturn in the financial markets.

The technique involves asking "what if" questions, and an investor answering them honestly. Here is a simple example of such a question:

> Assume that you invested half of your life savings in a total U.S. stock market index fund and the other half in a total U.S. bond market index fund. By the end of the year, the stock fund had collapsed by 30 percent, while the bond fund was up by 10 percent. You planned to rebalance the portfolio back to a 50 percent stock and 50 percent bond position annually. However, given the large loss in the stock portion, what action would you take?
>
> 1. Rebalance the portfolio back to the 50 percent stock and 50 percent bond target.
> 2. Do nothing until you have a clearer picture of market direction.
> 3. Sell part of the stock fund and buy more of the bond fund to reduce your risk.

If the 50 percent stock and 50 percent bond allocation was at a level below your risk tolerance, you would choose answer 1, sell bonds and buy stocks to rebalance back to the original target. On the other hand, if you would let the portfolio remain out of balance or if you were inclined to sell stocks, then a 50 percent stock and 50 percent bond allocation is beyond your tolerance for risk.

I find that most people have a risk tolerance that is lower than what they are willing to admit in public or in a risk tolerance questionnaire. Perhaps that is a cultural phenomenon that some behavioral finance researcher will study. Nevertheless, at our firm we have a policy of proposing an asset allocation to a client that is below the risk level that the client says he or she can handle. That policy has served our clients well over the years.

It does not matter how low your level of risk is, as long as you know what it is. Understanding your tolerance for risk significantly increases the probability of your maintaining an asset allocation strategy over the long term, and that is the essence of a successful investment plan.

AN EXAMPLE OF THE STRESS TEST

The following is a detailed example of an Asset Allocation Stress Test. It suggests an initial asset allocation to an investor, and then stress-tests the allocation to observe how the investor reacts to a volatility shock. If an emotional reaction to loss occurs, a change in asset allocation is needed to bring the portfolio into line with the investor's true tolerance for risk.

Consider a single woman in her mid-fifties who decides to retire after being offered early retirement from her employer. The woman will receive a small monthly pension as well as a $300,000 IRA rollover from a 401(k). She meets with a financial planner to ask for assistance in investing the $300,000 IRA rollover.

The planner concludes that the woman will not make enough from the pension to cover her living expenses and travel plans. She will need to withdraw $1,000 per month from the IRA to supplement her pension income. After determining the woman's cash-flow needs, the conversation turns to asset allocation. The advisor explains the historical returns and risks of each asset class, how modern portfolio theory works, and the necessity for annual rebalancing. The advisor asks the woman to complete a risk tolerance questionnaire to find the maximum level of risk she can tolerate.

The woman completes the risk tolerance questionnaire, and the financial planner calculates the results. He concludes that the woman has the risk tolerance to handle an aggressive portfolio. The advisor suggests an asset allocation of 70 percent in stocks and 30 percent in bonds.

Before recommending individual investments, the planner wishes to ensure that a 70 percent stock and 30 percent bond portfolio is not above the woman's risk tolerance. Therefore, he asks her to take an Asset Allocation Stress Test.

A hypothetical portfolio is created to simulate the month-by-month value of a 70 percent stock and 30 percent bond portfolio between the years 2000 and 2002. Two investments are selected for the study: the Vanguard Total Bond Market Index fund and the Vanguard Total U.S. Stock Market Index fund.

The planner assumes that the woman starts with $300,000 in December 1999, withdraws $1,000 per month starting at the end of January 2000, and rebalances the portfolio back to a 70 percent stock and 30 percent bond mix at the end of each year. Table 13-1 is a summary of the investment results over the three-year period.

As the financial planner works through the year 2000 results with his client, the woman is relatively accepting of the results. Although the loss in 2000 is $11,745, and the withdrawals are $12,000 during the period, she is comfortable with the performance and with rebalancing the portfolio at the end of 2000.

The year 2001 starts with a rebalanced target allocation of 70 percent in stocks and 30 percent in bonds. However, in 2001 the stock market continues lower. By the end of that year, the woman has $249,769 in her portfolio, which is $50,231 below its starting value of $300,000. The woman is no longer smiling. She acknowledges that $24,000 has been withdrawn from the portfolio over the last two years, and she reluctantly agrees that she will still rebalance the portfolio back to the target of 70 percent in stocks and 30 percent in bonds for the start of 2002.

As the financial planner works through 2002, a flag goes up that ends the exercise. In June 2002, the portfolio value falls to $225,355, and the woman becomes very concerned. By September, the portfolio value falls below $200,000 to $199,619. That is a breaking point for the woman. She becomes emotional about the 70 percent stock and 30 percent bonds allocation, which is evident when she comments, "At this rate I will be broke in five years."

When answering questions on a questionnaire, it is easy for people to mistakenly assume that they can handle more risk than they are capable of handling. Despite the woman's young retirement age and her desire to take risk, she is not capable of handling the risk of a 70 percent stock and 30 percent bond portfolio.

The financial planner explains to the woman that if she is inclined to abandon her investment plan after losing money, then the 70 percent stock and 30 percent bond portfolio asset allocation is too aggressive. A less aggressive asset allocation should be implemented from the start. The financial planner suggests a moderate allocation using a 50 percent stock and 50 percent bond portfolio.

TABLE 13-1

Stress Test 1: 70 Percent Stocks and 30 Percent Bonds, 2000–2002; Start with $300,000

Quarter End	Vanguard Total U.S. Stock Fund	Vanguard Total Bond Fund	70% Stocks	30% Bonds	Total Investment Gain/Loss	Total Withdrawn @ $1,000/ Month	Ending Value
Dec. 1999			210,000	90,000			300,000
Mar. 2000	3.84%	2.42%	216,564	90,678	10,242	(3,000)	307,242
June 2000	−4.39%	1.48%	205,557	90,520	2,077	(6,000)	296,077
Sept. 2000	0.27%	3.07%	204,612	91,799	5,411	(9,000)	296,411
Dec. 2000	−10.17%	3.98%	182,303	93,953	(11,745)	(12,000)	276,255
Mar. 2001	−12.27%	3.24%	168,151	84,062	(32,787)	(15,000)	252,213
June 2001	7.47%	0.79%	179,212	83,226	(19,562)	(18,000)	262,438
Sept. 2001	−15.93%	4.29%	149,164	85,296	(44,540)	(21,000)	234,460
Dec. 2001	12.32%	−0.08%	166,041	83,728	(26,231)	(24,000)	249,769
Mar. 2002	0.97%	0.06%	175,034	73,476	(24,490)	(27,000)	248,510
June 2002	−12.69%	2.80%	151,322	74,033	(44,645)	(30,000)	225,355
Sept. 2002	−16.84%	3.71%	124,340	75,279	(67,381)	(33,000)	199,619
Dec. 2002	7.82%	1.47%	132,563	74,886	(56,551)	(36,000)	207,449

Table 13-2 is a replay of the stress test. This time it is bench-marked to a 40 percent stock and 60 percent bond portfolio. The woman starts with $300,000 in December 1999, withdraws $1,000 per month, and the portfolio is expected to be rebalanced back to a 50 percent stock and 50 percent bond target allocation at the end of each year.

At its low point in September 2002, the market value of the 40 percent stock and 60 percent bond portfolio is $249,585. However, only $17,415 of the reduction is due to poor market conditions. The rest is the cumulative withdrawals from the portfolio. The woman is more comfortable with the portfolio and decides that a 40 percent stock and 60 percent bond mix is appropriate for her risk tolerance.

Effective investing involves having realistic expectations about market volatility, then coupling those expectations with an understanding of your tolerance for risk. If you assume too much risk in a portfolio, there is a high probability that you will abandon your investment strategy during severe market downturns. In con-trast, investors who have taken the stress test and are emotionally prepared for the risk they have elected will be able to maintain their allocation during all market conditions. Discipline in main-taining strategy is an essential element of investment success.

REBALANCING FINANCIAL RISK

Portfolio rebalancing is a fundamental part of asset allocation. Rebalancing reduces portfolio risk and creates a diversification benefit in the form of a higher long-term return.

There are many methods of rebalancing. The most common type is on a regular time interval, such as monthly, quarterly, or annually. A second method is based on percentages. A portfolio's fixed target allocation is compared to its current allocation. A rebal-ancing occurs when the asset classes are off target by a predefined percent. Other strategies for rebalancing can become quite com-plex. They involve a sophisticated mix of differential percentages and time elements that take a long time to implement and involve more trading costs.

I recommend avoiding sophisticated rebalancing strategies. For simplicity, annual rebalancing is used throughout this book.

TABLE 13-2

Stress Test 2: 40 Percent Stocks and 60 Percent Bonds, 2000–2002; Start with $300,000

Quarter End	Vanguard Total U.S. Stock Fund	Vanguard Total Bond Fund	40% Stocks	60% Bonds	Total Investment Gain/Loss	Total Withdrawn @ $1,000/Month	Ending Value
Dec. 1999			120,000	180,000			300,000
Mar. 2000	3.84%	2.42%	123,108	182,856	5,964	3,000	302,964
June 2000	–4.39%	1.48%	116,204	184,062	3,266	6,000	297,266
Sept. 2000	0.27%	3.07%	115,017	188,213	9,230	9,000	300,230
Dec. 2000	–10.17%	3.98%	101,820	194,204	5,024	12,000	293,024
Mar. 2001	–12.27%	3.24%	101,328	180,011	(6,661)	15,000	278,339
June 2001	7.47%	0.79%	107,397	179,933	2,330	18,000	284,330
Sept. 2001	–15.93%	4.29%	88,789	186,152	(7,059)	21,000	271,941
Dec. 2001	12.32%	–0.08%	98,228	184,503	3,731	24,000	279,731
Mar. 2002	0.97%	0.06%	111,478	166,439	1,917	27,000	274,917
June 2002	–12.69%	2.80%	95,831	169,599	(7,570)	30,000	262,430
Sept. 2002	–16.84%	3.71%	78,193	174,391	(17,415)	33,000	249,585
Dec. 2002	7.82%	1.47%	82,808	175,455	(8,737)	36,000	255,263

A study of the different methods concluded that annual rebalancing captures most of the diversification benefit without spending a lot of time or money in the process.

There are other situations when your portfolio may require rebalancing to get it back to its asset allocation target. When money is added to a portfolio, this is an ideal time to check the asset allocation and invest that cash where it is needed. If you are taking withdrawals from your portfolio, this is creates another opportunity to rebalance. In a taxable account, I recommend that interest and dividends from investment flow into a money market fund rather than being automatically reinvested (see Chapter 14). Cash income created by current investments can be reinvested if it is not withdrawn.

Consistent rebalancing is also a good test of risk tolerance. If a portfolio is within a person's risk tolerance, that investor will rebalance at the appropriate time without hesitation. If there is hesitation about rebalancing, then the portfolio's asset allocation may be too aggressive. Hesitation normally occurs after a couple of bad years in the market. If you are hesitant about rebalancing your portfolio to its target mix after a market downturn, it may be time to rethink your plan and make a permanent adjustment to the stock and bond mix.

WHEN TO USE RISK AVOIDANCE

Risk avoidance is a different concept from risk tolerance. Risk avoidance is a conscious decision not to invest up to your risk tolerance level. It is important to know your maximum pain threshold, and it is equally important to know when to invest at that level and when not to.

There are many good reasons not to hold a risky portfolio. Once you have accumulated enough assets to provide adequate cash flow throughout your life, there is no need to invest at the peak of your risk tolerance level. Keeping a higher level of risk in a portfolio when there is no need to can have a negative effect. It can take a portfolio that is large enough to retire on and change it into a portfolio that is not. There is nothing worse than having enough money to retire and then losing it.

Many former employees of Enron Corporation know firsthand the dangers of taking risk needlessly. As you recall from

Chapter 2, many preretirees at Enron invested a significant portion of their 401(k) savings in company stock. When the company collapsed, these people not only lost their jobs but lost most of their retirement savings. Enron is just one example of individuals being overallocated to risk. During the last market downturn, hundreds of thousands, if not millions, of individual investors were invested above an appropriate risk level.

If you have a good plan to accumulate and maintain the wealth you will need in order to live comfortably in retirement, the most you can accomplish by taking a high level of risk is to potentially accumulate more wealth for those who will inherit your money. If that is your goal, then some extra risk may be appropriate. However, in this investment advisor's opinion, investing at a maximum risk tolerance level is rarely appropriate for anyone who is in retirement or nearing retirement.

The risk avoidance pendulum can swing too far in the conservative direction as well. It is not prudent to eliminate all potential risk from a portfolio, even after you have accumulated enough wealth to meet your financial goals. First, there is no such thing as a risk-free portfolio. All investments face the corrosive effects of inflation and taxes. Retaining some risky assets in the portfolio has the advantage of earning a real after-tax return. Second, if a portfolio is properly managed during your lifetime, the assets will probably be around long after you are gone. A surprisingly large number of people leave behind more money than they had on the day they retired. In that sense, an appropriate asset allocation may go beyond your lifetime to include children and other heirs.

Table 13-3 is an example of a minimum-risk portfolio. At least 20 percent of a portfolio should be allocated to growth assets, such as common stock and real estate. At least half of the fixed-income portion should be in intermediate-term bonds to capture a higher return.

Risk reduction below one's risk tolerance is purely a business decision, although it should not rest on a stock market prediction or the word of some Wall Street analyst. Risk avoidance should be based on your known assets and an assessment of your future liabilities. Reducing risk when the time is appropriate ensures that the markets will not take away the financial security you have worked years to achieve.

TABLE 13-3

Minimum-Risk Portfolio

Investment Class	Percent
Diversified common stock funds	15%
REIT mutual fund	5%
Intermediate-term bond fund	40%
Short-term bond fund	35%
Money market fund	5%

CHAPTER SUMMARY

Successful asset allocation requires that you act rationally and methodically when managing your portfolios. The best asset allocation is one that an investor is comfortable with during all market conditions and will have the discipline to maintain even during prolonged downturns. That is easier said than done. Most investors are not entirely rational in their decision-making process. Researchers in the field of behavioral finance have uncovered a large number of irrational behaviors and errors in judgment that lead to lower investment returns.

Many portfolio failures occur when investors take on more risk than they are capable of handling. Too much portfolio risk results in adverse investor behavior during market downturns. The right amount of risk is a level where an investor does not become emotional about the portfolio when the markets are poor.

There are several personality tests that investors can take in an attempt to find their true tolerance for investment risk and an appropriate asset allocation. One assessment of maximum risk is the use of risk assessment questionnaires. A portfolio stress test can help investors find an appropriate asset allocation that is right for their needs. Finally, portfolio management is as much common sense as mathematics. Erring on the side of prudence never sent anyone to the poorhouse.

Once a portfolio asset allocation has been set, rebalancing will occur on a regular basis to capture the diversification benefits and to control risk. Rebalancing strategies can be simple or elaborate. Rebalancing once per year is simple and provides good diversification benefits.

SAMPLE RISK TOLERANCE QUESTIONS

(This is not a complete questionnaire)

1. When making a long-term investment, I plan to hold the investment for

❑ 1–2 years
❑ 3–4 years
❑ 5–6 years
❑ 7–8 years
❑ 9–10+ years

2. In October 1987, stocks fell more than 20 percent in one day. If I owned an investment that fell by 20 percent over a short period, I would: (If you owned stock in 1987, check the answer that corresponds to your actual behavior.)

❑ sell all of the remaining investment.
❑ sell a portion of the remaining investment.
❑ hold onto the investment and sell nothing.
❑ buy more of the investment.

3. My previous investment experience in asset classes is (check all the apply):

❑ short-term assets (cash, money markets).
❑ U.S. government/corporate bonds or bond mutual funds.
❑ large stocks and stock funds.
❑ small-company stocks and stock funds.
❑ international stocks and stock funds.

4. Generally, I prefer investments with little or no fluctuation in value, and I'm willing to accept the lower return associated with these investments.

❑ Strongly disagree
❑ Disagree
❑ Somewhat agree
❑ Agree
❑ Strongly agree

5. During market declines, I tend to sell portions of my riskier assets and invest the money in safer assets.

❑ Strongly disagree
❑ Disagree
❑ Somewhat agree
❑ Agree
❑ Strongly agree

6. I would invest in a mutual fund based solely on a brief conversation with a friend, coworker, or relative.

❑ Strongly disagree
❑ Disagree
❑ Somewhat agree

❏ Agree

❏ Strongly agree

7. During the first half of 1994, some bond investments fell by more than 10 percent. If I owned an investment that fell by 10 percent over a short period, I would: (If you owned bonds in 1994, check the answer that corresponds to your actual behavior.)

❏ sell all of the remaining investment.

❏ sell a portion of the remaining investment.

❏ hold onto the investment and sell nothing.

❏ buy more of the investment.

8. My current and future income sources (for example, salary, social security, pension) are

❏ very unstable.

❏ unstable.

❏ somewhat stable.

❏ stable.

❏ very stable.

The answers to these questions and more will help develop a general asset allocation based on your tolerance for risk. However, more work will be required to develop an appropriate portfolio for your needs.

NOTE

[1] Olivia S. Mitchell and Stephen P. Utkus, *Lessons from Behavioral Finance for Retirement Plan Design*, Wharton School and Vanguard Center for Retirement Research, November 24, 2003.

CHAPTER 14

Investment Expenses and Professional Advice

KEY CONCEPTS

- Fund expenses have a direct impact on investment returns.
- Taxes are an investment expense that can be controlled.
- Proper asset location reduces the effects of taxes on a portfolio.
- Professional investment advisors can provide assistance.

Successful asset allocation is all about planning, implementation, and investment discipline. It involves proper investment selection based on your needs, regular rebalancing, and effective cost controls. All of these elements together form a no-nonsense, businesslike approach to managing your money.

The purpose of this chapter is to explain cost control, tax management, and the selection of professional help if needed. Controlling costs is an important part of any investment strategy. The more you pay in fees and commissions, the less you earn in return. In a taxable account, cost control includes a good tax strategy. Paying unnecessary taxes can be your biggest cost of all. The final part of the chapter discusses the advantages and disadvantages of hiring a professional investment advisor.

INVESTMENT COSTS

"A penny saved is a penny earned." That old axiom applies particularly well to investing. Every penny spent on unnecessary mutual fund fees, custodial charges, commissions, advisor's fees, and other expenses is one penny less that you have for retirement. One simple way to increase your investment performance is to lower your investment costs. Investors should scrutinize their portfolio and rid it of high-priced investment products that erode long-term performance.

How does investment cost affect investment performance? High costs could take thousands of dollars in income away from you every year. Consider this example.

Assume that a young man of age 24 starts saving 10 percent of his $36,000 salary. Over his 40-year career, the man receives a 3 percent annual pay increase and saves 10 percent of that increase. He then retires at age 65 and begins to withdraw 4 percent of his retirement savings each year. Assume that he can invest in either a low-cost mutual fund family or a high-cost fund family. The low-cost funds have expenses of 0.5 percent per year, and the high-cost funds have expenses of 1.5 percent per year.

Assume that the markets earn 7.5 percent per year. Table 14-1 shows the difference between a low-fee mutual fund portfolio that earns 7.0 percent after fees and a high-fee mutual fund portfolio that earns only 6.0 percent.

In this example, the lower-expense funds accumulated 32 percent more money in 40 years. The cash benefit that resulted

TABLE 14-1

What a Difference 1 Percent in Fees Makes

	6% Return	7% Return	Difference	% Increase
Retirement account value	$1,471,394	$1,943,699	$472,305	32%
Annual withdrawal @ 4%	$58,856	$77,748	$18,892	32%
Monthly withdrawal	$4,905	$6,479	$1,574	32%

was over \$472,000. That is an enormous amount for someone in retirement. The extra money increased this person's annual retirement income by almost \$19,000 per year based on a 4 percent withdrawal rate.

COMPARING FUND EXPENSES

The December 2004 edition of the Morningstar Principia database lists 15,736 mutual funds of all types and share classes that reported fund expenses (about 1,500 did not). About 70 percent of those funds were equity investments, and about 30 percent were in bonds and balanced portfolios. The median annual expense for all funds was 1.42 percent. In addition, more than 10,000 of those funds have a sales charge that adds to the overall cost.

Low investment costs are not difficult to find. It just takes some willpower. About 6 percent of all mutual funds reported expenses below 0.5 percent per year. Figure 14-1 illustrates the breakdown between higher-cost funds and lower-cost funds.

Fund expenses have a consistently negative effect on fund performance. The more you pay in expenses, the less you will earn in

FIGURE 14-1

The Universe of Mutual Fund Fees

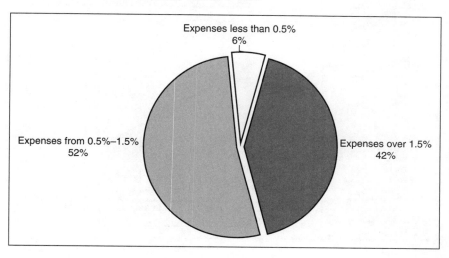

return. Figures 14-2 and 14-3 illustrate how much fees matter in investment returns. The data were compiled from the Morningstar Principia database. Figure 14-2 is the 10-year return for 302 equity growth and income funds that have been in existence since 1995. The bar chart is the average equity mutual fund return for high-fee funds and low-fee funds. The line is the expense ratio for the two categories.

Figure 14-3 is the 10-year return for 234 general corporate bond funds that have been in existence during the same period. The bar chart is the average bond mutual fund return for high-fee funds and low-fee funds. The line is the expense ratio for those two categories.

Clearly, low-cost stock and bond mutual funds have a significant advantage over high-cost funds. Virtually every study of mutual fund performance done by every leading academic researcher has come to the same conclusion: Mutual fund fees not only matter, they matter a lot.

There is no reason to pay high fees and commissions when putting together a portfolio. There are several low-cost, no-load fund companies available. One such company is the Vanguard

FIGURE 14-2

Growth and Income Funds
Ten-Year Returns since 1995

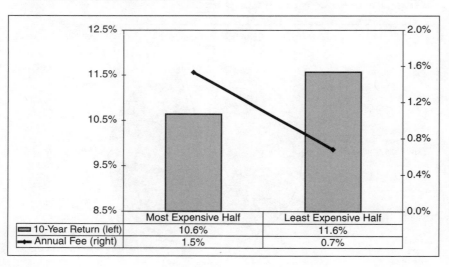

	Most Expensive Half	Least Expensive Half
10-Year Return (left)	10.6%	11.6%
Annual Fee (right)	1.5%	0.7%

FIGURE 14-3

General Corporate Bond Funds
Ten-Year Returns since 1995

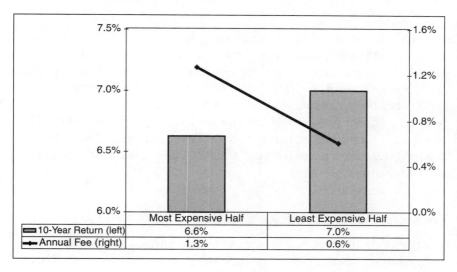

	Most Expensive Half	Least Expensive Half
10-Year Return (left)	6.6%	7.0%
Annual Fee (right)	1.3%	0.6%

Group, located in Valley Forge, Pennsylvania. Vanguard has 193 low-cost mutual funds listed in the Morningstar database. The average expense for a Vanguard fund is only 0.22 percent. That is 1.2 percent lower than the Morningstar average!

Many investors are unaware of the amount they are paying in investment fees. That fact is not entirely the fault of the investor. Fund companies cleverly hide mutual fund costs. For example, mutual funds routinely pay brokerage firms "soft dollars" for access to research, computers, and software that may or may not help investors in those funds. Soft dollars are commission costs and trading spreads granted to the brokerage firm. These extra costs are typically not reported to investors.

Hidden mutual fund costs are widely known. Even President George W. Bush mentioned them in his 2005 State of the Union address when speaking about personal savings accounts for social security:

> The goal here is greater security in retirement, so we will set careful guidelines for personal accounts. We will make sure the

money can only go into a conservative mix of bonds and stock funds. We will make sure that your earnings are not eaten up by hidden Wall Street fees.

George W. Bush

In the past few years, the Securities and Exchange Commission (SEC) and New York Attorney General Elliot Spitzer have been crusading to stop investment firms from abusing their customers through hidden fees and expenses. Several investigations have been opened focusing on trading improprieties and the payment of soft dollars. No sooner do investment firms settle one charge than another abuse surfaces. There seems to be no end to the lengths some investment firms will go to separate investors from their money.

TAXES ARE AN EXPENSE

In addition to expenses, investors who buy mutual funds in a taxable account may incur another cost, one that can dwarf all others. That is the cost of taxation. There are four different events that can trigger a tax on mutual fund shareholders. Three of these events are created by cash distributions by the mutual fund. In addition, investors can trigger a fourth taxable event by selling mutual fund shares.

Mutual fund companies routinely distribute ordinary interest, dividend income, and realized capital gains to shareholders. The interest income is subject to ordinary federal income taxes at an individual's rate of up to 35 percent. Dividends incur a lower tax rate that is capped at a maximum of 15 percent. Capital gains are also a taxable event. They are divided into short-term gains on investments held one year or less, and long-term gains on investments held for more than one year. Like dividends, long-term capital gains are taxed at a maximum of 15 percent. Short-term gains are taxed as ordinary income, which is an investor's highest tax rate of up to 35 percent. Mutual fund distributions are subject to income tax even if a shareholder automatically reinvests the cash in more shares.

Mutual fund managers do not hesitate to distribute all income and realized capital gains. If the fund manager did not distribute the income and gains, the fund itself would have to pay a 35 percent tax on those amounts.

Income and capital gains distributions are reported to taxable shareholders annually on Form 1099-DIV. The report is sent in late January for the previous tax year. Not all cash distributions shown on Form 1099-DIV represent taxable income. Municipal bond funds distribute mostly tax-free interest income that is not taxable at the federal level. The exceptions are certain municipal bonds that pay taxable income, and possibly bonds subject to the alternative minimum tax (ATM). In addition, some mutual funds return capital each year. That is your own investment coming back to you. Both tax-free income and capital distributions are also listed on Form 1099.

The fourth event that triggers a tax liability is the personal sale or exchange of mutual fund shares that have an unrealized capital gain. All investors are required to track the purchase and sale price of their mutual fund shares and report realized gains or losses to the IRS on Schedule D of their tax returns. If you exchange one mutual fund for another fund within the same fund family, you are required to report the sale of the first fund and pay a tax on any realized gain.

The IRS has ruled that it is your responsibility to track the gains and losses on the sale of mutual fund shares. At a minimum, you should keep a separate folder for each mutual fund, and at the end of each year match up any share sales with a purchase price. Mutual fund and brokerage firms may provide you with gain and loss information, but it is still your responsibility to ensure that the data are correct and to report this information to the IRS.

ASSET LOCATION REDUCES TAXES

Asset *allocation* is the percentage of your overall portfolio that you invest in different investment categories. Asset *location* is the type of account in which each investment is placed. Some types of accounts are taxable, some are tax-deferred, and at least one is tax-free. Different categories of investments are taxed at different tax rates. Therefore, with proper placement of your investment choices in the various types of accounts, you can reduce the tax burden on the overall portfolio.

The proliferation of tax-deferred and tax-free savings opportunities has added a new dimension to the traditional asset allocation equation. Tax-deferred accounts include, but are not limited to, Individual Retirement Accounts (IRAs), 401(k) plans, Keogh plans, and 403(b) plans. The investments in tax-deferred accounts are subject to taxation only when the money is withdrawn.

Roth IRAs allow tax-free growth and tax-free withdrawals. They can also be passed on to future generations without incurring an income tax. Roth IRA accounts are always funded with after-tax contributions.

Some investments are less tax-efficient than others. Corporate bond interest is taxed at a higher rate than stock dividend income. Short-term capital gains are taxed at a higher rate than long-term capital gains. Since different investments are taxed differently and different types of accounts are taxed differently, investors can reduce their annual tax burden by placing the right investments in the right accounts. Investments that distribute a high level of taxable income should be placed in tax-deferred or tax-free accounts, and investments with low-tax dividend distributions and long-term capital gains should be placed in taxable accounts.

Examples of investments that you should consider placing in a tax-deferred or tax-free account include

- Corporate bonds and bond funds
- Certificates of deposit, agency bonds, and mortgages
- Mutual funds that have a high turnover of securities
- REITs and REIT mutual funds
- Commodities funds

Examples of investments that you should consider placing in a taxable account include

- Low-turnover equity funds, including equity index funds
- Municipal bonds and municipal bond funds
- Preferred stocks that pay a 15 percent DRD-eligible dividend

Saving on taxes is a good idea; however, nothing is as easy as it seems. Tax location strategies have side effects that may hinder investment strategy. Here are issues to consider:

- Tax location strategies make rebalancing difficult. Having different investments stretched across several accounts may create a rebalancing quagmire.

- Your personal tax rate is not consistent. The ideal tax location strategy today may not be the ideal strategy five years from now.
- Tax rates today are not likely to be the tax rates in the future. Any change may affect your strategy.

One more concern with asset location that is worth mentioning deals with human behavior. Investors sometimes compare the performance of the accounts they own to one another rather than looking at the entire picture from the top down. By mistakenly focusing on the performance of each account separately, investors can turn an asset location strategy into a ticking bomb. When one account performs badly compared to another, an investor may decide to switch investments in the underperforming account without considering the overall asset allocation. Investors who practice asset location need to remember that it is the big asset allocation picture that matters, not each individual account.

TAX SWAPS FOR HIGHER AFTER-TAX RETURNS

Stock and bond prices change every day. Occasionally, there will be a loss in one of the mutual funds in a taxable account. When a loss occurs, "swapping" mutual funds can increase after-tax performance. Tax swapping involves selling one investment and incurring a tax loss while simultaneously buying another investment that is very similar to the one sold but not "substantially identical" to it. That keeps your overall asset allocation on target while harvesting the loss. The tax loss can then be used to offset gains from other parts of the portfolio, to offset mutual fund distributions, or to offset up to $3,000 per year in ordinary income. Harvesting tax losses when they are available helps turn lemons into cherries.

Here is an example. Assume that you hold the Vanguard Total U.S. Stock Market (VTSMX) fund at a loss. Sell VTSMX and buy the TIAA-CREF Equity Index (TCEIX) fund. The two funds have nearly identical returns, but they are not substantially identical because they are managed by different mutual fund companies and are benchmarked to different stock indexes (VTSMX tracks the MSCI U.S. Broad Market Index and TCEIX tracks the Russell 3000).

FIGURE   14-4

Total Return Analysis of TCEIX and VTSMX since TCEIX
Inception on 4/3/2000

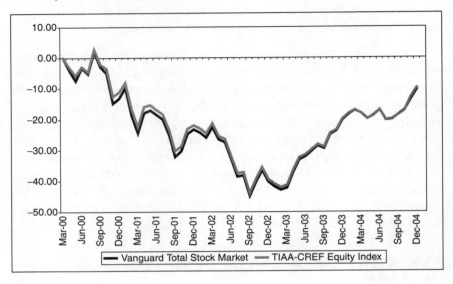

Figure 14-4 illustrates the tracking between the two funds.
Since the funds are not substantially identical but are very close in
performance, a swap from VTSMX to TCEIX allows you to capture
the loss while staying 100 percent invested in the stock market.

ESTABLISH TAX LOTS BY DOLLAR COST AVERAGING

Most people buy mutual funds over time when they have excess
capital. Rather than simply investing when the money is available,
I recommend saving your taxable dollars and making regularly
scheduled quarterly investments. This strategy is commonly
known as dollar cost averaging. One reason dollar cost averaging
makes sense is because it establishes different "tax lots" for
your shares. Each quarter you buy shares at a different price,
thereby establishing different tax positions. For example, instead
of investing $1,000 one month, $500 the next, and $1,500 the next,

instead invest $3,000 once per quarter on a regular basis. That makes tax swapping much easier.

To see how tax swapping works, let's look at an example. Assume that you are buying $3,000 worth of VTSMX each quarter on the first day of the quarter. From January through July, the purchases would be those shown in Table 14-2.

Assume that during the third quarter, the stock market suffers a 10 percent correction, and on August 1, the VTSMX is trading at $108 per share. Your account value and tax lot values are now those shown in Table 14-3.

In this example, the overall account has a gain of $180; however, the 25 shares bought on July 1 had a loss of $300. If you track specific tax lots, you can take the $300 loss by designating on Schedule D of your tax return that the 25 shares sold on August 1 were bought on July 1. If you do not designate the July 1 tax lot, the

TABLE 14-2

Purchases for January through July

Purchase Date	Index Fund NAV	Number of Shares	Cost	Value on July 1
Jan. 1	$100	30	$3,000	$3,600
Apr. 1	$100	30	$3,000	$3,600
July 1	$120	25	$3,000	$3,000
Account shares and value, July 1		85		$10,200

TABLE 14-3

Values on August 1

Purchase Date	Cost	Number of Shares	Value on August 1	Gain/Loss
Jan. 1	$3,000	30	$3,240	+240
Apr. 1	$3,000	30	$3,240	+240
July 1	$3,000	25	$2,700	(300)
Account shares and value, August 1		85	$9,026	+180

IRS will assume that the shares being sold were the first ones bought, or those bought on January 1; thus, you will owe tax on a short-term capital gain of $240. That would be a tax of $84 based on a 35 percent federal tax bracket.

By designating on Schedule D the tax lot sold as the one bought on July 1, the portfolio would realize a loss of $300 rather than a short-tem gain of $240. A capital loss can be deducted from ordinary income up to $3,000. That means that the loss would reduce your tax liability for the year by about $105, assuming a 35 percent tax bracket. The total difference in taxes between selling short-term shares at a $240 gain and selling short-term shares at a $300 loss is $189 ($84 + $105).

To maintain your former equity exposure, on the same day you sell VTSMX, you buy $2,700 of TCEIX. The net result of the transaction is to harvest a tax loss of $300 that you can write off against income taxes while remaining 100 percent invested in a broad market index fund.

There are a couple of issues surrounded tax-swapping that you should consider before you try this strategy. First, depending on where you trade, commissions and other fees may reduce the effectiveness of a tax swap. Second, since the IRS has not addressed tax swapping in mutual funds, there is no clear definition of what "substantially identical" means to mutual fund investors. Accordingly, consult your tax advisor before using tax swaps in a portfolio. His or her interpretation of the tax code may differ from mine.

INDEX FUNDS—LOW FEES AND LOW TAXES

Throughout this book, I have made numerous mentions of index mutual funds. An index fund is a mutual fund that seeks to replicate the return of a particular market index. They have low expenses compared to actively managed funds and have lower turnover of securities in the portfolio, which also keeps costs low.

Index funds have a large following among institutional investors such as pension funds and insurance companies. Ironically, one of the most vocal advocates of index funds for individual investors is Warren Buffett, self-made billionaire and chairman of Berkshire Hathaway, Inc. Although Buffett made his fortune through individual stock selection, in the 2004 annual report of Berkshire Hathaway, he explains in no uncertain words why individual investors should be buying and holding index funds:

> Over the [past] 35 years, American business has delivered terrific results. It should therefore have been easy for investors to earn juicy returns: All they had to do was piggyback Corporate America in a diversified, low-expense way. An index fund that they never touched would have done the job. Instead many investors have had experiences ranging from mediocre to disastrous.
>
> There have been three primary causes: first, high costs, usually because investors traded excessively or spent far too much on investment management; second, portfolio decisions based on tips and fads rather than on thoughtful, quantified evaluation of businesses; and third, a start-and-stop approach to the market marked by untimely entries (after an advance has been long underway) and exits (after periods of stagnation or decline). Investors should remember that excitement and expenses are their enemies. And if they insist on trying to time their participation in equities, they should try to be fearful when others are greedy and greedy only when others are fearful.

Index funds are available in a variety of asset classes and categories. There are many U.S. stock index funds, international stock index funds, bond index funds, and even a couple of gold index funds. If you are considering an investment in a particular asset class, chances are that there is an index fund available, or that one will be available shortly.

The Morningstar Principia database lists close to 700 index funds that trade in the United States, and many new funds are added each year. These funds cover a wide variety of markets and are issued by several competing companies. The Standard & Poor's 500 is the most commonly used index. There are over 100 funds listed in the Principia database that attempt to mirror the performance of the S&P 500 Index.

There are three reasons that index mutual funds are an ideal choice for those pursuing an asset allocation strategy in their portfolio:

1. *Low tracking error with the indexes.* The data used in almost all asset allocation analysis come directly from the return

on the market. Accordingly, market-matching index funds are a logical investment choice for people who want to make the most of asset allocation analysis. Any deviation from index funds adds an element of risk that was not captured in the asset allocation analysis.

2. *Index funds have low fees.* In general, stock and bonds index funds have the lowest investment fees in the industry. The lowest-cost index funds charge about 0.1 percent per year, which is well below the mutual fund industry average of 1.4 percent. One word of caution: not all index funds have low fees. Some investment companies charge over 1.0 percent for their index funds, even though those funds invest in the exact same indexes as very-low-cost funds. Let the buyer beware.

3. *Low tax liability.* Index funds generally have very low turnover of securities compared to actively managed funds. Low turnover results in low capital gains distributions to taxable shareholders. That means low tax liability.

For more information about index funds, including a detailed analysis of indexes and their construction, see my previous book, *All About Index Funds* (McGraw-Hill, 2002). The marketplace for index funds is growing rapidly. New funds are being added weekly as fund companies expand into new and exciting markets. Check for current news on index funds by going to the www.Morningstar.com Web site. A second Internet source for current information on index funds is www.Indexuniverse.com.

TIPS ON HIRING AN INVESTMENT MANAGER

The process of asset allocation can be difficult for some investors and an unwelcome chore for others. The design, implementation, monitoring, rebalancing, tax management, and occasional reassessment of strategy can take a lot of effort, and that is not how many people want to spend their free time.

If an investor would rather not manage his or her own portfolio, or cannot manage the account for health or legal reasons, one solution is to hire a professional investment manager. A competent manager can help you formulate an asset allocation, implement the plan, monitor the results, rebalance when needed, and modify the asset allocation when your needs dictate that it is appropriate to do so.

There are several benefits of employing the services of an investment manager if you believe you should have one. Here is a partial list of the benefits:

1. *Planning and implementation.* Managers can help clients understand their cash-flow needs, then design, implement, and maintain a specific asset allocation to meet those needs. As a person's situation changes, the manager will suggest appropriate changes in the asset allocation.

2. *Consistency of strategy.* Discipline is critical to investment success. Investors need to follow their plan and rebalance their portfolios on a regular basis. It is the job of an investment manager to ensure that this process happens.

3. *Create a circuit breaker.* During uncertain market conditions, some investors need to talk with someone about their concerns. A call to an advisor or financial planner usually calms an investor's nerves and stops the investor from making an emotionally incorrect decision.

4. *Place someone on duty 365 days per year.* There are times when all investors get sidetracked. An investment manager is there to do the investment chores for you all day every day.

The biggest concern about hiring an investment manager is finding a good one. Advisors come in all shapes, sizes, and levels of competence. Make sure you check the background information on a potential advisor on the Securities and Exchange Commission Web site at www.SEC.gov. If you have any question in your mind as to what a particular advisor's competence level is, go on to the next one.

Advisors generally charge a fee based on a percentage of the account's value. The fee can range from reasonable to expensive.

Make sure you are not paying too much to have your portfolio managed. An acceptable fee for asset management services is 0.5 percent per year with a minimum annual fee per household. If you are considering the services of an advisor that charges more, then negotiate the price. There is nothing to gain from paying a lot of money for investment management services when those services are available elsewhere for far less.

Be careful whom you go to for advice. Some people in the investment business claim to be investment advisors, but they are actually selling investment products on commission. By definition, anyone who is compensated by commissions cannot be offering unbiased advice. It is unrealistic to think that you will be offered low-fee investments when the recommendation is coming from a person whose livelihood is rooted in the high-fee products that he or she is paid to distribute.

If you are considering an advisor, make sure you know *exactly* how that advisor is paid and *all* the fees that will be charged to your portfolio. Advisor's fees should be fair, and there should be no conflicts of interest. An advisor should put all cost information in writing. If an advisor hesitates to do this, then you should not hire that advisor. Caveat emptor—let the buyer beware.

CHAPTER SUMMARY

Low investment fees and tax control play an important role in the success of an investment plan. The more you pay in fees and taxes, the lower your long-term investment performance. How you allocate your investments across different accounts goes a long way toward keeping taxes low. In addition, swapping out of losing funds and harvesting losses can increase your after-tax return.

The heart of a successful asset allocation strategy relies on the investor's confidence that a multi-asset-class, low-cost approach to portfolio management is right for him or her. With confidence comes a commitment to maintaining an asset allocation during all market conditions. A properly designed portfolio of low-cost investments that is within an investor's tolerance for risk will help ensure that the plan is followed in good times and bad.

All About Asset Allocation has covered a lot of ground. The tools and strategies discussed in this book provide a no-nonsense, businesslike approach to managing your portfolio effectively. Learn the principles of asset allocation, design an investment plan that fits your needs, implement and maintain that plan, and keep your costs low. You will be further ahead in the future for doing so.

Low-Cost Mutual Fund Providers*

American Century Investments	Phone: 800-345-2021
AON Funds	Phone: 800-266-3637
Armada Funds	Phone: 800-342-5734
Barclays Global Investors	Phone: 800-474-2737
Bridgeway Funds	Phone: 800-661-3550
California Investment Trust Group	Phone: 800-225-8778
Deutsche Asset Management	Phone: 800-730-1313
Dreyfus	Phone: 800-373-9387
E*TRADE Funds	Phone: 800-786-2575
Fidelity Group	Phone: 800-544-8888
Financial Investors Trust	Phone: 800-298-3442
Galaxy Funds	Phone: 800-628-0414
Harris Insight Funds	Phone: 800-982-8782
Nationwide Funds	Phone: 800-848-0920
Schwab Funds	Phone: 800-435-4000
Scudder Funds	Phone: 800-621-1048
StateStreet Global Advisors	Phone: 800-843-2639
Strong Funds	Phone: 800-368-1030
T. Rowe Price Funds	Phone: 800-638-5660
Transamerica Premier Funds	Phone: 800-892-7587
USAA Group	Phone: 800-382-8722
Vanguard Group	Phone: 800-662-7447
Vantagepoint Funds	Phone: 800-669-7400
Wachovia Funds	Phone: 800-994-4414
TD Waterhouse Funds	Phone: 800-934-4448
DJ Wilshire Target Funds	Phone: 888-200-6796

*Mutual fund companies that have at least some funds with fees less than 0.50 percent and no sales load.

Research Web Sites

INVESTMENT ADVICE SITES

Morningstar.com   This site provides news and analyses of markets, stocks, and mutual funds for the individual investor.

Vanguard.com   Besides being one of the best places to shop for index funds, Vanguard has an "Education, Planning, and Advice" section that is one of the best on the Web. There is lots of good information in the "Plain Talk® Library."

EfficientFrontier.com   William J. Bernstein and Susan F. Sharin edit "Efficient Frontier: An Online Journal of Practical Asset Allocation." Bernstein's quarterly online journal is a must read for all serious index fund investors.

Dfafunds.com   Dimensional Fund Advisors offers unique index funds through investment advisors. Its three-factor approach to portfolio construction is gaining acceptance worldwide.

iShares.com   You can learn about exchange-traded funds and use the helpful portfolio management tools on Barclay's iShares Web site.

Ssga.com   State Street Global Advisors manages many exchange-traded funds around the world. Its site offers tools and information.

PortfolioSolutions.com   The Web site of Portfolio Solutions, LLC, a leading investment advisor specializing in asset allocation and low-cost investment management, offers useful information.

OTHER INFORMATIONAL SITES

Indexinvestor.com   Provides comprehensive asset allocation and index fund information.

IndexUniverse.com   Provides news, information, and analysis of markets and index funds.

Spglobal.com   Standard & Poor's offers comprehensive analyses of and commentary on all of its global indexes.

Barra.com   Barra is a leading provider of index data on the U.S. equity market. It has teamed up with S&P to provide many of the popular growth and value index fund benchmarks.

DowJones.com   Dow Jones offers lots of great information on the markets and has a wonderful historical section featuring charts that include major economic and world events.

MSCI.com   Morgan Stanley Capital International (MSCI) covers the globe with its Web site. It includes methodology and analysis.

Russell.com   This site provides comprehensive information about all the Russell indexes and methodology.

Wilshire.com   Dow Jones Wilshire indexes are explained, with past returns available.

Recommended Reading

The Intelligent Asset Allocator, by William J. Bernstein. An analysis of sensible asset allocation strategies for intermediate and advanced investors.

The Four Pillars of Investing: Lessons for Building a Winning Portfolio, by William J. Bernstein. An easy-to-read guidebook on asset allocation for all levels.

Common Sense on Mutual Funds, by John C. Bogle. A low-cost mutual fund icon shares his views on investing.

The Art of Asset Allocation, by David M. Darst. Asset allocation information for intermediate to advanced investors.

Winning the Loser's Game, by Charles Ellis. A classic book on how investors can increase their returns and decrease their risk.

All About Index Funds, by Richard A. Ferri, CFA. A guide to low-cost index fund investing that complements this book.

Protecting Your Wealth in Good Times and Bad, by Richard A. Ferri, CFA. A sensible lifelong saving and investing handbook for all investors.

Asset Allocation: Balancing Financial Risk, by Roger C. Gibson. Asset allocation concepts made understandable.

A Random Walk Down Wall Street, by Burton G. Malkiel. A comprehensive look at today's market and what is driving it.

The Coffeehouse Investor, by Bill Schultheis. An asset allocation book for those who want to keep their life simple.

Stocks for the Long Run, by Jeremy Siegel. A classic book about investing, with market data going back 200 years.

Mutual Funds: Profiting from an Investment Revolution, by Scott Simon. An investment advisor shares his views on the asset allocation of low-cost index funds.

12b-1 Fee   An annual fee charged by some mutual funds to pay for marketing and distribution activities. The fee is taken directly from fund assets, which reduces a shareholder's total return.

Active Management   An investment strategy that seeks to outperform the average returns on the financial markets. Active managers rely on research, market forecasts, and their own judgment and experience in selecting securities to buy and sell.

Alternative Minimum Tax (AMT)   A separate tax system designed to ensure that wealthy individuals and organizations pay at least a minimum amount of federal income taxes. Certain securities that are used to fund private, for-profit activities are subject to the AMT.

Annualize   To make a figure for a period of less than a year apply to a full year, usually for purposes of comparison. For instance, a portfolio turnover rate of 36 percent over a six-month period could be converted to an annualized rate of 72 percent.

Ask Price   The price at which a security is offered for sale. For a no-load mutual fund, the ask price is the same as the fund's net asset value per share. Also called offering price.

Automatic Reinvestment   An arrangement by which the dividends or other earnings from an investment vehicle are used to buy additional shares in the investment vehicle.

Average Coupon   The average interest rate (coupon rate) on all the bonds in a portfolio.

Average Effective Maturity   A weighted average of the maturity dates for all securities in a money market or bond fund. (The maturity date is the date when the buyer of a money market instrument or a bond will be repaid by the security's issuer.) The longer the average maturity, the more a fund's share price will move up or down in response to changes in interest rates.

Back-End Load   A sales fee charged by some mutual funds when an investor sells fund shares. Also called a contingent deferred sales charge.

Benchmark Index   An index that correlates with a fund, used to measure a fund manager's performance.

Beta   A measure of the magnitude of a portfolio's past share-price fluctuations in relation to the ups and downs of the overall market (or an appropriate market index). The market (or index) is assigned a beta of 1.00, so a portfolio with a beta of 1.20 would have seen its share price rise or fall by 12 percent when the overall market rose or fell by 10 percent.

Bid-Ask Spread   The difference between what a buyer is willing to bid (pay) for a security and the seller's ask (offer) price.

Blue Chip Stocks   Common stocks of well-known companies with a history of growth and dividend payments.

Bond Covenant   The contractual provision in a bond indenture. A positive covenant requires certain actions, and a negative covenant limits certain actions.

Book Value   A company's assets, minus any liabilities and intangible assets.

Broker/Broker-Dealer   An individual or firm that buys or sells mutual funds or other securities for the public.

Capital Gain/Loss   The difference between the sale price of an asset—such as a mutual fund, stock, or bond—and the original cost of the asset.

Capital Gains Distributions   Payments to mutual fund shareholders of gains realized during the year on securities that the fund has sold at a profit, minus any realized losses.

Cash Investments   Short-term debt instruments—such as commercial paper, banker's acceptances, and Treasury bills—that mature in less than one year. Also known as money market instruments or cash reserves.

Certified Financial Planner (CFP)   An investment professional who has passed exams administered by the CFP Board of Standards on subjects such as taxes, securities, insurance, and estate planning.

Certified Public Accountant (CPA)   An investment professional who is licensed by a state to practice public accounting.

Chartered Financial Analyst (CFA)   An investment professional who has met competency standards in economics, securities, portfolio management, and financial accounting as determined by the Institute of Chartered Financial Analysts.

Closed-End Fund   A mutual fund that has a fixed number of shares, usually listed on a major stock exchange.

Commodities   Unprocessed goods, such as grains, metals, and minerals, traded in large amounts on a commodities exchange.

Consumer Price Index (CPI)   A measure of the price change in consumer goods and services. The CPI is used to track the pace of inflation.

Correlation Coefficient   A number between -1 and 1 that measures the degree to which two variables are linearly related.

Cost Basis   The original cost of an investment. For tax purposes, the cost basis is subtracted from the sale price to determine any capital gain or loss.

Country Risk   The possibility that political events (a war, national elections), financial problems (rising inflation, government default), or natural disasters (an earthquake, a poor harvest) will weaken a country's economy and cause investments in that country to decline.

Coupon/Coupon Rate   The interest rate that a bond issuer promises to pay the bondholder until the bond matures.

Credit Rating   A published ranking, based on a careful financial analysis, of a creditor's ability to pay the interest or principal owed on a debt.

Credit Risk   The possibility that a bond issuer will fail to repay interest and principal in a timely manner. Also called default risk.

Currency Risk   The possibility that returns for Americans investing in foreign securities could be reduced because of a rise in the value of the U.S. dollar against foreign currencies. Also called exchange-rate risk.

Custodian   Either (1) a bank, agent, trust company, or other organization responsible for safeguarding financial assets or (2) the individual who oversees the mutual fund assets of a minor's custodial account.

Declaration Date   The date when the board of directors of a company or mutual fund announces the amount and date of the entity's next dividend payment.

Default   Failure to pay principal or interest when it is due.

Depreciation   A decrease in the value of an investment.

Derivative   A financial contract whose value is based on, or "derived" from, a traditional security (such as a stock or bond), an asset (such as a commodity), or a market index (such as the S&P 500 Index).

Discount Broker   A brokerage firm that executes orders to buy and sell securities at commission rates lower than those of a full-service brokerage.

Distributions   Either (1) withdrawals made by the owner from an individual retirement account (IRA) or (2) payments of dividends and/or capital gains by a mutual fund.

Dividend Reinvestment Plan   The automatic reinvestment of shareholder dividends in more shares of the company's stock.

Dividend Yield   The annual rate of return on a share of stock, determined by dividing the annual dividend by the current share price. In a stock mutual fund, this figure represents the average dividend yield of the stocks held by the fund.

Dollar Cost Averaging   Investing equal amounts of money at regular intervals on an ongoing basis. This technique ensures that an investor buys fewer shares when prices are high and more shares when prices are low.

Earnings per Share   A company's earnings divided by the number of common shares outstanding.

Enhanced Index Fund   An index fund that is designed to generally track an index, but also to outperform that index through the use of leverage, futures, trading strategies, capital gains management, and other methods.

Exchange-Traded Fund   An index fund that trades on the stock market. Some common ETFs are the Nasdaq 100 Index Tracking Stock (QQQ), which tracks the Nasdaq 100, and Standard & Poor's Depositary Receipts (SPY), which tracks the S&P 500.

Efficient Market   The theory (disputed by some experts) that stock prices reflect all market information that is known by all investors. It also states that investors cannot beat the market because it is impossible to determine future stock prices.

Equivalent Taxable Yield   The yield needed from a taxable bond to give the same after-tax yield as a tax-exempt issue.

Exchange Privilege   A shareholder's ability to move money from one mutual fund to another within the same fund family, often without additional charge.

Ex-Dividend Date   The date when a distribution of dividends and/or capital gains is deducted from a mutual fund's assets or set aside for payment to shareholders. On the ex-dividend date, the fund's share price drops by the amount of the distribution (plus or minus any market activity). Also known as the reinvestment date.

Expense Ratio   The percentage of a portfolio's average net assets used to pay its annual expenses. The expense ratio, which includes management fees, administrative fees, and any 12b-1 fees, directly reduces returns to investors.

Federal Reserve   The central bank that regulates the supply of money and credit throughout the United States. The Fed's seven-member board of governors, appointed by the president, has significant influence on U.S. monetary and economic policy.

Fee-Only Advisor   An arrangement in which a financial advisor charges a set hourly rate or an agreed-upon percentage of assets under management for a financial plan.

First-In, First-Out (FIFO)   A method for calculating taxable gain or loss when mutual fund shares are sold. The FIFO method assumes that the first shares sold were the first shares purchased.

Front-End Load   A sales commission charged at the time of purchase by some mutual funds and other investment vehicles.

Full Faith and Credit   A pledge to pay interest and principal on a bond issued by the government.

Fund Family   A group of mutual funds sponsored by the same organization, often offering exchange privileges between funds and combined account statements for multiple funds.

Fundamental Analysis   Examining a company's financial statements and operations as a means of forecasting stock price movements.

Futures/Futures Contracts   Contracts to buy or sell specific amounts of a specific commodity (such as grain or foreign currency) for an agreed-upon price at a certain time in the future.

Global Fund   A mutual fund that invests in stocks of companies in both the United States and foreign countries.

Gross Domestic Product (GDP)   The value of all goods and services provided by U.S. labor in a given year. One of the primary measures of the U.S. economy, the GDP is issued quarterly by the Department of Commerce. Formerly known as the Gross National Product (GNP).

Hedge   A strategy in which one investment is used to offset the risk of another.

High-Yield Fund   A mutual fund that invests primarily in bonds with a credit rating of BB or lower. Because of the speculative nature of high-yield bonds, high-yield funds are subject to greater share price volatility and greater credit risk than other types of bond funds.

Index Providers   Companies that construct and maintain stock and bond indexes. The main providers are Standard & Poor's, Dow Jones, Lehman Brothers, Morgan Stanley, Russell, and Wilshire.

Indexing   An investment strategy designed to match the average performance of a market or a group of stocks. Usually this is accomplished by buying a small amount of each stock in a market.

Inflation Risk   The possibility that increases in the cost of living will reduce or eliminate the returns on a particular investment.

Interest-Rate Risk   The possibility that a security or mutual fund will decline in value because of an increase in interest rates.

International Fund   A mutual fund that invests in securities traded in markets outside of the United States. Foreign markets present additional risks, including currency fluctuation and political instability. In the past, these risks have made the prices of foreign stocks more volatile than those of U.S. stocks.

Investment Advisor   A person or organization that makes the day-to-day decisions regarding the investments in a portfolio. Also called a portfolio manager.

Investment Grade   A bond whose credit quality is considered to be among the highest by independent bond-rating agencies.

Junk Bond   A bond with a credit rating of BB or lower. Also known as high-yield bonds because of the rewards offered to those who are willing to take on the additional risks of a lower-quality bond.

Large-Cap   A company whose stock market value is generally in excess of $10 billion, although the amount varies among index providers.

Liquidity   The degree of marketability of a security; that is, how quickly the security can be sold at a fair price and converted to cash.

Load Fund   A mutual fund that levies a sales charge, either when shares are bought (a front-end load) or when they are sold (a back-end load).

Long-Term Capital Gain   A profit on the sale of a security or mutual fund share that has been held for more than one year.

Management Fee   The amount a mutual fund pays to its investment advisor for the work of overseeing the fund's holdings. Also called an advisory fee.

Market Capitalization   A determination of a company's value, calculated by multiplying the total number of shares of the company's stock outstanding by the price per share. Also called capitalization.

Maturity/Maturity Date   The date when the issuer of a money market instrument or bond agrees to repay the principal, or face value, to the buyer.

Median Market Cap   The midpoint of the market capitalization (market price multiplied by the number of shares outstanding) of the stocks in a portfolio. Half the stocks in the portfolio will have a higher market capitalization and half will have a lower market capitalization.

Mid-Cap   A company whose stock market value is between $2 billion and $10 billion, although the range varies among index providers.

Municipal Bond Fund   A mutual fund that invests in tax-exempt bonds issued by state, city, and/or local governments. The interest obtained from these bonds is passed through to shareholders and is generally free of federal (and sometimes state and local) income taxes.

Mutually Exclusive   A situation in which the occurrence of one event excludes the possibility of another event. If an investment is a member of one index, this precludes membership in others.

National Association of Securities Dealers (NASD)   An organization of brokers and dealers designed to protect the investing public against fraudulent acts.

Negative Correlation   A situation in which the value of one of two investments moves opposite to the value of the other.

Net Asset Value (NAV)   The market value of a mutual fund's total assets minus its liabilities, divided by the number of shares outstanding. The value of a single share is called its share value or share price.

No-Load Fund   A mutual fund that charges no sales commission or load.

Nominal Return   The return on an investment before adjustment for inflation.

Noncorrelation   A situation in which the changes in the value of two different investments are completely independent of each other.

Open-End Fund   An investment entity that has the ability to issue or redeem the number of shares outstanding on a daily. Prices are quoted once per day, at the end of the day, at the net asset value of the fund (NAV).

Operating Expenses   The amount paid for asset maintenance or the cost of doing business. Earnings are distributed after operating expenses are deducted.

Option   A contract in which a seller gives a buyer the right, but not the obligation, to buy or sell securities at a specified price on or before a given date.

Overlap   The situation that arises when two indexes or mutual funds are not mutually exclusive. The degree to which two funds or indexes have similar holdings, as measured in percentage of market value.

Payable Date   The date when dividends or capital gains are paid to shareholders. For mutual funds, the payable date is usually within two to four days of the record date. The payable date also refers to the date on which a declared stock dividend or bond interest payment is scheduled to be paid.

Portfolio Transaction Costs   The expenses associated with buying and selling securities, including commissions, purchase and redemption fees, exchange fees, and other miscellaneous costs. In a mutual fund prospectus, these expenses would be listed separately from the fund's expense ratio. They do not include the bid/ask spread.

Positive Correlation   A situation in which the value of one of two investments moves in unison with the value of the other.

Premium   An amount by which the price of a security exceeds the face value or redemption value of that security or the price of a comparable security or group of investments. It may indicate that a security is highly favored by investors. Also refers to a fee for obtaining insurance coverage.

Price-to-Book Ratio   The price per share of a stock divided by the stock's book value (i.e., its net worth) per share. For a portfolio, the ratio is the weighted average price-to-book ratio of the stocks it holds.

Price-to-Earnings (P/E) Ratio   The share price of a stock divided by its per-share earnings over the past year. For a portfolio, the weighted-average P/E ratio of the stocks in the portfolio. P/E is a good indicator of market expectations about a company's prospects; the higher the P/E, the greater the expectations for a company's future growth in earnings.

Prospectus   A legal document that gives prospective investors information about a mutual fund, including discussions of its investment objectives and policies, risks, costs, and past performance. A prospectus must be provided to a potential investor before he or she can establish an account and must also be filed with the Securities and Exchange Commission.

Proxy   Written authorization by a shareholder giving someone else (such as fund or company management) authority to vote his or her shares at a shareholders' meeting.

Quantitative Analysis   In securities, an assessment of specific measurable factors, such as cost of capital; value of assets; and projections of sales, costs, earnings, and profits. Combined with more subjective or qualitative considerations (such as management effectiveness), quantitative analysis can enhance investment decisions and portfolios.

Real Estate Investment Trust (REIT)   A company that manages a group of real estate investments and distributes at least 95 percent of its net earnings annually to its stockholders. REITs often specialize in a particular kind of property. They can, for example, invest in real estate, such as office buildings, shopping centers, or hotels; purchase real estate (an equity REIT); or provide loans to building developers (a mortgage REIT).

Real Return   The actual return received on an investment after factoring in inflation. For example, if the nominal investment return for a particular period was 8 percent and inflation was 3 percent, the real return would be 5 percent (8 percent − 3 percent).

Record Date   The date used to determine who is eligible to receive a company or fund's next distribution of dividends or capital gains.

Redemption   The return of an investor's principal in a security. Bond redemption can occur at or before maturity; mutual fund shares are redeemed at net asset value when an investor's holdings are liquidated.

Redemption Fee   A fee charged by some mutual funds when an investor sells shares within a short period of time after their purchase.

Registered Investment Advisor (RIA)   An investment professional who is registered—but not endorsed—by the Securities and Exchange Commission (SEC) and may recommend certain types of investment products.

Reinvestment   Use of investment income to buy additional securities. Many mutual fund companies and investment services offer the automatic reinvestment of dividends and capital gains distributions as an option to investors.

Return of Capital   A distribution that is not paid out of earnings and profits. It is a return of the investor's principal.

Risk Tolerance   An investor's ability or willingness to endure declines in the prices of investments while waiting for them to increase in value.

R-Squared   A measure of how much of a portfolio's performance can be explained by the returns on the overall market (or a benchmark index). If a portfolio's total return precisely matched the return on the overall market or benchmark, its R-squared would be 1.00. If a portfolio's total return bore no relationship to the market's returns, its R-squared would be 0.

Sector Diversification   The percentage of a portfolio's stocks that is placed in companies in each of the major industry groups.

Sector Fund   A mutual fund that concentrates on a relatively narrow market sector. These funds can experience higher share-price volatility than diversified funds because sector funds are subject to issues specific to a given sector.

Securities and Exchange Commission (SEC)   The federal government agency that regulates mutual funds, registered investment advisors, the stock and bond markets, and broker-dealers. The SEC was established by the Securities Exchange Act of 1934.

Sharpe Ratio   A measure of risk-adjusted return. To calculate a Sharpe ratio, an asset's excess returns (its return in excess of the return generated by risk-free assets such as Treasury bills) is divided by the asset's standard deviation. It can be calculated versus a benchmark or an index.

Short Sale   The sale of a security or option contract that is not owned by the seller, usually to take advantage of an expected drop in the price of the security or option. In a typical short sale transaction, a borrowed security or option is sold, and the borrower agrees to purchase replacement shares or options at the market price on or by a specified future date. Generally considered a risky investment strategy.

Short-Term Capital Gain   A profit on the sale of a security or mutual fund share that has been held for one year or less. A short-term capital gain is taxed as ordinary income.

Small-Cap   A company whose stock market value is less than $2 billion, although the amount varies among index providers.

Spread   For stocks and bonds, the difference between the bid price and the ask price.

Standard Deviation   A measure of the degree to which a fund's return varies from its previous returns or from the average return for all similar funds. The larger the standard deviation, the greater the likelihood (and risk) that a security's performance will fluctuate from the average return.

Style Drift   When a fund moves away from its stated investment objective over time.

Swap Agreement   An arrangement between two parties to exchange one security for another, to change the mix of a portfolio or the maturities of the bonds it includes, or to alter another aspect of a portfolio or financial arrangement, such as interest-rate payments or currencies.

Tax Deferral   Delaying the payment of income taxes on investment income. For example, owners of traditional IRAs do not pay income taxes on the interest, dividends, or capital gains accumulating in their retirement accounts until they begin making withdrawals.

Tax Swapping   Creating a tax loss by the simultaneous sale of one investment or fund and purchase of a similar investment or fund that is not substantially identical to it.

Taxable Equivalent Yield   The return on a higher-paying but taxable investment that would equal the return on a tax-free investment. It depends on the investor's tax bracket.

Tax-Exempt Bond   A bond, usually issued by a municipal, county, or state government, whose interest payments are not subject to federal, and in some cases state and local, income tax.

Total Return   A percentage change, over a specified period, in a mutual fund's net asset value, with the ending net asset value adjusted to account for the reinvestment of all distributions of dividends and capital gains.

Transaction Fee/Commission   A charge assessed by an intermediary, such as a broker-dealer or a bank, for assisting in the sale or purchase of a security.

Treasury Security   A negotiable debt obligation issued by the U.S. government for a specific amount and maturity. Income from Treasury securities is exempt from state and local tax but not from federal income tax. Treasury securities include Treasury bills (T-bills; 1 year or less), Treasury notes (T-notes; 1 to 10 years), and Treasury bonds (T-bonds; over 10 years).

Turnover Rate   An indication of trading activity during the past year. Portfolios with high turnover rates incur higher transaction costs and are more likely to distribute capital gains (which are taxable to nonretirement accounts).

Unit Investment Trust (UIT)   An SEC-registered investment company that purchases a fixed, unmanaged portfolio of income-producing securities and then sells shares in the portfolio to investors, usually in units of at least $1,000. Usually sold by an intermediary such as a broker.

Unrealized Capital Gain/Loss   An increase (or decrease) in the value of a security that is not "real" because the security has not been sold. Once a security is sold by the portfolio manager, the capital gains/losses are "realized" by the fund, and any payments to the shareholder are taxable during the tax year in which the security was sold.

Volatility   The degree of fluctuation in the value of a security, mutual fund, or index. Volatility is often expressed as a mathematical measure, such as a standard deviation or beta. The greater a fund's volatility, the wider the fluctuations between its high and low prices.

Wash Sale Rule   The IRS regulation that prohibits a taxpayer from claiming a loss on the sale of an investment if that investment or a substantially identical investment is purchased within 30 days before or after the sale.

Yankee Dollars/Bonds   Debt obligations, such as bonds or certificates of deposit, bearing U.S. dollar denominations and issued in the United States by foreign banks and corporations.

Yield Curve   A line plotted on a graph that depicts the yields of bonds of varying maturities, from short-term to long-term. The line, or "curve," shows the relationship between short- and long-term interest rates.

Yield to Maturity   The rate of return an investor would receive if the securities held in his or her a portfolio were held until their maturity dates.

Active retirees, 222, 232–238
Advisor, professional
    management, 7, 16–17,
    274–276
Agarwal, Vikas, 188
Alternative investments, 171–193
    collectibles, 189–192
    commodities, 173–184
    hedge funds, 172, 184–190
    mutual funds list, 192–193
Arbitrage hedge strategies,
    185–186
Asset allocation, 33–52
    correlation analysis, 38–41,
        46–50
    diversification goal, 33
    history of, 34–35
    rebalancing, 35–38
    risk and return, 42–45
    success of, 15–16, 50–52
    two-asset-class model, 42
    (*See also specific topics*)
Asset classes, 69–193
    alternative investments,
        171–193
    fixed-income investments,
        131–153
    framework for selection, 71–82
    international equity
        investments, 109–131
    real estate investments and
        REITs, 155–170
    summary, 61
    U.S. equity investments, 83–107
Asset location, 267–269
"Average miss," 28–30
Avoidance of risk, 256–258

Banz, Rolf, 91
Beebower, Gilbert, 15
Behavioral finance, 243–260
    asset allocation stress test,
        250–254, 255
    finance impact, 248
    rebalancing, 254, 256
    research on, 244–247
    risk avoidance, 256–258
    risk tolerance, 247, 249
    skill self-assessment, 246–247
Bernstein, William, 67
Bias, hedge funds, 187
Bonds and bond market
    early savers (life), 225–228
    mid-life accumulators, 228–232
    pre- and active retirees, 235–238
    mature retirees, 238–242
    credit risk, 133–139
    economic forecasting, 209–210
    fixed-income investments,
        139–140
    global bond structure, 132–133
    maturity, 133–135
    multi-asset-class investing,
        59–61, 74
    in multi-asset-class portfolio, 62
    risk-adjusted returns, 201
    risk premiums, 206–207
    structure of, 132–133
    vs. U.S Treasury notes, 59–60
    (*See also* Fixed-income
        investments)
Brinson, Gary, 15
Buffett, Warren, 9, 272–273
Bush, George W., 266–267
Buy and hold, 4

Canada, 122
Casterline, Gordon, 7
Categorization of investments,
    95–96
Center for Research in Security
    Prices (CRSP)
  collectibles, 190, 191
  fixed-income investments, 139,
    146
  market expectations, 200
  real estate investments, 161,
    162, 163, 164, 171
  U.S. equity measurement,
    91–93, 104
Collectibles, 189–192
Commercial REITs, 157–158
Commodities, 173–184
Commodity Research Bureau
    (CRB) indexes, 176, 178–183
Corporate bonds, 144–147
  (*See also* Bonds and bond
    market)
Correlation
  asset allocation, 38–41, 46–50,
    77–79
  commodities, 180–181
  hedge funds, 185
  multi-asset-class investing, 67
  real estate investments and
    REITs, 163–166
Costs and fees, 261–277
  alternative investments, 171
  asset allocation framework,
    79–80
  control, 261
  equity investments, U.S., 106
  expenses comparison,
    264–266
  hedge funds, 172
  of investment, 262–263
  mutual funds, 16–17
  taxes, 266–274

CRB (Commodity Research
    Bureau) indexes, 176, 178–183
Credit risk, 133–139
CRSP (*See* Center for Research in
    Security Prices [CRSP])
Currency risk, 110–111

Default risk, 145–147
Developed markets and indexes,
    112–113, 114–119
DFA (Dimensional Fund
    Advisors) index, 122–126
Dimensional Fund Advisors
    (DFA) index, 122–126
Dimson, Elroy, 155–156
Directional hedge strategies, 186
Diversification, 33, 35–38
  (*See also specific topics*)
Dividends, 210, 212–215
DJ-AIGCI (Dow Jones-AIG
    Commodity Index), 182–183
DJIA (Dow Jones Industrial
    Average), 248
Dodd, David, 95
Dollar cost averaging, 270–272
Dow Jones-AIG Commodity
    Index (DJ-AIGCI), 182–183
Dow Jones Industrial Average
    (DJIA), 248

EAFE (Europe, Australia, and
    the Far East) Index, 114–128
Early savers, life-cycle, 222,
    224–228
Earnings growth method model,
    209–215
Emerging markets, 112–113,
    122–125, 147–149
Equity investments (*See*
    International equity
    investments; U.S. equity
    investments)

Equity REITs, 160
Europe, Australia, and the Far
    East (EAFE) Index, 114–128
European equities, 56–59, 62,
    115–118, 120–121
Event-driven hedge strategies, 186
Expectations for market returns,
    197–219
    dividends and market
        valuation, 212–215
    earnings growth method
        model, 209–215
    Federal Reserve growth, 212
    fixed income forecasting,
        215–217
    forecast creation, 218–219
    forecasting returns, 198–199
    inflation effects, 203–204
    risk-adjusted return model,
        199–209
    stacking risk premiums, 204–209
    volatility model, 199–209
Expenses, comparison of, 264–266
    (See also Costs and fees)

Fama, Eugene, 96, 103, 125
Fama and French (FF) factors,
    96–105
Fear of regret, 246
Federal Reserve, market
    forecasting, 210, 212, 216
Fees (See Costs and fees)
Ferri, Richard A., 106, 128, 152, 169
FF (Fama and French) factors,
    96–105
Fitch investment rating, 136,
    137, 144
Fixed-income investments, 131–153
    credit risk, 135–139
    emerging debt market, 147–149
    global bond market structure,
        132–133

high-yield corporate bonds,
    144–147
investment-grade bonds,
    139–140
market forecasting, 215–217
maturity structure, 135
municipal bonds, 151
mutual funds list, 151–152
portfolio building, 149–151
returns, 133–135
risk, 133–135, 201
TIPS, 21–22, 139–144, 205, 216
Forecasts, 198–199, 203–204,
    218–219
Framework, asset allocation
    selection, 71–82
    asset classes, summary, 61
    correlation analysis, 77–79
    cost, 79–80
    fundamental differences in,
        74–75
    global markets, 80–82
    guidelines for, 73–74
    securities overlap, 75–77
French, Kenneth, 96, 98, 103, 125
Fundamental differences, asset
    allocation framework, 74–75
Futures, commodities, 173, 177–179

GDP (gross domestic product),
    198, 209–212, 214–215, 218
Gibson, Roger C., 55, 67
Glassman, James, 248
Global markets
    asset allocation framework,
        80–82
    fixed-income and bond
        investments, 132–133
    international equity
        investments, 111–113
        (See also International
        equity investments)

Gold commodities, 174, 175
Goldman Sachs Commodity
    Index (GSCI), 182–183
Government bonds, 132–133
Graham, Benjamin, 95
Greenspan, Alan, 11
Growth stocks, 96
Guidelines for asset allocation
    framework, 73–74

Hassett, Kevin, 248
Hedge funds, 172, 184–190
Historical view
    asset allocation, 34–35
    equity investments, U.S., 84–85
    market returns, 198–199, 202
    real estate investments, 158–159
Home ownership, REITs, 166–169
Hood, L. Randolph, 15
Hot stocks and poor returns, 10–11
House Price Index (HPI), 166–169
Hybrid REITs, 160

Ibbotson, Roger, 15
iBonds, U.S. Treasury, 21–22, 144
Index funds, 272–274
Individual Retirement Accounts
    (IRAs), 267–269
Individualized plan, 4–5
Inflation
    commodities, 176–177
    economic forecasting, 209–210
    forecasting, 216
    House Price Index (HPI),
        166–169
    market forecasting, 203–204
    real estate investments,
        161, 162
    returns and performance,
        20–22, 84
Information, investment selection,
    8–10, 11–12

Interest rates, 135, 164–165, 168,
    216–217
International equity investments,
    109–131
    early savers (life), 225–228
    mid-life accumulators, 224–232
    pre- and active retirees, 235–238
    mature retirees, 238–242
    Canada, 122
    currency risk, 110–111
    developed markets and
        indexes, 112–113, 114–119
    emerging markets, 112–113,
        122–125
    global markets, 111–113
    mixes, 119–121
    multi-asset-class investing,
        55–59, 74–75
    mutual funds list, 128, 129
    sample allocation, 127–128
    size, 125–127
    value factors, 125–127
Investment manager, 7, 274–276
Investment style, 87–91, 95–106
IRAs (Individual Retirement
    Accounts), 267–269

Jaeger, Robert A., 189
Junk bonds, 136

Kadlec, Charles W., 248
Kahneman, Daniel, 244

Large-cap stocks, 56–59, 62, 209
Lehman (Brothers) indexes
    fixed-income investments, 137,
        139–141, 144–146, 148–150
    international, 132, 139–141,
        145–149
    real estate investments, 163, 165
    U.S., 22, 42, 59
Liability matching, 229

Life-cycle investment, 13–14,
221–242
Limited partnerships (LPs), 80,
157–158

Margin, futures, 178–179
Market risk factors (beta), 97
Markowitz, Harry, 34
Mature retirees, life-cycle
investing, 222, 238–242
Maturity, 133–135
Mei, Jianping, 190
Mei Moses Fine Art Index, 190–191
Micro-cap stocks, 88–95
Mid-life accumulators, 222, 224–232
Mitchell, Olivia, 246
Models, 42, 199–209, 210
Modern Portfolio Theory (MPT),
34–35, 171
Money management importance,
5–8
Moody's investment rating, 136,
137, 144
Morgan Stanley Capital
International (MSCI) indexes,
55–56, 87, 106
Morningstar classification system,
87–91, 96
Morningstar Principia, 263–265, 273
Mortgage-backed securities, 133,
160
Moses, Michael, 190
MPT (Modern Portfolio Theory),
34–35, 171
MSCI EAFE (Europe, Australia,
and the Far East) index,
114–128
MSCI Emerging Market indexes,
122–126
MSCI (Morgan Stanley Capital
International) indexes, 55–56,
87, 106

Multi-asset-class investing, 53–68
adding classes, 54–55
corporate bonds, 59–61
correlation analysis, 67
design, 67–68
example, 62–66
international equities, 55–59
portfolio building, 61–62
Munger, Charlie, 9
Municipal bonds, 151
Mutual funds
alternative investments,
192–193
in asset allocation, 16–17
commodities and futures,
192–193
for early savers, 222, 227–228
expenses, 263–266
fixed-income investments,
151–152
international equity
investments, 128, 129
low-cost providers, 279
mature retirees, 239–242
mid-life accumulators,
230–232
for preretirees and active
retirees, 235–238
real estate investments and
REITs, 169–170
retirement, 235–238, 293–242
value investments list, 106
Myth, risk-free investment as,
20–22

Naik, Narayan, 188
National Association of Real
Estate Investment Trusts
(NAREIT), 159, 161–165
Negative correlation, 38–41, 72
Northwest Quadrant, 43–45, 54,
66–67

OFHEO (U.S. Office of Federal
   Housing Enterprise
   Oversight), 166, 168
Oil commodities, 174, 175
Overanalysis, 17

P/E ratio, 210, 212–214
Pacific Rim equities, 56–59, 62,
   115–118, 120–121
PCGS (Professional Coin Grading
   Service) index, 191–192
Performance (*See* Returns and
   performance)
Planning for success, 3–18
   asset allocation process, 12, 14–16
   buy and hold, 4
   hot stocks and poor returns,
      10–11
   individualized, 4–5
   information and skill, 8–10,
      11–12
   investment mix selection, 16–17
   life span investment, 13–14
   money management
      importance, 5–8
   overanalysis, 17
   "seat of the pants," 3–4
   written plan, 4
Political risk, 147–148
Portfolio building, 221–242
   early savers, 224–228
   fixed-income investments,
      149–151
   life-cycle investing overview,
      221–223
   mature retirees, 238–242
   mid-life accumulators, 224–232
   minimum risk, 258
   multi-asset-class investing, 61–62
   preretirees and active retirees,
      232–238
   volatility, 25–30
Positive correlation, 38–41

Pre- and active retirees, 222,
   232–238
Professional advice/management,
   7, 16–17, 274–276
Professional Coin Grading Service
   (PCGS) index, 191–192

Real estate investment trusts
   (REITs) (*See* Real estate
   investments and REITs)
Real estate investments and
   REITs, 155–170
   asset class, 158–159
   commercial opportunities,
      157–158
   correlation analysis, 163–166
   direct ownership, 157
   equity REITs, 160
   history of, 158–159
   home ownership, 166–169
   hybrid REITs, 160
   limited partnerships (LPs),
      157–158
   mortgage-backed securities, 133
   mortgage REITs, 160
   mutual fund list, 169–170
   performance, 160–163
   returns, 155–157, 160–163
Realistic market expectations
   (*See* Expectations for market
   returns)
Rebalancing, 35–38, 254, 256
Reinganum, Marc, 91
Research, 244–247, 279, 281–282, 283
Retirement
   active retirees, 222, 232–238
   asset allocation, 235–238, 239–242
   mature retirees, 222, 238–242
   preretirees, 222, 235–238
Returns and performance
   asset allocation, 42–45
   commodities, 180–181, 184
   correlation analysis, 38–41

factors in, 97
fixed-income investments,
    133–135
hot stocks and poor returns, 10–11
inflation, 20–22, 84
in multi-asset-class portfolio,
    56–59
real estate investments and
    REITs, 155–157, 160–163
risk-adjusted, 19–20
tax swaps, 269–270
(*See also* Expectations for
    market returns)
Reuters CRB, 182, 183
Rickey, Wesley Branch, 63–64
Risk, 19–31
    asset allocation, 42–45
    avoidance of, 256–258
    currency risk, 110–111
    default risk, 145–147
    defined, 23–25
    fixed-income investments,
        133–135, 217
    in multi-asset-class portfolio,
        56–59
    political risk, 147–148
    rebalancing, 254, 256
    and return, 19
    risk-free investment as myth,
        20–22
    stacking premiums, 204–209
    tolerance for, 247, 249
    volatility, 25–30
Risk-adjusted return model,
    19–20, 199–209
Russell, Frank, 94
Russell indexes, 87, 91–92,
    98–100, 106

"Seat of the pants" investing, 3–4
Securities and Exchange
    Commission (SEC), 10, 172,
    184, 266, 275

Securities overlap, 75–77
Security Analysis (Graham and
    Dodd), 95
Selection of stocks (*See* Asset
    allocation, selection
    framework)
September 11, 2001, attacks, 67, 72
Sharpe, William, 91
Shiller, Robert J., 244
Singer, Brian, 15
Size and performance, 87–89,
    91–102, 125–127
Skill, investment selection, 8–10,
    11–12, 246–247
Small-cap stocks, 102–105, 208, 209
S&P 500 (Standard and Poor's)
    vs. GDP growth, 211
    as large-cap equities, 62
    percent of GDP, 214, 215
    professional advice, 273–274
    risk-adjusted returns, 199–200,
        202
    U.S. Treasury T-bills correlation,
        46–50
S&P investment rating, 136,
    137, 144
Spitzer, Elliot, 266
Spot price, commodities, 173
Stacking risk premiums, 204–209
Standard and Poor's (*See* S&P 500
    [Standard and Poor's])
Standard deviation, risk, 25–30,
    199–201
Statman, Meir, 244, 246
Stock exchanges, 85
Stress test, asset allocation,
    250–254, 255
Structure of equity investments,
    U.S., 85–86
Style, investment, 87–91, 95–106

Tactical hedge strategies, 186
Tax lots, 270–272

Tax swaps, 269–270
Taxes, 266–274
    asset location, 267–269
    collectibles, 189
    deferred accounts, 267–269
    dollar cost averaging, 270–272
    as expense, 266–267
    index funds, 272–274
    mid-life accumulators, 231
    REITS, 158–159
    returns impact, 20–22
    tax lots, 270–272
    tax swaps, 269–270
    U.S. Treasury notes and
        inflation, 203–204
Test, asset allocation stress,
    250–254, 255
Thaler, Richard, 244
TIPS (Treasury Inflation Protected
    Securities), 21–22, 139–144,
    205, 216
Tolerance for risk, 247, 249
Treasury Inflation Protected
    Securities (TIPS), 21–22,
    139–144, 205, 216
Tversky, Amos, 245
Two-asset-class model, 42

U.S. equity investments, 83–107
    early savers, 225–228
    mid-life accumulators, 224–232
    pre- and active retirees,
        235–238
    mature retirees, 238–242
    broad market, 86–87
    history of, 84–85
    investment style, 87–91
    low cost funds, 106
    micro-cap stocks, 88–95
    Morningstar classification
        system, 87–91
    opportunities, 87–88
    returns, 20–22, 84
        size and performance, 87–89,
            91–102
        S&P 500 index as proxy for, 42
        structure of, 85–86
        value investments, 95–106
        (See also U.S. Treasury T-bills)
U.S. Office of Federal Housing
    Enterprise Oversight
    (OFHEO), 166, 168
U.S. Treasury iBonds, 21–22, 144
U.S. Treasury notes
    corporate bonds, 59–61
    vs. corporate bonds, 59–60
    credit risk, 136
    economic forecasting, 209–210
    inflation effects, 203–204
    maturity, 135
    in multi-asset-class portfolio, 62
    returns, 20–22, 84
    risk-adjusted returns, 199–201,
        202
    S&P 500 correlation, 46–50
    stacking risk premiums, 204–209
Utkos, Stephen, 246

Value investments, 95–106
    categorization, 95–96
    FF factors, 96–105
    international equity
        investments, 125–127
    mutual fund list, 106
    return factors, 97
    small-caps, 102–105
    U.S. equity investments, 95–106
Value risk factors, 97
Volatility, 25–30, 199–209

Web sites for research, 281–282
Wilshire indexes, 91, 101–106, 167
Written plan, 4

Yield, 60, 144–147 (See also Bonds
    and bond market)

Richard A. Ferri is the president of Portfolio Solutions, LLC, an investment advisor firm in Troy, Michigan. He is a financial analyst, a portfolio manager, a college professor, an author, and a nationally recognized speaker on investment topics.

Ferri earned a Bachelor of Science degree in Business Administration from the University of Rhode Island in 1980. Over the next eight years, he served as an officer and fighter pilot in the U.S. Marine Corps. He eventually retired from the Marine Corps Reserves in 2001. After leaving full-time active duty in 1988, Ferri worked as a stockbroker with a major Wall Street firm for 10 years. During that period, Ferri earned the designation of Chartered Financial Analyst (CFA), offered through the CFA Institute, and also holds a Master of Science degree in Finance from Walsh College of Accountancy and Business, where he currently serves as an adjunct professor of finance.

In 1999, Ferri founded Portfolio Solutions, LLC. The firm manages accounts for individuals, high-net-worth families, foundations, and corporate pension plans. The firm's management strategy is based on the topics covered in this book. The Web site for Portfolio Solutions, LLC, is www.PortfolioSolutions.com.

In March 2000, Ferri self-published his first book, *Serious Money, Straight Talk about Investing for Retirement*. In August 2002, McGraw-Hill published his second book, *All About Index Funds*, which is an essential guidebook for all fee-conscious mutual fund investors. In 2003, *Protecting Your Wealth in Good Times and Bad* was also published by McGraw-Hill. In addition to books, Ferri also writes for several investment magazines and online investment sites. He has been interviewed by and quoted in several major financial publications, including the *Wall Street Journal, Money, Barron's*, and *Kiplinger*. Ferri has spoken at numerous investment conferences and meetings around the country and is available for future speaking engagements. For speaking requests, contact Portfolio Solutions, LLC.